2005

To Ja[...]

Hope th[...]
interest to you and
Alix — can I
borrow it after !

love

Lynn + Mariel

# THE LOST
# KINGDOMS
# OF AFRICA

# THE LOST KINGDOMS OF AFRICA

*Through Muslim Africa
by Truck, Bus, Boat
and Camel*

## Jeffrey Tayler

LITTLE, BROWN

A *Little, Brown* Book

First published in the United States of America in 2005 by
Houghton Mifflin Company
First published in Great Britain in April 2005 by Little, Brown

Note: Certain names and minor identifying characteristics have been
changed to protect the privacy and prevent the embarrassment of people
described in this book. Specifically, the names of Ahmad and Madame X in
Chapter 4, Hussein and Isa in Chapter 6, Ezekiel in Chapter 9, Mustafa in
Chapter 10, Ahmad in Chapter 12, Moussa in Chapter 16 and Oumar in
Chapter 17 are pseudonyms.

A CIP catalogue record for this book is available
from the British Library.

ISBN 0 316 72607 9

Typeset in Caslon by M Rules
Printed and bound in Great Britain by
Mackays of Chatham plc

Little, Brown
An imprint of
Time Warner Book Group UK
Brettenham House
Lancaster Place
London WC2E 7EN

www.twbg.co.uk

*To my wife, Tatyana*

HARMATTAN (from the Twi *haramata,* a derivation of the Arabic *haram,* forbidden, evil, accursed):

a parching easterly wind that originates above the wastes of the Sahara and blows for days over Central and West Africa. Fills the sky with reddish-brown dust, reduces the sun to a pale orb. Exacerbates drought, cracks the trunks of trees, defoliates vegetation, prompts the acacia to ooze gum arabic. In humans, the Harmattan may aggravate respiratory illnesses and cause splits in the skin, dryness of the eyes and lips. Under certain conditions, the Harmattan fosters the spread of dust-borne diseases, including lethal strains of meningitis.

# CONTENTS

# CONTENTS

# THE LOST KINGDOMS OF AFRICA

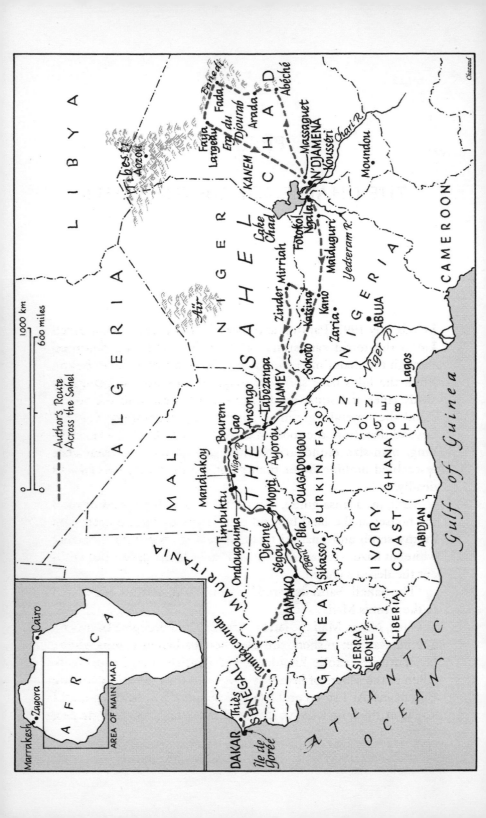

# Prologue

## THE CHALLENGE OF THE SAHEL

It was July 1997. Panting and dizzy from the heat, I clambered atop the torrid sandstone brow of Dala Hill and squinted through the noontime glare at the Nigerian city of Kano below. From the hill's base spread a rough-hewn maze of zigzagging sandy lanes and squat mud hovels. Farther away, to the south, stood the emerald green minaret of a great walled mosque; beyond that, from the roofs of distant earthen houses, rose stabbing, man-size crenellations that, though molded from clay, resembled nothing other than giant sharks' teeth, curved and deadly.

Sarki, my Hausa guide, spread his arms and gestured beyond the houses at the land beyond: flat, tawny barrens, dotted with thorny scrub and gnarled trees, sweeping away into a blazing whiteout haze – terrain as sere and harsh as the desert but without the desert's charm.

'The Sahel!' Sarki declared. 'East is Chad, north is Niger, and to the west is Mali.'

Chad, Niger, Mali . . . lands of famine and drought, Islam and guerilla warfare; in short, sun-bleached, barbarous realms where, for centuries, exotic kingdoms had flourished and eventually fallen to the sabers of invading Arabs and the guns of colonizing Europeans. As I stood on Dala Hill that day, that was about all I knew, or thought I knew, of those countries, but their names, conjuring up alien peoples and vague perils, stirred and intrigued me. They even seemed to present me with some sort of challenge.

Sarki's name in Hausa meant 'king,' and he had the look of royalty about him. In his early forties, wearing long white robes and a crested white turban, with the tight skin on his gaunt cheeks and aquiline nose glistening like oiled mahogany, he possessed the imperious mien of an Islamic suzerain. As I looked at him, a flood of unfamiliar words came to mind: khedive, dey, nabob, emir – legend-laden titles of Arab and Turkish potentates of whose likes I had only read. Sarki was a Muslim, but he was black, a speaker of an African language peppered with Arabic loan words, a member of the Hausa – a people about whom I knew little, except that they had resisted Western influence during Nigeria's colonial days and afterward, and were among the most fervent Islamic fundamentalists pushing for the imposition of shari'a, or Islamic law, in the northern states of the country.

With sweat dripping into my eyes, I followed Sarki off the hill and into the maze of old Kano. The assault on my heat-addled senses was immediate and relentless. Shrouded lepers with leaking sores and yellowed eyes swarmed around me, sticking their stumps in my face and whining for alms. Hordes of barefoot children in smocks came running to tug at my shirt and shout 'Masta! Masta!' and rattle their tins. I winced at the sight of a man in rags ambling by, jaw agog, his teeth sprouting horizontally through his cheeks. From the dark innards of alley-side workshops came the ear-shattering pounding of hammers and the screechy creaking of looms; from the open doors of Islamic schools resounded Qur'anic chants as deafening as they were monotonous. Pushing my way through the crowd, clinging close to Sarki and unable to understand a word he shouted to me, I inhaled air heavy with sweat and the cloying reek of wet clay and open sewers; often I stumbled, my eyes failing to adjust to the flaming pools of white sun alternating with columns of black shade cast by the beams stretching over the alleys. I wanted nothing more than to escape.

Once we were out of the alleys and past the beggars, Sarki, strolling at ease, expounded in his bass, pidgin-inflected English on the history of Kano, or, rather, on the legend of Kano's birth. The people of Kano, like the rest of the Hausa in Nigeria's mostly Muslim north, were not really Africans, he contended, but traced their lineage to a renegade Arab prince from Baghdad, Bayajida, who came here, killed a fearsome snake, married the queen, and fathered the children who would establish seven Hausa city-states, of which Kano would become the most prominent. This legend granted the Hausa a bloodline leading back to the pro-genitors of Islam, a religion the Hausa began accepting only in the fifteenth century after their king converted. What is certain is that the king's conversion brought close ties with Arabia and the North African Arabs who ran the trans-Saharan trade on which Kano and the other Hausa states would flourish. It also brought the Arabic language, in which the Hausa chronicled their cities' history and whose alphabet they later adopted to write their own tongue.

Talking to Sarki, I would never have guessed that Islamic Kano belonged to the same country as did the city from which I had just arrived, Lagos – a festive but violent, mostly Christian, and definitely African shantytown of 13 million people built on the malarial swamps and jungle lagoons of the Gulf of Guinea, seven hundred miles to the southwest. Within the walls of old Kano alcohol was forbidden and crime was rare. Kano's Hausa inhabi-tants, aloof and dressed in robes of green, white, and blue, exchanged formulaic Arabic greetings and mingled with indigo-robed Nigériens and visiting Libyan traders. A mercantile spirit ruled: Christian workers (Yoruba and Igbo from the south) loaded donkey carts for hectoring Muslim bosses, and every corner bus-tled with commerce. Only when Kano's emir, or traditional Islamic ruler, appeared on horseback to deliver his Friday sermon at the central mosque would the din stop.

'The emir's word is our law,' said Sarki. 'The federal govern-ment must get his approval before it acts in Kano.'

We wandered through the dust-choked lanes in search of 'lion oil' to cure the backache of one of Sarki's friends. Sarki intro-duced me to all sorts of Hausa traders and relatives. They expressed disdain for Christian southerners and blamed them for

Nigeria's most notorious problems – armed robbery, drug trafficking, and fraud.

'Because of Islam, sons of Hausa would be afraid and ashamed to steal. Armed robbers come from the south,' Sarki said. All agreed.

We stopped by a poster of Mu'ammar al-Gaddafi, bearing the Arabic inscription AL-AKH QA'ID AL-THAWRA [Our Brother and the Leader of the Revolution] MU'AMMAR AL-GADDAFI. Sarki looked up at the turbaned Libyan. 'We feel solidarity with Gaddafi, a true power-man who tells the truth. He calls for us Muslims to unite!'

When Sarki spoke, it was easy to forget that he was a citizen of a country where those he dismissed as 'thieving southern Christians' make up 40 percent of a population of 130 million. Listening to him, one might also forget that his ethnic and religious group had done much, through malfeasance, corruption, and outright theft, to reduce to penury, civil strife, and decay what could be, thanks to huge oil and natural gas deposits, the wealthiest country in Africa. Four of Nigeria's six military dictators (the last of whom died in 1998) have been Muslims from the north. Northern Nigeria needs southern Nigeria for its oil, its farmlands, and its ports, so Nigerian dictators have been bent on keeping united the fractious country, a designation that even a famous Nigerian nationalist called 'a mere geographical expression.' Conflicts between the Muslims of the north and the Christians of the south frequently erupt into deadly riots and outright insurrections that federal security forces quell with much loss of life.

On a crowded street just off Kofar Mata Road, the old town's main thoroughfare, we finally found a shop selling 'lion oil.' The merchant used a knife to spear gobs of the honeylike substance and slip them into a plastic bag. What was it, exactly? I asked. Sarki couldn't – or wouldn't – say. (Perhaps it was some sort of secret folk medicine an infidel like me should know nothing about.) Smiling, he paid, and we stepped back out into the din and said goodbye.

Under a rattling air conditioner, I lay in my hotel bed that night and reflected on the disorienting, disturbing nature of what I had seen, smelled, heard, and felt during the day. I had been traveling and living abroad for half my life and had spent several years in North Africa and the Middle East, but everything in Kano seemed as new, frightening, and shocking as it was intriguing. The Muslim-Christian animosity; the African language studded with Arabic words; the crowds of desperate mendicants dwelling in medieval squalor in the middle of the second-largest city of what should have been Africa's wealthiest country; and beyond the shark-tooth crenellations, the infinity of sunbaked wasteland stretching away into turbulent countries of which I knew so little – all this left me with the prefatory burn of a new obsession for which I would be willing to risk my life, a challenge I would one day return to take up.

I did not make it back to sub-Saharan Africa before September 11, 2001, but the terrorist attacks of that day rekindled my fascination with the Sahel (still largely ignored by the Western media, despite all their newfound interest in the Islamic world) and prompted me to begin reading up on the region with renewed urgency. The Sahel, whose name comes from the Arabic *sahil*, or 'coast,' is an expanse of badlands, semidesert, and parched savanna that forms the southern shore of the Saharan sand sea and spreads some 3,000 miles across Africa from Ethiopia west to the Atlantic Ocean. My history books told me that in the countries of the Sahel – specifically in Sudan, Chad, Nigeria, Niger, and Mali – once thrived some of Africa's wealthiest, if obscurest, kingdoms and empires, whose borders bore no relation to modern-day frontiers. The kingdoms of Wadai and Kanem, the Hausa emirates, the sultanate of Zinder and the Sokoto caliphate, and the Malian and Songhai empires prospered on the trans-Saharan trade in gold, salt, ivory, and slaves.

Arab chroniclers tell us what is known about the region's precolonial history. In the seventh and eighth centuries, as Arab merchants began navigating ancient trade routes south across the Sahara, they encountered flourishing and orderly Sahelian kingdoms whose inhabitants regarded themselves as superior to outsiders. The Sahelians were practical, however, and to facilitate trade began adopting Islam, and with it the Arabic alphabet and much Arab culture. (The Arabs had a lot to teach in the Middle Ages: to them at that time belonged the most advanced literature, medicine, science, and law in the Eastern Hemisphere.) Hence, its predominantly Muslim faith makes 'Sahel' a cultural as well as a geographic designation. One might as well just call it Muslim black Africa.

Just as before September 11 Afghanistan drew few Western journalists, the Sahel, for decades beset by ethnic rebellion, sectarian violence, and banditry, receives little attention from the media today. Few areas of the world are as difficult to travel, to be sure, but there is another reason for the dearth of coverage: the countries of the Sahel don't appear to affect the West. With the exception of oil-rich Nigeria, they play a negligible role in the global economy. Poverty in the Sahel is some of the worst on earth: between 45 percent (in Nigeria) and 80 percent (in Chad) live below the poverty line. Niger is the second-poorest country in the world, after Sierra Leone. Most Sahelians survive – or don't – on half a dollar a day or less. Desertification (which stems from a combination of overgrazing and climate change and by some estimates is pushing the Sahara south at the rate of 3.5 miles a year) menaces what agriculture there is. The armies of the Sahel threaten no one beyond its borders, and no cold war now exists to spark great power rivalry over the region's resources, which, besides uranium in Niger and oil in Nigeria, are minimal. AIDS is less of a problem in the Sahel than elsewhere in sub-Saharan Africa: population-wide infection rates range from 1.4 percent in Senegal to 5–7 percent in Chad, high by Western standards, but not enough to make the news. When one hears of the Sahel at all, it is usually in connection with donor fatigue or drought. In short, for most Westerners, the Sahel is not on the map.

We can no longer afford such ignorance, for men dwelling in caves in a failed state as destitute as any in the Sahel orchestrated attacks that killed thousands of Americans on September 11. Al-Qa'ida has been active in Africa, perpetrating acts of terrorism in

Kenya, Tanzania, and Tunisia that have cost the lives of hundreds of people. One Sahelian state, Sudan, sheltered Osama bin Laden until 1996. Al-Qa'ida and similar organizations are now believed to be operating in nine countries of sub-Saharan Africa, three of which are in the Sahel, where terrorist dollars go a long way in bribing officials for support, where government control of vast regions is minimal, where ill-trained police forces and ragtag armies can do little more than oppress their own people, and where local populations, Muslim and poor and increasingly anti-Western, may sympathize with Islamic radicals. Under the auspices of a program called the Pan-Sahel Initiative, the U.S. military is already helping Mali, Niger, and Chad pursue Islamic militants operating on their territories.

Any state in the Sahel could serve as a base for Al-Qa'ida, but Nigeria deserves special attention in this connection. The U.S. alliance with the Saudi regime rests largely on oil – just as does America's relationship with Nigeria, possessor of the tenth-largest reserves of crude in the world, and Washington's new strategic energy partner. For years Nigeria has been the fifth-largest supplier of crude oil to the United States. By 2007, thanks to deals the Bush administration is concluding with Abuja, it will be the third.

Growing uncertainty over the future of the Saudi monarchy has prompted the United States to search for more stable sources of energy; hence its interest in Nigeria. But the U.S.-Nigeria relationship is fraught with perils similar to, or worse than, those bedeviling the Saudi alliance. For more than forty years Western multinationals have pumped oil from the Niger River Delta as the Nigerian government has battled villagers demanding their fair share of the wealth. Enter Osama bin Laden, who in February 2003 called Nigeria 'ripe for liberation' – an ominous declaration, given the spread of Islamic extremism in the country. Ever since the death of the dictator General Sani Abacha in 1998 and the introduction of new freedoms, Islamic fundamentalism has threatened the secular principles of the Nigerian state, and even the unity of the country. Over the past four years, twelve northern Nigerian states have adopted shari'a law, to the rising fury of the country's Christians. Since 1999 more than ten thousand Nigerians have died in vicious tribal and intercommunal clashes. The latest explosion came in November 2002 when women gathered in Abuja to compete in the Miss World pageant. A (Christian) Nigerian journalist contended in a national newspaper that the prophet Muhammad would have been pleased to choose a wife from among its contestants – a remark that legions of Nigerian Muslims took as an anti-Islamic outrage and an insult that implied, they said, that the Prophet would have approved of Western debauchery. The four days of rioting that erupted between Muslims and Christians left 220 dead, 1,000 injured, and 11,000 homeless, and twenty churches and eight mosques burnt to the ground. Unfortunately, this mayhem stands out only because the Western press reported it; worse bouts of religiously inspired rioting in Nigeria have resulted in much higher death tolls.

Religious ire mixed with hatred for corrupt Arab rulers partly motivated the hijackers of September 11 to attack their regimes' main ally, the United States. The people of oil-rich Nigeria are much, much poorer, and corruption is worse. In 2001 Transparency International rated Nigeria the second most corrupt country in the world. Despite $280 billion worth of oil revenues (as of the year 2000), per capita income over the past twenty years has dropped from $1,000 to $290 a year and continues to fall. Gas stations run dry for weeks at a time as officials divert fuel to the black market to be sold at a 300 percent markup. Electricity and running water fail for as long as twelve hours a day; roads have decayed; the phone system barely functions; and crime is widespread and violent. Now ranking number 148 on the United Nations' Human Development Index (behind Bangladesh and Haiti), oil-rich Nigeria may justly be called the largest failed state on earth, dwarfing Afghanistan in every miserable respect; it is the ground zero of African despair and rage. We ignore what happens there, and in the rest of the Sahel (which is poorer and, in places, even more conflict-ridden), at our peril.

So, the September 11 attacks and a macabre enchantment with Kano impelled me to travel the Sahel and find out what was going on there. In 2002 I began researching a 4,000-mile journey that would take me throughout its fabled domains (or most of them; I excluded Sudan from my itinerary for two reasons: the civil war in its south had closed the border with Chad, and I expected difficulty in obtaining a visa). My eyes swam over the bizarre names of remote towns on my maps and in my history books: Abéché of the Wadai kingdom in windswept eastern Chad; Fada and Faya Largeau, war-battered oasis settlements deep in the land-mined north of the Chadian Sahara, near Libya; Sokoto, once the seat of the first Muslim fundamentalist caliphate in Africa and now the spiritual capital of Nigerian Islam; Zinder in Niger, for a long time the bastion of a slave-trading sultanate; Gao and Timbuktu, lodestars of some of Europe's most daring and ill-starred adventurers, and the main cities of the Songhai empire in Mali. But would I make it to Timbuktu? Flights had been suspended; the Niger would be too low for navigation by the time I could arrive (in the winter dry season); and bandits were said to haunt the desert tracks leading there. Djenné, the jewel of the Sahel, was on my itinerary, and from there I hoped to move on to Mali's capital, Bamako. At the end of this sand-blown, heat-hazed route stood Dakar, the whitewashed, seabreezy capital of prosperous Senegal, gleaming in my mind's eye brighter than it ever could on earth.

I knew three languages of the Sahel: French, Arabic, and English. All three tongues were introduced by the region's invaders and conquerors, and, though not always spoken fluently, they still provide many of the Sahel's diverse peoples with vital lingua francas. In some ways Arabic, the most 'native' (that is, spoken before the arrival of the Europeans) of the three, could be considered the most controversial. The Arabs began penetrating the Sahel in the eighth century, both as traders and as warriors bent on Islamicizing the region by force. The Arab influx reached its peak when in the sixteenth century Moroccans crossed the desert and vanquished the Songhai empire, seizing control of the trans-Saharan trade and subjugating much of the region.

Would my speaking Arabic, coupled with my American nationality, provoke hostility, especially since the United States was declaring ever more loudly its intentions to invade Iraq?

I didn't know. But I wanted to hear out the people of the Sahel, to record and transmit their grievances, and to learn their views on the conflict between the West and the Islamic world. Now as never before, we on this planet find our lives interconnected, wherever we are. As September 11 showed, those whom power, distance, means, and circumstance would exclude from discourse can, suddenly and with consummate ferocity, emerge from the remotest redoubts to make their voices heard.

Apart from religion, one other thing characterizes the Sahel: the Harmattan. From east to west, the Harmattan blows, parching these unruly barrens, uniting the Sahel under a thrashing veil of red dust. Had the gales of the Harmattan buried the last traces of the empires and kingdoms of which I was reading? I longed to find out.

# 1

# MAHAMAT OF N'DJAMENA

It was the afternoon rush hour in N'Djamena. Over the craters and potholes of the dirt-track avenue Charles de Gaulle, alongside gutters gurgling with iridescent waste, moved brass bed frames and soapwood bookcases on carts dragged by sweating boys, their toes curling into the dust, the long white cotton kadmuls wrapped around their heads fluttering in the breeze like banners of surrender. Following the boys, donkeys dragged wheeled tables stacked with tottering pots and rattling pans, swaying bolts of silk. Next came plump women swathed in blue and yellow milhafa wraps and flamboyant floral scarves, ululating and clapping; after them danced ebony-skinned striplings in ankle-length caftans. The parade, a dowry procession heading to a Muslim bride's new home, held up traffic – hand-levered tricycles carrying polio victims with shriveled legs; beeping mopeds backfiring exhaust; Peugeot taxis with cracked windshields and sagging fenders; tall Hausa butchers balancing sides of beef atop their turbaned heads; short Sara Christians in trousers and T-shirts. Over all, columns of rising dust roamed in the coppery light of the failing sun and melted away into the haggard canopies of roadside neem trees.

Facing the avenue, Mahamat and I sat cross-legged at the Champion d'Afrique *jizara* – a butcher's stand restaurant consisting of a brazier, a bast mat, a straw roof, and one straw wall in back. This airy arrangement let in the breeze but also the dust and the flies and the squawking, querulous birds and the occasional runty, flea-chewed dog of the type so common in African cities. Using our fingers, we dipped chunks of freshly grilled beef in a bowl of *shatta* (red pepper sauce) and popped them into our mouths. Sitting in the warm shade, intoxicated with the aroma of meat roasting on the brazier, I felt myself relaxing for the first time since my arrival. Just twenty-four hours before I had been hurrying around fogbound, frigid Paris, running errands and checking e-mail. Now that dismal clime and its worries belonged to another life.

'What decent colonial power would make a dirt road the main boulevard of their colony's capital?' Mahamat demanded in his baritone. 'It's a disgrace! The French left nothing behind here, nothing!'

Chad just never got any respect. Scorching hot, battered by the Harmattan, and mostly desert, with a population enamored of slaving and raiding, Chad inspired dread in French colonial officers, who regarded a posting in Fort Lamy (as N'Djamena was known then) as tantamount to banishment to one of the more unfashionable outer planets. Accordingly, the outcasts and losers of French officialdom found themselves posted here, and at least one historian has noted that it was impossible to be too demented or depraved to evade service in Chad. In fact, Fort Lamy's lieutenant governors had little to do here but pat the sweat from their brows and swig tepid Chablis: *Tchad utile* (the more fertile land in the south) was really ruled from Brazzaville, in the French Congo; and a military administrator in the desert outpost of Faya Largeau ran the rebellious Saharan regions to the north. The French administrators never managed to tame Chad's warlike tribes, and contented themselves with exporting the territory's two resources – raw cotton and unskilled laborers – before being reassigned to more agreeable colonies.

Those, however, turned out to be the good old days. Since independence, Chad's history has been a chronicle of chaos and slaughter relieved by famine and drought. Muslims and Christians have massacred one another and fought for power; the

Libyans have invaded and been driven out; there have been assassinations and coups, droughts and locust plagues and more droughts. The current president, Idriss Déby, came to power in a French-supported coup in 1990 but 'legitimized' himself through elections in 2001. The violence has mostly stemmed from one underlying fact: the 'country' of Chad is really a mess of mutually hostile regions united by the French to serve the interests of Paris. Muslims make up about half the population and live mostly in the north, while the Christian third of the population inhabits the south; N'Djamena, situated roughly in the middle, is mixed.

I had met Mahamat the previous day after asking my hotel receptionist to call me a cab. Into the lobby marched a broad-shouldered black man with a sparse beard and receding hairline. He appeared to be in his late thirties. With his imperious flair and prominent belly, and dressed in an immaculate white caftan and baggy white sirwal trousers, he looked more like an Islamic potentate than a taxi driver, and I found him somewhat intimidating.

I knew most Chadians spoke a dialect of Arabic, but having just dealt with the hotel clerk in French, I addressed him in French, too, asking what it might cost me to rent his taxi for the day. Looking down his nose at me, he struggled for words and answered gruffly that his fee was *discutable*.

Realizing my error, I switched to Arabic, greeting him with '*As-salam 'alaykum!*' (May the peace be upon you!) and telling him that my name in Arabic was Jelal.

His eyes shone. 'Are you Lebanese?'

'No, American. But I've spent a long time living in the Arab world.'

'American?' He clasped my hands and shook his head. 'Jelal, it's wonderful to speak Arabic to you! No one would even believe you *could* be American, since you all think of us Arabs as evil and wouldn't speak our language. Come, *ya khay* [my brother], let me show you to my car.'

Mahamat swaggered out the hotel door, his caftan billowing in the breeze. Just outside stood an old brown Peugeot. He opened the door for me.

'So does everyone speak Arabic here?' I asked, climbing in.

'Pretty much. But our Arabic has been influenced by the *'ajam* [non-Arabs, barbarians] we have living with us.' Here he cast a glance at a pair of passing Sara Christians, recognizable by their Western dress. 'They adopted the language after we Arabs arrived, so you may have trouble understanding some people here.' Mahamat spoke correct classical Arabic as well as the Chadian dialect.

We drove out of the hotel lot. Now that Mahamat had called me 'brother,' his bulk and demeanor comforted me, which was good: I was nervous about touring N'Djamena – a seething dusty slum of 700,000 people, mostly dirt roads, one-story tin shacks, and low cement buildings riddled with bullets from years of civil war. With its poverty, high population growth, and history of violence, much of N'Djamena was said to be unsafe in the daytime and all of it dangerous at night, even for locals. The matronly hotel clerk who had sold me a map (a useless investment, I soon learned: streets had no signs) warned me, 'Wherever you go here, walk like a man, or thugs will strip you naked and steal your shoes! You're white, after all!' My skin would not evoke racist animosity, but it would announce to thieves the presence of a relatively rich man in a country where the CFA (Communauté financière africaine) franc equivalent of two hundred dollars a year made for a decent wage.

Mahamat, I sensed, had the sort of charge-ahead charisma one feared rather than admired. This aura even extended to his ancient Peugeot. As we drove through the Christian crowds near the hotel, he maintained his speed and a steady banter about his life as people jumped and skipped in panic out of our way. He told me he operated a taxi only because salaries were sporadically paid at the high school where he practiced his true profession: teaching Arabic. If his skin was black, his language was Arabic and his religion was Islam, so he considered himself Arab. (Only 15 percent of Chad's population is ethnically Arab, though Arabic is spoken by a majority.) But most important, he was the son of the former chief imam of N'Djamena and traced his lineage back to the arrival of the Babiliya tribe from Iraq in the ninth or tenth century. Ancestry, faith, and language determined status and identity here, not profession or even talent: he was a noble. The '*ajam* to whom he had referred had had 'only' nine centuries to master Arabic, but in his view this wasn't enough.

'We came to Chad,' Mahamat said, 'to conquer and proclaim the *da'wa* [the call to Islam]. We found the natives worshiping idols, so we defeated them and converted them. We've married them, but we've kept our '*uruba* [Arabness].'

I told Mahamat I had to register with the police – a requirement about which the officer at airport customs had informed me with some urgency. 'Very necessary,' Mahamat said. 'They're suspicious of foreigners here.'

We took a turn for the police station as a wind raised clouds of dust that blew over the herds of goats and cattle meandering down the dirt road.

'Is this the Harmattan?' I asked.

'No. By the way, we call the Harmattan 'Garwa' in Chadian Arabic.' The wind, I was to learn, has local names throughout its domain. 'Harmattan is what the Nasranis' – Nazarenes or Christians, but more generally white people – 'call it. When the Garwa blows, the sky turns dark with dust and the nights are cold. It's a curse, the Garwa.'

As we trundled toward the police station, I told Mahamat my plans for Chad: I wanted to travel to Abéché, 450 miles to the northeast, and from there head due north into the Sahara to the oasis settlements of Fada and Faya Largeau. He listened to me but said nothing, and I thought I saw his brow furrow. His silence made me feel that I was talking nonsense.

We drove onto the sandy lot in front of the police station, a low, unremarkable cement building.

'If you manage to make it to Abéché,' Mahamat said, 'you'll have to protect yourself from the Garwa. It will freeze you solid at night.'

'Why do you say if I "manage to make it"?'

'My brother Jelal, you're in Chad. You're white, and when we see a white person, we think of money. You'll have to be very careful. I spent four years working in Abéché, so I know the situation out there. Always when we Chadians leave the capital, we say, '*Tawakkalna 'ala Allah!*' [We rely on God!] There're bandits and rebels out there, and our soldiers are a menace. We know only war. War is the way of Chad.'

'But what about the truce the government just signed with the rebels?'

'It won't last. How could it? Before the French made us one country, we were four different kingdoms with four separate rulers. No, peace will not last, *ya khay.*' His voice hoarsened. 'I've seen people killed in front of me in the streets here, when N'Djamena was split between two guerilla groups. I know what people are capable of.'

I got out and walked into the station, easing my way into an office crowded with men in white turbans (kadmuls, as Chadians called them) and white caftans. The men were indifferent to my presence, which I found comforting. A notice in French on the wall read, WE ARE ALL CITIZENS OF THE WORLD, OF THE SAME EARTH, OF THE SAME BLOOD. IT MAKES NO SENSE TO HATE SOMEONE BECAUSE OF HIS SKIN COLOR OR BECAUSE OF WHERE HE WAS BORN.

Three stern officers in caftans sat behind desks in front of sagging shelves stacked with yellowed documents. One man, looking dyspeptic and fatigued, took my passport and recorded its details in a register, and then passed it over to the next man, who examined it with glum assiduity, never glancing at me, and emitted an irritated sigh. I handed him the required photograph. He returned my passport with an elaborate stamp placed next to my visa, showing the head of a scarved woman encircled with the words, in French, REPUBLIC OF CHAD – MINISTRY OF THE INTERIOR AND ADMINISTRATION OF TERRITORY. DEPARTMENT OF THE EXPLOITATION OF FOREIGNERS.

'Exploitation of foreigners'? Beneath that was marked, SEEN AND REGISTERED on 19-12-02 – a notation that I could, if stopped, show to authorities as proof that I had complied with the law.

Back in the car, I showed the stamp to Mahamat. He remarked on the woman. 'The French scoured the country to find that woman to model for our national stamp – she really existed. But we as Muslims would have *never* put a woman's face on our symbol. It's against Islam. Our state is secular now, so they kept her, and of course we were run by a bunch of Christians in the beginning.'

It was already noon and I had not breakfasted, so I told Mahamat I would like to eat. He suggested Champion d'Afrique, a *jizara* run by Hausa butchers 'brought here by the French to cut meat. We Chadians don't know much about butchering.' With the sun dousing the dusty streets in a glare that hurt my eyes, we set off down the chopped-up dirt roads, fording crowds in caftans and kadmuls, honking to scatter goats, our destination avenue Charles de Gaulle. The gusty wind kept all the kadmuls and caftans trailing and flapping. I marveled at the scene: this was black Africa in Arab garb, something new and exciting to me.

After lunch we drove back toward my hotel, passing through the center of town, where, unlike elsewhere, buildings rose above one story and there was a slapdash but well-patronized Lebanese-run shop called Wissam's that Mahamat referred to as the *supermarché* – the best, and one of the few, such stores in Chad.

We drove onto a paved road, another rare sight here. Soon, on the left appeared a yellow-walled compound with soldiers squatting and chatting in front of a barred gate, their rifles on their knees. Mahamat pulled into the far-right lane and slowed, as did everyone else. Without turning his head he spoke through clenched teeth.

'That's the president's compound.'

'That?' I asked, pointing to the gate.

'Don't point!' he said, teeth still clenched, eyes forward. 'For God's sake, don't point! And look straight ahead!'

We bounced slowly past the compound, sitting stiffly in our seats.

Afterward, Mahamat relaxed. 'It's illegal to point at it. They could stop me and demand to know why I'm showing a foreigner the compound. Worse, worse . . . the American ambassador's wife once made the mistake of stopping near there. The soldiers opened fire on her car. It was bulletproof, but the incident threw the city into an uproar.'

More than three decades of civil war, coups, and assassinations, plus the violence of the colonial era and centuries of raiding, had instilled a trenchant atmosphere of fear between rulers and ruled. I was reminded of a paradoxical truth I had observed in other perennially troubled countries: even years of peace can seem an unreal interlude, with war the natural, comprehensible, and thus recurring state of affairs.

We continued toward my hotel. But all at once soldiers were waving their guns and billy clubs and shouting, directing traffic onto a dirt road. Cars ahead bounced off the tarmac, and so did we; pedestrians jumped out of the way, and the resulting mayhem threw up so much dust we could barely see.

'What's going on?'

'The president's motorcade must be coming. They're clearing the road. No one must see him.'

At every turn amid the neems and squat houses more soldiers were waving. The sun was setting, the dust swirling in dense gilt clouds. Finally, more soldiers motioned us off the dirt road, and our column of cars made tracks through dusty fields. The Hotel Tchadienne loomed ahead. The cars slowed into a bottleneck.

Ahead of us a young woman teetered on white high heels among the cars, swearing at the drivers, swatting the dust from her olive green pantsuit. Her braided, hennaed mane reached to her waist; her breasts and hips were round and bouncy. She clutched a white purse that was rapidly browning with the dust.

She caught the eye in a city where even Christian women went about covered up. A little boy on a bicycle stopped next to us and, winking at me, licked his lips with a lasciviousness far too advanced for his years. '*C'est bon! C'est bon, comme le bonbon!*' ('She's sweet! She's sweet as candy!')

'An '*azaba* from Cameroon,' said Mahamat flatly, ignoring the boy, his eyes steadily following the woman.

'An '*azaba*?' A similar word in classical Arabic meant, roughly, 'unmarried girl.'

'An '*azaba* . . . you know, a *qahba*' – a whore.

A soldier ordered her to retreat the way she had come. We backed up and began looking for a free road to the hotel.

The next day the sun rose quickly above the Chari River, turning its cool dark waters into panes of molten glass, hardening into stark silhouettes the misty shadows of fishermen casting nets from dugout canoes. On the low banks a giant lizard scampered out of dry grass into the warming light. Above, doves hurtled by on whistling wings, hawks lazed on updrafts, mounting the deepening azure. Across the water, where the fulvous barrens of Cameroon (with which the Chari forms Chad's border) spread to a crisply cut western horizon, herds of cattle driven by boys in smocks were on the move, lumbering along with heads and horns lowered, kicking up low clouds of dust. Looking at the river from my hotel room balcony, I sensed that whatever has happened elsewhere on the planet, here the river and the land have always awakened this way; and this scene offered me peace.

Mahamat was waiting for me in the lobby. His brows were furrowed for real now.

'I've been doing some asking around,' he said. 'This trip you want to make to Abéché – it's not so easy. Before we even see how you can get there, you'll need to get a permit to leave the capital.'

'Where?'

'At the police.'

It turned out that I had to apply to the government body that had been recently created to handle such matters and held jurisdiction over foreigners: the Ministry for the Development of Tourism.

With its shady neems and the pensive, clucking guinea fowl perched on its stucco walls, the Ministry, a couple of two-story stucco buildings near the river, looked to be a place to grow old and die in, an idyll well removed from the dangers either within or beyond N'Djamena's boundaries. We approached the guard who handled permits, and he directed us to the office of the director of hotels, on the second floor.

Mahamat flung open the door and strode in ahead of me, his

caftan flaring into a cape, and greeted the director with a boisterous 'As-salam 'alaykum!' The director, a stately middle-aged
Muslim in blue robes and a blue fez-shaped cap, seemed not to
mind this brashness and motioned us to have a seat. We then all
exchanged the usual pleasantries – lengthy formulaic inquiries
about health and male members of the family. In Arabic, only the
most trivial matters are conducted without ceremony; real business must appear to be an afterthought tacked on to elaborately
expressed concerns for the health and relations of people one
might not know at all. This ritual slows life down to a pleasant and
humane pace, the advantages of which Westerners often discount.

After the greetings, I mentioned to the director offhandedly
that I wanted to go to Abéché and, if possible, north into the
Sahara.

He nodded and smiled and nodded again. 'Well, our president
is from Fada, and he's resting out there, since the weather's now
so cool.'

'That sounds reassuring.' I smiled and digested his words. The
president's presence in the region would mean extra troops and
police; that is, real and present danger. In Africa the security
forces are often thieves and bandits, as Mahamat had reminded
me.

'How do you want to travel?' he asked.

'I'd like to rent a Land Rover and a driver.'

'I'm sorry, but that's not the best idea. You shouldn't go alone
like that. You see, well, people have this idea based on our past
that Chad is a place where bandits kill people on the roads, out in
the desert . . . Ah, anyway, you should go with others. There's a
piste, so there should be a bus.'

'I'll find out about that for him,' said Mahamat.

'Thank you,' said the director. 'But you will need a permit, or
our soldiers could create problems for you, real trouble. That's the
way it is here. We've had war for a long time.' He stood up. 'Mai
will be happy to help you with the permit.'

The director led us downstairs and around the side of the
building and pointed out Mai's office. It was marked DIREC-
TORATE OF THE PROMOTION OF TOURISM.

We knocked and opened the rickety screen door. Inside a dusty yellow room was a thin avuncular man with a flat nose and a pointy chin. He sat with his ankles together and knees apart, his toes splayed on the crossbeam beneath his desk. He had salt-and-pepper hair and wore Western dress (slacks and a long-sleeved shirt). He looked as absorbed as Gauguin at his easel as he daubed whiteout onto a piece of paper, huffed on the wet splotches, and daubed again.

'*As-salam 'alaykum!*' I said.

He glanced up at us and then back at the paper. Huff-huff, another daub, and a sniffle. He squinted at the splotches, and I half expected him to judge their scale with his thumb. He cleared his throat and looked up.

'*Oui?*'

Mahamat pushed past me and swaggered into the room. 'This American needs a permit to go to Abéché, Fada, and Faya. The director says you issue permits.'

Lowering his head again, the man wiggled his toes, took the brush out of the whiteout bottle and licked it, and continued with his splotching. He cleared his throat and sniffled, making a persnickety grimace as he did so.

He responded in French. 'Excuse me. There are procedures to be followed. It's not quite so simple as that.' Huff. Sniffle. 'Not so simple at *all*.' Huff-huff, daub.

'Well, could you please tell me what these procedures are?' I asked, starting in Arabic but switching to French. My words sounded abrupt to me, and I wondered what had happened to the greeting ritual.

I glanced over at Mahamat. Disdain washed over his face as he towered over the barefoot man.

'I'm *quite* busy,' Mai answered. 'As you *may* have noticed.'

'I understand, but if you could spare a moment to explain what I need to do . . .'

He motioned for us to sit in the chairs in front of his desk and then undertook ten minutes of huffing and splotching. Mahamat shifted in his seat and sighed loudly, rubbed his face with fatigue, and sighed again.

Finally Mai looked up. 'For *personal* reasons,' he said, 'my boss, who is the minister herself, isn't here today. You file a request for an *autorisation de circuler*, which must be approved at the highest levels. The *highest*. Travel here is not so easy. The minister of public security himself will issue the permit, *if* you are approved and *if* he so desires.'

I asked him what filing a request entailed.

'Writing a *personal* letter, in your name, asking for permission to travel, and stating your itinerary and mode of transport. The wording must be as follows' – here he closed his eyes and spoke as if quoting scripture – '"To Her Excellency: I am honored to solicit through the good offices of your intermediary a permit to circulate between N'Djamena, Abéché, Fada, and Faya Largeau, traveling by local means of interurban transport. Thanking you in advance, I request that you please accept my most distinguished sentiments."' He sniffled. '*Voilà*.'

Mahamat rolled his eyes, and I feared Mai might notice and take offense and then refuse to deal with me. But his epistolary apostrophe completed, Mai looked down, took up his whiteout again, licked the brush, and asked us to please return in the morning.

Back at the car, Mahamat was steaming. 'He's a very inefficient man and he's just trying to delay us, to cause you problems, and to get you to pay a bribe. That, that *janubi!* [southerner!] For us, southerners here are like *dogs!*'

Now I understood what was bothering Mahamat, and it went far beyond this particular persnickety, splay-toed bureaucrat. The Muslims of the desert north had historically preyed on the pagans of the south, raiding them and enslaving them all the way until the 1920s. During the French occupation, the southerners thus chose to cooperate with the colonial powers against the north, and also to adopt Christianity, which made them even more despicable in the northerners' eyes. Chad's first president, Ngarta Tombalbaye, had been a Sara Christian southerner who had received initial (and hasty) plaudits from the West to the effect of, 'Look how a Christian can rule in a mainly Muslim country!

Pluralism and tolerance and reconciliation!' However, it soon transpired that tolerance was not among Tombalbaye's virtues: he filled the jails and torture chambers with his political opponents; he banned all political parties except his own; he began 'Africanizing' the government, or, as Muslims said, 'southernizing' it, outlawing turbans and beards; he imposed arbitrary taxes on all; and he sent Christians to govern territories in the north that had never before been ruled by southerners. Proud northerners couldn't bear the affronts visited on them by infidel southerners whom they still considered little better than chattel. Or dogs.

As we were getting into the car, Mahamat spotted a cousin who worked in the ministry and called him over. The cousin told us we should have come to him in the first place. He took us back up to the director of hotels and exchanged a few words with him. The director came out and again greeted us warmly and exclaimed, 'Follow me!' He addressed Mahamat. 'Please forgive me! I didn't know you were family!'

He led us back to Mai's office and commanded in Arabic from the doorway, 'This American must have his permit immediately. Get to work on it.'

'Yes, sir,' answered Mai, popping the whiteout brush back into its bottle.

The director watched the southerner begin to indite the text of the official letter that would accompany my personal request for a permit. After a few minutes he wished us well and returned to his office.

No sooner had his footsteps pattered back up the stairs than Mai set aside the letter, took out his whiteout, and began splotching and huffing on another document. He wobbled his head. 'Yours is not the *only* request I have to deal with,' he said in a piqued tenor.

An hour later, after endless sniffles and huffs, Mai finished my letter. He said that if we wanted the permit today, we would have to drive him to the Ministry of Public Security for the requisite ministerial signature. Fine.

A ten-minute ride around a few corners and down a dirt road brought us to another placid compound under more neems. As we walked into the reception room, I asked Mai if his name meant 'king' in Sara, as I had heard. It did. Mahamat snorted derisively. Behind the desk, under a twirling fan, sat the secretary – a neat, light-skinned Muslim in a blue caftan and blue cap, apparel that apparently constituted the uniform of distinction here. He was typing on a computer. A bottle of whiteout sat on his desk next to a copy of a letter. Now and then he applied splotches of the liquid to a letter and huffed on them, then went on pecking at his keyboard.

Mai asked us to wait by the door, and walked up to the desk. Speaking French, Mai asked for the secretary's attention.

Huff-huff, tap-tap-tap on the computer, daub-huff-daub. Without looking at Mai, the secretary slowly extended his hand and wiggled his fingers. Mai handed him his letter.

The secretary read it and began shaking his head. He spoke in Arabic. 'This is all wrong, all wrong. First of all, the minister has left for Friday prayers and so naturally won't be able to sign anything until next week. But moreover and most of all, your letter is from director to *director*, whereas it should be from minister to *minister*. How could you have made this mistake? How? This is the most elemental rule: *your* minister requests the permit from *my* minister, and then my minister takes the appropriate decision at his *ministerial* level, and signs or not, as the case may be, and according to his judgment of documents presented . . .'

Mai squirmed. 'Yes, but . . .'

'But what? This is obvious. This is a rule accepted all over the world.' He looked to me for confirmation. I glanced away, not wanting to give Mai more reason to resent me. 'No, no, no. Unacceptable.' He thrust the letter away. '*Absolutely* unacceptable. You'll have to redo it.' He took the whiteout and returned to his daubing and huffing.

We walked out. The permit would have to wait until Monday morning.

# 2

## PARI-VENTE

Mahamat told me that the name *N'Djamena* was the
Africanized version of the Arabic *irtahna* ('We rested/had a
good time'). After all, had not his tribe, driven by a God-granted
zeal to spread Islam and conquer scorners of the *da'wa*, earned its
repose on the banks of the Chari River, following such a long
trek across the desert from Iraq? His tribe's sacred mission, executed a thousand years ago, plus his faith and status as the son of
the city's former chief imam, endowed him with an impregnable
self-confidence and determined his behavior toward the people
around us. I grew up with no such certainties and no mission; I
spread no holy word and heeded no *da'wa*; I possessed no
immutable criteria by which to judge people. Believing myself to
be a child of the Enlightenment, I told myself that I wanted no
certitudes beyond those determined by reason for the good of
people, but spending time with Mahamat and enjoying both the
spectacle he provided as he sauntered through the crowds, ever
commanding, and the protection he offered me as his charge, I
soon came to see that his world was a grand one: my 'enlightened'
malleability could not match his faith-based surety. I could not be
certain and he could be; if there was a conflict, I might doubt and
fret, but he would seize the sword and slash.

His certainty led me to extrapolate: Might there not have been
something almost Darwinian about Islam's advance in the Sahel?

The faith-ordained rewards and punishments motivated Muslims to fight their enemies hard, perhaps much harder than the pagans they confronted. Maybe fervid faith was a cultural trait that furthered the survival of its bearers. *Irtahna* did, however, suit the spirit of the city. Even before arriving, I had heard that, despite a tragic past and poverty and the ever-present threat of civil war, or perhaps on account of them, a party spirit ruled N'Djamena on weekends, and people there rested and had a good time.

I soon had evidence of this in hand: a xeroxed flier in French festooned on one side with images (apparently lifted from a 1950s Western movie theater advert) of ducktailed revelers clutching buckets of popcorn and sitting goggle-eyed, as if at a drive-in theater watching a Godzilla flick, and on the other side with black stick figures dancing with a distinctly African, bandy-legged aplomb. The text read:

### INVITATION

Madame Christine will be very very *hyper*-happy to count you among her illustrious *invités* at the reopening party of the general store B., which will take place the 25th of December 2002 starting at 10:00 a.m. and last till dawn in the Moursal district.

*Voilà!* An occasion you won't want to miss! Fresh beer and hors d'oeuvres and a warm welcome await you!

*Merci d'avance*

The flier announced a curious tippling tradition peculiar to N'Djamena: that of the *pari-vente*. Local women (Christians, of course), to make money and have fun, get together and rent out a premises, usually a bar or nightclub, invite their friends, and advertise among people they know to be safe as well as moneyed. The women serve the drinks and food themselves at marked-up prices, which, along with the limited guest list, keeps out the riffraff.

I wanted to attend this *pari-vente*, but since I hoped to be in Abéché by Christmas, I asked Mahamat to find me another. He did. Since he was Muslim, I invited him to join me with some hesitation (I feared he might take offense, since alcohol would be served), but he agreed immediately, saying he would sip a Coke while I enjoyed a beer.

Under a cobalt canopy jeweled with diamond stars and the bulkier gems of planets, Mahamat and I bounced down dark and deserted alleys in his Peugeot in search of the Zamzam Club – the site of one of the three *pari-ventes* to be held that evening in town. Traveling around a huge, unlit city at night is an experience to which I was not accustomed. However much I admired the sky, we were riding through crowded and collapsing warrens of anger and poverty and despair, and I was afraid; I strained nervously to discern whether shadows swaying at the roadside were threatening thugs or peaceable palms.

We rounded a corner. Wild-eyed men jumped out into the road, blocking our way and brandishing clubs and shouting. But not to worry: they were just soldiers out doing their road-closing duty; the vice president was going to pass by. We turned off onto a narrow side street and kept going.

Clouds of dust kicked up by cars drifted through our head-lights, giving us, or me, the sensation of being lost in the desert under a brown fog. Finally, a restaurant-club glowed with bright green neon lights: the *pari-vente*.

We pulled up next to the open sewer opposite the club. Two youths in rags wandered over, stopped just behind Mahamat's door, and started a casual conversation in Sara, or feigned one. There seemed to be something forced about their mannerisms and talk, even to me, who could not understand their language.

Mahamat cut the engine. 'Don't get out just yet,' he said, look-ing at the teenagers in his rearview mirror.

'Why?'

He kept his eyes on the mirror. A moment later he took a deep breath and rolled down the window. 'Hey, you!'

'*Oui?*'

'Get away from my car.'

'We're just having a talk.'

'Talk somewhere else.'

'Oh? Who're you to —'

Mahamat swung open the door, jumped out, and thrust his bulk toward them, his caftan whooshing into a V. 'I said, GET AWAY FROM MY CAR!'

'*On y va! On y va!*' They skittered off into the velvety dark, their sandals flapping.

'You have to be careful,' Mahamat said calmly, opening the door for me. 'In the Christian quarters there're a lot of thieves.'

I got out and followed the V of Mahamat's caftan into the club. This was a simple arrangement of cement rooms around a sandy courtyard, where benches were scattered next to a concrete dance floor tinted green and blue by pale neon lights. Dancers swayed to Kinshasan pop, the tinny, salsa-sounding music so beloved in Africa. Though there were a few Muslim men about (recognizable by their caftans), most people were Christians in Western dress, chatting and sipping beers from foot-tall brown bottles, and now and then shooing away mosquitoes. Immediately I felt relaxed: the warm breeze, the stars, the lilting music, the smiles, and the hazy green light all gave the place the atmosphere of an episode from the past remembered in a dream.

In fact, I felt as though I had seen this or something like it before. But where?

I soon remembered: in Zaire, along the Congo River, in a bar at the jungle's edge, on the equator. Besides the music, the smiles and easy atmosphere seemed the same. But in the Zairean bar I was terrified of my impending solo descent of the river in a dugout canoe. Now, here in N'Djamena, in an open-air bar among bullet-riddled shacks, I felt I could relax and enjoy Africa the way I had hoped to for so long. Mahamat had much to do with this, and the dry desert air helped too. The muggy heat of the jungle makes fear stickily, sickly palpable.

A plump *janubiyya* came over to take our order. I ordered a beer for myself and a Fanta for Mahamat. I paid her in advance, as was the custom.

She returned the change to me. Mahamat grabbed it from my palm, checked the amount, and nodded his approval. 'I spent many good years as a student in places like this, you know? I haven't come to a *pari-vente* since 1990. I'd forgotten how relaxing they are. But now, with a wife and a daughter, I have responsibilities. I think of my family first.' He smiled as he said this: the responsibility was not a burden but something he valued.

Earlier that day we had stopped by his house – four cement rooms around an immaculate sandy courtyard. To my surprise, he introduced his wife to me, and did so proudly. In most traditional Islamic households male guests would not meet female members of the family. Her name was 'Aisha, and she was a shy and slender teenager with exquisite features who, when she saw me, slowly, with amazement, pulled her veil to her face. The daughter on her arm, Fatima, was already two. 'Aisha gave me Fatima to hold, but the child recoiled from my white face and began crying.

'You really love your wife, don't you?' I asked, thinking of the visit.

'I do – I married for love, unlike most Muslims. And I waited to get married until I had money enough to support her. She's my cousin – we marry our cousins to keep money in our family – and she's only sixteen. But, ah, I have a question. She was thirteen when I brought her from our village and married her. Could I have married her in your country at that age?'

'No, I think not.'

'I didn't think so. But here, that's the marrying age. There's nothing lustful about marrying such a young girl. But I know you Nasranis don't do it.' He paused and looked at his Fanta. 'All the same, it's most important to me to support the family and be honest. You see, with age, men change. At twenty-five I could think of only one thing. Now, at thirty-seven, I'm calmer, the blood cools, and I take my responsibilities seriously.'

'I know what you mean. I never expected to marry, but now that I have I'm very happy.'

'I help my brothers and my mother,' he went on to say. 'I even . . . I even think of death. I'm of that age, you know.' The breeze turned chilly, and he clutched his caftan. 'You see, I lost my father not long ago. Just before he died, at one hundred and five, I saw him staring into the sky. I said, 'Father, what are you looking at?' He didn't answer for a while, but then he turned and looked at me. 'Don't worry. I'm thinking of the next life.' He was looking beyond this life into the heavens, and he was pleased. He was, in a way, already beyond us all.'

Mahamat evinced no sadness in recounting this: his father, a man of piety and Islamic erudition, had merited a place in paradise and was only to be envied now. Death for him was a topic solemn but not grievous.

The music turned to slower, wailing Sudanese tunes. I shuddered, partly on account of the cold, but mostly because his words, aided by the music, awakened dormant memories. In 1987 I had been called to the bedside of my dying grandfather. He looked at me with something like benumbed astonishment, as if he were already on his way and there was nothing left here for him, not even me, and too much distance separated us – the distance between an elder relinquishing life for oblivion and a youth for whom death was just a word. I belonged to the past he was about to lose. He did not look pleased, as Mahamat said his father had.

Mahamat's voice returned me to the *pari-vente*. 'So, you and I have reached the middle of our lives. We will die when God wills.'

I nodded agreement, but I didn't believe in an end determined by Providence, or in Providence, for that matter. How often during my travels I had felt unbridgeable gaps of culture and faith and worldview between myself and others. Even though I have spoken Arabic for almost two decades, I have felt this alienation especially strongly in Arab countries. The concepts of life and death and love and family assume, in Arabic, verbal garb so embroidered with religion as to seem nearly unrecognizable to Westerners.

Still, listening to Mahamat, and knowing his world could have hardly differed more from mine, I understood that our objective experiences were the same – we had lost loved ones who carried parts of our pasts to their graves, and that hurt. We diverged in how we dealt with the loss. He could accept the death and perhaps even take comfort in thinking that his father was now beyond the pale of N'Djamena's poverty and violence, reclining in the ethereal pavilions of paradise. About my grandfather's passing I still ached with bereavement, though it was now softened somewhat by the years. So, my beliefs would have had little to offer him, should I have shared them. Again, wasn't there something Darwinian about his faith, which comforted him with notions of eternity? My barren eschatological speculations left me with no hope of outlasting my own breath and heartbeat. After a few moments of silence, Mahamat spoke. 'My brother Jelal, no American ever spoke Arabic to me before you. Nasranis always want to live apart from us Africans. They don't want to talk our language or know us . . . Listen, if you get your permit and *do* take a bus or a truck to Abéché, you're going to have to be careful. Can you pray?'

'I'm not Muslim. So, no, I can't.'

'Remember, we say, *'Tawakkalna 'ala Allah!'* when heading out of the capital. People are not going to understand how you can speak Arabic but not be a Muslim. It will arouse suspicion. I want you to make good friends with your driver, whoever he is. Once you leave the capital, you are in the wilds, and you may need his help.'

I did not want to think about this yet. I sipped my beer and looked up at the sky, now a brilliant wash of stars against a black infinity; these same stars looked down, I thought, on my wife in Moscow and my family in the States. The same stars would gleam over me as I traveled east across the Sahel to Abéché. Comforting notions, these, but Mahamat's words reminded me that life happens here and now, and that one must think ahead to survive.

I finished my beer. The music switched back to Congolese pop, but the tunes now offered me nothing, after so much dismal rumination. We left the *pari-vente* and headed back into the dark street, where ragged youths still loitered near the walls and set hungry eyes on us; they too had to eat. But this time they left us alone.

# 3

# THE PISTE TO WADAI

'The bus to Abéché might not be running,' Mahamat announced grimly the next day as we drove out of the hotel lot into a wearying wash of hot sun and floating dust. 'You may have to go to Abéché by way of Faya, and atop a truck. Not many trucks make the trip, so we should ask now at the *teshsha*.'

'What's that?'

'That's dialect for "road station."'

His frown reminded me of what I would have to face on leaving N'Djamena.

'Is it true the desert is still mined?'

'Mined? Remember, when we leave the capital we say, "*Tawakkalna 'ala Allah*!"'

The *teshsha* turned out to be a walled-off dirt lot on the edge of town next to a sun-seared dump-heap dune on which scampering goats and squawking vultures tussled over shreds of offal. As I stepped out of the car, the stench hit me like a blow to the head, and the heat struck me with a sort of hopelessness, as did the glare-infused vista of the Sahel beginning just beyond: sandy wastes studded with thorny, twisted acacias and shards of broken black rock. I quailed at the thought that this was all I'd see from here to Dakar.

At the head of the lot, in the shade of the wall, we found a young man in washed-out indigo robes and a black turban curled up and dozing on a sheet of cardboard. Nothing was exposed except his feet, hands, and eyes. His posture recalled one huddled up against the cold. Then I remembered we were in the cool season.

'*As-salam 'alaykum, ya khay!*' shouted Mahamat.

He sat up. From the slit in his turban two hard eyes, brown and long-lashed, blinked and with some difficulty focused on us.

'This brother needs to go to Faya. Can you take him?'

'I don't speak much Arabic,' the man said in a voice hoarse with sleep. 'I'm a Gorani.' (The Gorani are one of the many bellicose ethnic groups inhabiting the Chadian Sahara.) He looked at me and narrowed his gaze with apparent contempt. 'I do own a truck,' he continued in broken Arabic, 'but my cabin space is already sold. He'll have to ride on top. It's six or seven days to Faya, God willing. Water's on me. Can the Frenchman handle it?'

'I can handle it,' I said. 'But I'm not French.'

'You an Arab?'

'No, American.'

'Oh ho!' He opened his eyes wide and rose nimbly to shake my hand. His hand felt as coarse as hemp. 'American! Well, there'll be no filtered oxygen for you aboard *my* truck! The trip is dangerous and hard on us all. You'll sleep on the ground like us and eat our food. I don't know whether you can take it.' He paused. 'Look, I'm a Chadian, a son of the desert. I respect you Nasranis. I've been colonized by the French, but I respect you all the same – *really*. But you're not tough like we are. The desert is hard on Nasranis, that much I know.'

'The African body can withstand anything,' said Mahamat. 'We're much stronger than Nasranis. This is a fact.'

'I've done a lot of desert travel,' I said, 'so I'm not too worried. I can handle it.'

In fact, I *was* worried: I had seen the giant trucks lumbering out of town belching smoke, overloaded with sacks of grain and dangling passengers and tied-on goats and strapped-on baskets and bundles. In a country without roads, desert-worthy trucks provided one of the few means of getting around. But sometimes they overturned or broke down or lost their way – with tragic results. Was I really ready to surrender myself to this arrogant driver and ride a week with him over land-mined terrain?

'Well,' the Gorani said, smirking, 'we'll see about *that*. Be here tomorrow if you want to ride with me. I am at your *service*, American!'

On that unfriendly note, we parted. As we drove back into town I asked Mahamat why the man had been so hard on me.

'You have to understand how northerners and southerners differ. The southerner fears death. He's civilized and educated. It is no disgrace for the southerner to flee when the northerner pulls his dagger. A northerner like this guy, however, fears nothing and is quick to fight and die. The northerners disdain everyone – everyone except the Arabs, whom they respect as warriors. *Zuruq* [blue men] they consider slaves, the lowest.'

'*Zuruq?*'

'That's what we call blacks here. Their skin makes them look blue to us.' Though Mahamat himself was black, his tone carried no hint of irony.

'But he seemed to look down on me and respect me at the same time, or at least he respected the French. Why?'

'He's *ignorant* to talk like that,' Mahamat spat back. '*No one* who knows the history of Chad could respect the French. The French are behind all our wars. They're after the riches in our earth. But you see, no matter what, he knows Nasranis are weaker and less manly than people of the desert. This unfortunately is the truth.'

I hoped I would find a bus to Abéché.

On Monday noon at Champion d'Afrique the lusty odor of burning flesh pervaded the air. The Hausa cook, his cheeks slashed with tribal scars, stood by his rusty grill, using a dagger to flip over chunks of bloody beef and gobs of sizzling guts, fanning away flies with a sheet of cardboard. Mahamat and I had visited Mai in the morning and found he had not prepared the permit as he had promised, so we came to Champion to have lunch before heading back to the ministry. Today I would either get my permit or not, find a bus or not, and things would be resolved. In the meantime,

sitting in the shade on the straw mat and chewing charred beef
spiced with pepper sauce, I decided I had tasted no finer meat
anywhere.

The pile of meat on the tray between us dwindled under
assault from our greedy fingers. Stretched out regally on the mat,
leaning on one elbow, Mahamat turned to me. 'Look, I told you
I'm worried about you going to Abéché alone, and I should explain
why exactly. We've had a lot of problems, and I won't say that the
imams don't preach against the United States in our mosques.
After your country attacked Afghanistan and killed so many innocent people, Chadians came out in the streets and protested. Then
our president forbade demonstrations and said we're with you in
the war against terrorism. Now people are too scared of the soldiers to protest, but that hasn't changed their hearts. It's natural
that we oppose America. After all, who suffers in the wars America
starts? Always the poor, the innocent. You have to remember that.'

'I'll be diplomatic and listen to people. I think this is just the
time to make such a trip, when people are angry. Their voices
have to be heard.'

He shook his head. 'I don't know about that. Anyway, you
shouldn't just turn up in a place like Abéché not knowing any-
body. I've decided I'm going to write a letter of introduction to
my former boss there and give it to you. He's a big man there, and
I want you to see him first thing. Whatever you do, don't try to
head north to Fada until you've asked him about the security situation. For your own safety.'

The cook set aside his cardboard fan and speared a leg of beef,
which he dropped on the plank next to his grill. He slashed and
hacked at it with his cleaver, and then piled a tray with blackened
beef, which he brought over and dumped into the bowl between
us.

'*Wayn ish-shatta, ya khay, wayn!*' Mahamat demanded.

The cook hurried off for more pepper sauce, and we dug in.

After the meal Mahamat tore a sheet of paper out of a school
notebook and penned a letter to his friend in elegant, loop-and-
slash Arabic. It began with, 'In the name of God, the Merciful,
the Compassionate! My distinguished professor, may the peace

and the mercy of God the Exalted be upon you!' and continued with a most respectful request that he see to the safety and well-being of his brother, Jelal Tayler, in Abéché.

After lunch we returned to the tourism ministry. We found Mai sitting behind his desk, squinting at a letter he was holding up to the light and sounding out the words. I greeted him in French; Mahamat saluted him in Arabic.

Without looking at us, Mai stopped mumbling and put down the letter. He muttered an unintelligible reply, sniffled, and reached for his whiteout.

'So,' I asked, trying to be more polite than last time, 'might my permit be ready?'

He began huffing and daubing. He held his letter up to the light again and said in a distracted way, almost as if talking to himself, 'The secretary is still attending to your permit. You're not the only one with a request.'

Mahamat barked, 'Look, he's traveling today. This morning you promised us his permit would be ready after lunch. Now where is it?'

Such aggressive words, I thought, were sure to provoke Mai to more sniffling obstinacy and daubing delay. But Mai set aside his whiteout and got up. 'Okay, okay. Let's go see if she's finished with it.'

On our way to the secretary's office, Mahamat whispered to me, 'These southerners have a slave mentality, you see. But they're spoiled by all the bribes they get. They don't work for nothing.' I understood him: we would have to boss this bureaucrat around and then pay him for the privilege of doing so.

In the secretary's office, a Muslim woman in a black milhafa sat plump and glum under a poster showing topless teenage girls – Christians from the south – dancing in a row, decked out in colored beads and feathery headdresses. It was captioned DANCE OF THE CIRCUMCISED GIRLS. Genital mutilation is a widespread and ancient practice in Chad (and across much of the Sahel) that most women have suffered. Perhaps, I thought, the secretary had ample reason to be glum.

Mai asked sheepishly, in French, 'So, ah, might you have finished his request?'

She tossed the flap of her milhafa over her shoulder and snapped back in Arabic, 'Don't you see how much work I have? Do you think you're the only one with permits to be typed?' She reached for a bottle of whiteout, unscrewed it, and began huffing and daubing.

Thus began the first round in a match that would include remonstrations with the secretary; the dispatch of the typed letter by 'interministerial courier' (a knock-kneed, runny-nosed boy on a beat-up bike) to various government offices around town; much subsequent huffing and daubing; and a crisis of stamps and seals that necessitated a new bout of blotting and more signatures and a repeat visit by the 'courier' to the Ministry of Public Security.

The ordeal ended with Mai's handing me the permit.

Under the letterhead UNITE! TRAVAIL! PROGRES! and the title AUTORISATION DE CIRCULER, the document issued by the Ministry of Public Security granted me permission to travel 'by land and by means of interurban transport' between N'Djamena, Abéché, Fada, and Faya Largeau on the condition that I present myself on arrival at said localities to the 'administrative authorities' and respect the 'rules of security *en vigueur.*' Notations at the bottom of the page indicated that four top ministers and President Déby himself had been apprised of my travel plans.

I thanked Mai for his efforts and said a polite goodbye to him. Leaving Mahamat in conversation with the secretary, I walked out and climbed into the Peugeot.

I heard the office door shut. In a half-minute Mai was standing by my window, shifting his weight from foot to bare foot.

'You've got to admit it, *monsieur.* I've done an *awful* lot for you.'

'Thank you.'

'You should be really grateful I was around to help you out.'

'I am.'

'I mean, what would you have done without my help? You should *recognize* the work I've done for you.'

'I *do*. I told you so.'

'As well you should have. Say, ah . . .'

Bribes in Third World countries are a form of payment for services *efficiently* rendered. Had Mai not huffed and daubed; or had he shown me anything but disdain, I would have handed him the standard dash. I knew his people had been abused by Mahamat's tribe, and suspected he might have identified me with the hated Muslims because Mahamat was my protector and we spoke Arabic, but these considerations ceded to sentiments of the moment, and his pestering only hardened my heart. After what he had put me through, it went against my gut feeling to give him anything, so I didn't.

Mahamat emerged from the office, pushed Mai aside, and got into the car. Mai remained rooted to his spot. We turned around, and as we were passing him, Mahamat slowed and deposited a few bills in Mai's outstretched palm.

We left the lot and headed for the bus station.

'Why did you give him anything?' I asked. 'You saw how he treated us.'

'Yes, but I can't have enemies in the government. You never know.'

NO ONE IS ABOVE THE LAWS OF OUR COUNTRY OR THE REGULATIONS OF OUR BUS STATION! proclaimed the chipped letters of a weathered sign in French at the entrance to the station – a scattering of crude cement storefronts on dirty sand. Only the occasional dust devil blowing by offered diversion from the general torpor. Here and there men were stretched out in patches of shade, their kadmuls hiding their faces from sun and flies. A few others waited, with tragic looks in their eyes, by ailing Toyota pickup trucks; they may have been there for days, hoping for enough passengers to make the trip worthwhile for the driver; and once they got under way, they would suffer the fears and hardships of the Chadian Sahara.

Not all were so grim here.

'Just in time!' said the manager in the storefront of Agence de Voyage Abou Islam. He had a bus leaving for Abéché at two o'clock. As he wrapped his seven-meter kadmul around and around his kinky-haired head, he enthused about the smooth trip that awaited me with such infectious cheer that I at once felt silly to have been worried and turned to smile at Mahamat. But Mahamat stuffed his hands in his caftan pockets and studied the oil stains on the floor.

'You'll drive *bila wuquf, wallah!* [nonstop, by God!] and get to Abéché around noon tomorrow!' he said, done with his wrapping.

'That's just twenty-four hours!'

'*Sixteen* hours!' said a teenager, peeking up from some sort of rustling labor behind sacks of sorghum. 'It'll take us *sixteen* hours!' He ducked back behind the sorghum.

'That sounds great,' I said. 'Why, if it only takes twenty-four hours —'

'*Sixteen!*' came another shout from the sorghum.

'— then we'll cover the four hundred and seventy miles at a rate of . . . wait a second.'

I calculated how slowly a bus had to go to cover 470 miles without stopping in twenty-four hours: less than twenty miles an hour. This hardly justified my optimism or the manager's enthusiasm. He just didn't want to upset me by stating the truth, which was most likely that the trip would involve countless stops and take who knows how long. How many times had I found people in Africa ready to say anything *but* the truth for fear of causing distress? I knew he meant well, so now, rather than ask questions that might prompt him to more baseless assertions, I dropped the subject of time and asked for the seat behind the driver, whom I planned to befriend as Mahamat advised.

The clerk set to work on my ticket. As I watched his hand and pen sweep gracefully right to left across the paper, leaving an inky trail of Arabic stabs and curlicues, I felt a shiver, a visceral rush surging through me: I was about to set off into the savage, heat-hazed terra incognita that had so intrigued me back on Dala Hill six years before.

Mahamat cleared his throat. 'Jelal, ah, let's see this bus.'

We walked outside. There it stood. Its silvery sides were streaked with the inscription, in schoolboy-sloppy Arabic letters,

*MA SHA' ALLAH!* (What [a wonder] God has willed!), beneath which ran a rainbow of blue, red, and yellow stripes – the colors of the Chadian flag. Under this patriotic flourish was another, smaller inscription informing us that the vehicle had in fact been made in Sudan. Still, I felt good about the bus: a six-wheeler of boxy, almost tanklike build, with small porthole windows of thick tinted glass, it was sturdy, Sahel-worthy, and certainly capable of traveling 470 miles.

Mahmat groaned. 'Torture. This is going to be sheer *torture*.'

'What? Why?'

'Oh, Jelal, every trip in my country is torture, from start to finish. My gut hurts for you already.' Tough Mahamat, my warrior, clenched his stomach and winced like a sick little boy.

'But . . . but I'm prepared.'

'*Tawakkalna 'ala Allah!*'

I walked back to the Peugeot to grab what Mahamat called essential gear for even the shortest voyage in Chad: a bast mat on which to sleep when the bus broke down; a woolen blanket made in Mecca to cover myself against the Harmattan that would likely begin out on the open Sahel; a down pillow to place over the seat that would inevitably be broken; a supply of dates, groundnuts, and bread to eat in hunger-stricken villages. I was as ready as I could be, and I tried to summon up the lucky feeling I had on arrival at the station.

But then I looked into Mahamat's eyes and pondered the pain I saw there. It reminded me of where I was: it was a miracle that buses here ran at all. The best I should hope for *was* torture, with a safe if late arrival. I felt a surge of gratitude for Mahamat's honesty: how many times had I been miserable during past trips, but feared admitting it lest I offend the people whose guest I was? If someone as tough as Mahamat could find travel here awful, then I could relax and suffer without guilt.

There was a cough and a snort. A middle-aged man in a safari suit steered his belly around a corner and waddled our way, swinging a key chain. He introduced himself as Hassan the driver. Bug-eyed and blubbery-lipped, unkempt and earnest and friendly, Hassan had the look of a grown-up schoolyard doofus whose appearance forced him to work extra hard to prove himself. He told us that he tolerated no delays and would not stop all the way to Abéché, except once or twice for meals. In fact, did I have food and water with me? Good, because he *might* not even stop for meals.

'What about sleep?' I asked.

'I sleep in Abéché.'

Such discipline! 'Well, it's almost two o'clock. We'll be leaving now, I suppose?'

'Certainly!'

He waddled back around the corner, swinging his keys.

The bus stood empty and locked up on the sandy lot, and the sun burned, driving us into the storefront for shade.

At four-thirty Hassan was still nowhere to be seen and the clerk had deserted his post. Mahamat and I dozed in the Peugeot (where the seats were comfortable), overcome with the heat. But then appeared a sluggish crowd dragging sacks of millet and satchels of bedding, followed by a few listless women in black, clutching veils to their faces. They looked like mendicants and hawkers and ruffians, lost people, N'Djamena's flotsam, but they gathered in the bus's shade.

Then came two skinny youths who hauled themselves up the bus's side ladder to the roof and gestured sluggishly for baggage so they could load the rooftop rack. The ruffians obliged. The women dozed, and their heads lolled in the heat.

An hour and a half later the bus was twice as tall with a dramatic crest of roped-down baggage, and the sun bled red through columns of dust whirling with the now-frequent departures of Toyota pickups from all around us. An air of mayhem came to reign, and people shouted and gestured and hurried about as if fleeing an advancing army. A turbaned boy came running and stabbed a key into the bus door's keyhole, wrestled open the door, and leaped aboard. He set about tooting the multitonal horn in deafening, maniacally elaborate peals with a ferocity that stirred the crowd to exclamations of grief and wonder. People jumped up and began hugging each other farewell. A breathless crush to board soon formed by the front door; there were grunts and gasps from shaggy kadmuls and shifting caftans; small children were passed over heads, hand to hand and through windows to mark seats.

Mahamat and I got out, and I grabbed my gear. I felt nervous about leaving. I dearly wished I could believe in the God whose protection he so avidly urged me to seek in his oft-repeated phrase. We embraced, and, dwelling on nothing, I turned and made for the bus. Carrying my gear above my head, I worked my way into a crevice in the writhing wall of cotton-clad elbows and shoulders, feeling knuckles in my ribs, knees in my thighs. Thrusting limbs forced me, breathless and choking, up the steps and into a dark, hot, red-plush interior, and I lurched toward the seat behind the driver. Seats were six to a row (divided into threes by a foot-wide aisle) and narrow, for the average Chadian male had all the hip girth of a twelve-year-old Russian gymnast.

Once all the seats were filled, stragglers forced their way into the aisles and door wells. From floor to ceiling we were stuffed; if someone sneezed, the bus would explode. I tried to wrangle six inches of floor space ahead of me to extend at least one leg at a time, but a turbaned tot squeezed into the slot between the gearshift and the driver's seat made sad eyes at me. I would go mad! Yet how stoic the Chadians were! Discomfort I found nearly unbearable for three minutes evoked no expression of distress from people who knew it would last a day or more. They just sat in silence and waited, listening to the crazy beeps of the horn. So I did the same.

Soon Hassan flung open the door next to the driver's seat, yanked the tooting boy down from his throne, and hauled himself in. There was now a need for great speed and merciless haste: after a roaring ignition, we blasted out of the station propelled by a fulminating cloud of fiery exhaust, and thundered into sunset-reddened dust clouds, barreling east down the paved road.

Twenty minutes later we passed the last stick-and-tin hovels on the outskirts of N'Djamena. I nodded greetings to my neighbor, an elder with the tan complexion of an Arab. His hard eyes locked on mine, but he did not respond.

*

Night fell as we trundled down ever more battered tarmac into a landscape of thorny soap trees and acacias and crooked baobabs, with straw teepee villages cropping up here and there in the bouncing beams of our headlights. Fifty miles out of N'Djamena, we pulled into Massaguet, a substantial hodgepodge of teepee huts, all black under the starlit sky except where lit by cooking fires.

The passengers filed out slowly and silently. Hassan called to me, '*Ta'al!*' Come.

I jumped down. He took me by the hand and began strolling into a dark lane leading away from the road. Although this sort of hand-holding was common among men in Muslim countries and usually meant nothing sexual, I found it uncomfortable, but not wanting to cause offense and remembering Mahamat's advice to be friendly, I let myself be so guided. He walked at a leisurely pace, as did the other passengers, who headed in different directions. Apparently, all had their own errands to accomplish here in this settlement where the paved road ended. We seemed to be going nowhere in particular except farther into the dark huts, away from the road and other people.

Relief: we heard a generator rumbling and rounded a corner to see fluorescent lights. Outside an aluminum shed a harsh-looking man in a kadmul that twirled upward from his head like a Mister Softee ice cream cone was frying eggs on a Buta-gas stove. His restaurant was of the *jizara* type, with, just in front of the shed, a straw awning over carpets spread on the sand.

Hassan pulled me down onto the carpet, and we sat cross-legged.

'In my country things are a hundred times, no, a *thousand* times better than this,' he said. He ordered eggs from the proprietor.

'Your country?'

'Why, the Sudan, of course. All our roads are paved. All our buses have video players and serve food. We have ancient ruins everywhere. And we're educated. Sudan is a *thousand* times better than Chad. It's the land of tourism.'

'Why are you working in Chad, then?'

'My company sent me. They built the bus we're in. See,

Chadians can't drive buses – they're too primitive and unedu-
cated – so they rent the buses and the drivers both from us.
Chadians are *very* inefficient.'

I remembered how Hassan had said we wouldn't stop. Scarcely
a half-hour from N'Djamena he called out, '*Salat al-maghrib!*'
(Sunset prayer!), slammed on the brakes, and swerved the bus to
a bumpy halt on the shoulder.

'We're stopping?' I had asked.

'No. Praying,' said Hassan. For the rest of the trip, every few
hours we would 'not stop, but pray' for twenty minutes.

Hassan now looked as though something had just dawned on
him.

'You from Lebanon?' he said, slurping water from a tin.

The waiter brought me three boiled eggs. As I began peeling,
I thought about how I should answer, and I wondered if telling
him my nationality might, as Mahamat had implied, lead him to
suspect I was some sort of spy, in view of my Arabic. But I didn't
want to lie.

'No. I'm from the United States.'

'The United States?' His eyes on mine, he slowly put down his
water tin.

Bin Laden had lived for years in Khartoum, and Sudan had
been on the United States' list of countries sponsoring terrorism.
The last significant episode in U.S.-Sudanese relations had
occurred in 1998, when Tomahawk cruise missiles slammed into
a Khartoum pharmaceuticals factory – a 'terrorist-related' facility
with links to bin Laden, according to President Clinton, who
ordered the strike in response to Al-Qa'ida's attacks on American
embassies in Kenya and Tanzania.

Hassan's eyes bugged out. He thrust forward his chest and
raised his head. 'The United States of *America?*'

Kadmuls turned all around and eyes fell on me.

'Yes,' I said quietly.

'Well, in that case . . . *welcome!* A thousand times *welcome!*' He
reached over and shook my hand, he kissed me on both cheeks,
he patted me on the back, and he shook my hand again. 'Please,
would you like more eggs? Let me order you more eggs! Let me

*pay* for your eggs! Cook, make more eggs for our guest! Would
you like water? A Coke? Name whatever you'd like!'

Each time I finished my eggs Hassan ordered more; when my
Coke dwindled he had the cook's son run out for another. I ate
and drank, with Hassan's eyes set warmly on mine. I wondered:
Would an Arab have been welcomed so warmly in the American
heartland?

After dinner we drove past the last shacks of Massaguet and
onto the piste (dirt track). Feeling sociable and relaxed, I tried
to talk to the old man next to me, but he wrapped himself in a
blanket and turned away to sleep. No one was speaking to
anyone aboard the bus. Night outside was dark and vast, the sky
brilliant with stars; a chill wind poured through the broken
window above me.

Our speed dropped to twenty miles an hour, and we creaked
and rattled over the piste, cut off from mankind and lost on a forgotten lunar sea of rock and dust. Our headlights bounced in the
black, falling on scrub trees and cracked ground and tufts of dead
grass, all bathed in a sterile pallor of moonlight. But the Sahel was
alive: gazelles bounded past, their cotton tails bobbing away into
the dark. Golden jackals froze in our lights and stared. Porcupines
ambled away from our noisy advance, their quills wobbling; vultures, gigantic and craggy-headed, raised befouled beaks from
rotting repasts and flapped their ponderous wings to escape. The
engine sputtered and roared, echoing loudly, with Hassan struggling now and then to shift gears as the bus bucked the crests and
hollows of baked earth.

I wrapped myself in my blanket and began dozing with the
warmth. Soon there was only the whir and roar of the engine, the
ghosts of gazelles, and the sense of rolling on breakers of clay,
rising and falling and rising again . . .

Angry voices. I started awake. We were stopped. Turbaned
men with automatic rifles were afoot outside the bus, moving
through the headlight beams. A murmur of alarm arose: we were
surrounded.

The side door slammed open. There was a moment of silence. A man in boots climbed slowly aboard, step by heavy step. He was wearing a khaki jacket over his caftan and his head was wrapped in a kadmul, the slit exposing only red drunken eyes. At the top of the steps he shone a flashlight about, his Kalashnikov swinging from his shoulder. He was a soldier of some sort, as were the other men outside.

He dropped the beam on my face. '*Wayn karta na'k!*' (Where is your identity card?) His voice was nasal and strident. He flicked the light on and off in my face. '*Yallah! Wayn karta na'k!*'

I pulled out my passport and handed it to him. He seized it and jumped down the steps into the black. The armed men surrounding the bus dispersed.

Ten minutes passed, and then fifteen. No one moved.

Hassan restarted the engine.

'Wait,' I said. 'That soldier has my passport!'

'You gave it to him? Why?'

'Why? He had a gun!'

'*Allah! Allah!*' Shaking his head, Hassan opened his door and jumped out into the night.

My thitherto uncongenial neighbor patted my arm and smiled reassuringly. But none of us was safe. The soldiers, who were probably unpaid, could loot, rape, or kill any of us – no one could stop them. For the first time since my days in Zaire, I felt the cutting blade of fear that comes with being at the mercy of men living outside the law, beyond restraint – fear that was startlingly new to me now but probably a tiring constant of everyday life for the others on the bus.

The wind blew colder and colder through the broken window slot, the stars shone in the icy air, and there was silence.

Fifteen minutes later footsteps sounded on the hard earth. Hassan climbed aboard, panting, flapping his arms and hugging himself from the cold.

'*Mashakil* [Problems]. Chad!' he exclaimed, waving my blue document.

I leaned forward. 'Thanks so much. What was wrong?'

He waved dismissively. 'You're my guest! Welcome!'

He must have paid a bribe, but it would be improper for me to ask, so I thanked him again and resolved to treat him at the next stop.

He threw the bus into gear and we were off again. We rolled east all night, bouncing along the piste, until the hour came when not a gazelle gamboled past, not a single pair of jackal eyes crossed our beams, and we were truly and, it seemed, irrevocably alone on the planet, under an infinitely receding black sky coruscating with stars so brilliant, they looked ready to break free of their mounts and drop to the earth.

Hassan welcomed the flat tire that forced us to stop at noon for a two-hour repair session: he hopped down groggily, and, clutching a blanket, staggered away to find a thornless patch of ground on which to stretch out as the baggage handler and the assistant set to work. The air out here was much, much cooler than it had been in N'Djamena, and it was cold in the shade.

I took the chance to repose in the sun. Past us marched single-file herds of cattle accompanied by tall men in pure white caftans and rakish kadmuls, only their black hands and dark eyes exposed. They carried ten-foot wooden spears tipped with twelve-inch blades of icy steel − out here no man traveled unarmed. None turned to look at us; we were outside their world, inconsequential, and perhaps, as city folk, unworthy of their desert-hardened gaze.

Whether those aboard my bus were armed I could not say; Mahamat said they would be. They were a mixed lot: most were black, Arabic-speaking Muslims, but others spoke French and must have been Christians from the south; my neighbor was an ethnic Arab. They all sat sullen and silent throughout the ride. Why? Did they feel as alien thrown together here as I did?

At around eleven that night a milky mist appeared in the sky ahead – Abéché. We rolled up to a branch hanging between crooked poles − the police checkpoint on the town's outskirts. We filed wearily off the bus, and I wondered about the gun-wielding troops surely dozing in the guard shacks ahead, and the identity-card check to come. Nevertheless, I felt something close to glee at having made it.

'Why don't we drive on in?' I asked Hassan.

'Chad! The government won't allow it. They're afraid the rebels might attack, so they close the town at dusk.'

My glee waned. With all our stops for prayer we had added enough hours to the trip to miss the closing hour and would have to sleep on the ground until morning.

No troops ever appeared. A row of palm-frond shelters had been erected at roadside to accommodate passengers thus caught out. Near the entrance to one of them I spread my straw mat and blanket on the sand and settled in for sleep, but the northerly wind hissed through the slats at my head. The Chadians silently arranged their bedding cocoons away from others and crawled in, with only their kadmuls or headscarves protruding. I had spoken little to anyone besides Hassan over the past thirty hours, and no one else had spoken to me.

It was Christmas Eve, and I huddled and shivered on the ground, my mat and blanket failing to protect me from the cutting, frigid wind. Gazing out at the stars, now mercilessly bright and nearer than ever, I fell asleep.

# 4

# ABÉCHÉ

Phlegmy honks, raspy coughs, and conspiratorial murmurs in Arabic seeped into my fading dreams. My cheeks, I vaguely sensed, were frozen and gritty with cold sand. I opened my eyes to a vault of radiant pearl, a gelid dawn sky so pure that I gasped, inhaling frigid air. I peeked over the flap of my blanket. The other passengers, squatting in circles of three or four at the back of the hut, turned to peer at me from under their kadmuls. Those seven yards of heat-saving cotton made sense. I would not leave Abéché without a kadmul.

Dressed in his safari suit, oblivious to the cold, Hassan popped out of an adjacent hut and walked up to me, loose-jawed and cheery in a way I found incredible, even irritating, given my stiff-boned discomfort.

'*Salam 'alaykum!* Sleep well?' he asked, his lower lip hanging and blubbery. He was impervious to the torments of the road, so no wonder we had spent so many hours 'not stopped but praying.' I returned his greeting and started gathering my things together.

From a mud hut just ahead on the road, on the other, forbidden side of the checkpoint, a flak-jacketed soldier with a towel wrapped around his head jogged out, clutching his sides from the cold. He daintily removed the tree-branch crossbeam from the gate hooks and tossed it aside. Abéché, former capital of the sultanate of Wadai, was now officially open.

In silence we piled aboard for the half-hour ride into town.

Abéché appeared to have been sketched by a meticulous artist with a few ochre-colored pencils on rough canvas: it was a clay and sand town of surprisingly clean, even sterile, lines and easy contours, with here and there a neem, a palm. A silence prevailed, and crystalline light showered down from the cloudless sky. Few people were about and shops were closed. The bus pulled into a lot and stopped by storefronts similar to those of the station back in N'Djamena.

We all filed out quietly, and the assistants climbed onto the roof to begin unloading baggage. This they accomplished almost wordlessly, and I felt I should observe silence, as if at a wake. But why?

Everyone seemed to have somewhere to go except me. No one looked friendly, so I approached Hassan, who was stretching his arms above his head in the bus agency's storefront. I asked him how I might find the *funduq* (hotel) of which I had heard, the Jus de Fruits.

'People visiting here stay with relatives,' Hassan said in an almost comedic way, as if delivering a line not to be believed by a sane person, but the others concurred with more nods of their heads. They all expressed vehement doubts that there was a single functioning hotel left in all Abéché; decades of civil war, they said, had killed such luxuries long ago.

'You should just come back to N'Djamena with me. Twenty-four hours, without a stop, *wallah*, sixteen if we're lucky . . .'

'I'd love to travel with you again,' I said. 'But really, how can there be no hotel here? There're supposed to be forty thousand people here. How can the biggest city in this part of Chad not have a single hotel?'

This time, I used the French loan word *uteel*.

'Oh, an *uteel!*' one of the clerks exclaimed with a frosty puff of breath, sitting wrapped in his blanket. 'I don't know the name, but we *do* have an *uteel!*' Through some sort of linguistic transmogrification the French word in Chadian Arabic had come to mean a lowly inn and not a hotel, for whose foreign grandeur they employed the classical Arabic *funduq*. He roused the lone moped driver around from his blanket and told him to take me to the *uteel*, and Hassan and I parted.

The *uteel* Jus de Fruits was an entirely decrepit assemblage of turquoise-painted stone rooms without running water or electricity, arranged around a pair of sandy courtyards and shaded by neems. The now-resurgent breeze moved the trees to shed their burdens of dust and dry leaves all over the place in a continual, sneeze-provoking shower. Heaven, as far as I was concerned. All I wanted was a safe place to stow my gear and sleep. The dusty-haired owner, a jolly middle-aged man in plastic flip-flops and a navy blue janitor's smock, welcomed me with a wide, dusty grin: I was to be his only guest. But then he found out I was American and with an equally jolly grin refused to accept me until I registered at the police station around the corner. I showed him my stamp from N'Djamena and asked for a stay of execution: couldn't I wash up first and settle in?

'Yes, of course, certainly. After you register!'

Still smiling, he hurried me toward the steel courtyard gates. I stepped outside and hoped to ask directions, but he slammed the gate and bolted it with a series of clanks and bangs.

I didn't take this personally: suspicion had to be a survival trait here. After three-quarters of Abéché's population had perished from plagues in the early twentieth century, the good times rolled: ferocious armed resistance to French invaders, the uncertainties of independence, ethnic clashes, civil war, drought, and now a new (or maybe the same) guerilla war somewhere along the Sudanese border. Bad neighbors didn't help: Next door in Sudan slavery is still practiced, and a decades-long civil war has killed hundreds of thousands and displaced millions. To the south is the Central African Republic, where, before things got really bad, a dictator named Jean-Bédel Bokassa had proclaimed himself emperor, spent $20 million on his coronation ceremony, and ordered the death by bludgeoning of eighty children whose parents had insolently refused to buy expensive school uniforms from his personal garment factory. To the north was Gaddafi. That I was free to walk around at all here seemed a small miracle, and I did not disparage it.

The police station turned out to be three cement rooms behind a high stone wall. I walked into its sun-heated courtyard and found three officers snoring on the sand, wrapped in blankets and kadmuls. One climbed grumpily out of his bedding, took my passport into a room, sniffled at it, and stamped it. After that, he abolished my miracle, telling me in kadmul-muffled words that I could not, in fact, walk around Abéché alone. I had to wait for a young fellow named Ahmad, an officer in the 'immigration bureau' (the desk across from his). At that, he rolled himself back into his blanket and dozed off.

I sat down on a bench in the sun and waited.

A short, emaciated man in his fifties walked into the courtyard and sat down next to me, examining me with benevolent, bewildered eyes. He wore a tattered blue windbreaker and a white shirt with a collar frayed into fluffy wisps; his hair was a dusty, Brillo-pad mop; he grinned to expose spiky teeth stained orange-red from chewing cola nuts, and slivers of nut inhabited his beard. He looked like a beggar, but his forwardness suggested he might be a minder of sorts. He introduced himself as a functionary in the local government, and his fluency in French attested to this.

'So,' he asked, 'how long will it take you to complete your mission in Chad? A year? Two years?'

Mission? I told him I was a tourist from the United States. He looked away, and when he turned again to me, I was surprised to see anger contorting his face and lighting his eyes.

'Your president, this Bush *fils*, he came to power by force.'

'By force?'

'I mean he manipulated the electoral process using his money. That's the same as force. Might makes right, in his eyes, or money makes right. Bush and his men see gold before their eyes, and that's what's driving them to attack Iraq. The whole world now suspects America's intentions. Look, how can it be, I ask you, how can it be that the world's cradle of democracy has a president who came to power by force? How?'

'The electoral process in Florida *was* manipulated. I —'

'Call it what you will – you know what I mean. His election was not democratic. Look, think of what this means to people in Chad who believed in America! Our leaders come to power by force and manipulation, and that's bad, but we expect it – this is Chad. But think of what it did to us, to those of us who cherished America as an ideal, as the hope for humanity, when we saw how *your* president came to power.' His eyes watered and his voice broke. 'Imagine how this hurt us and our faith in democracy!'

'You had such faith in America? A lot of Americans are more cynical.'

'It's a disgrace! It's shameful! Your system is corrupted just like in Chad: we would never have believed this possible, *never*. We *believed* in America. This belief was *all we had*.'

I didn't know what to say. I would not defend elections in which only 24 percent of Americans had voted for their president, who in the end was put in office by a Supreme Court that split along party lines just as civil war had divided Chad into Muslim and Christian factions. He had a right to his anger if all he had was faith in the American ideal.

'God always blinds men in power,' he went on to say, 'so that they can't see Him. When you have money and power, you think you don't need God. God blinded the Babylonians and He's now blinding Bush. Ever since Bush seized power, the whole world knows that God has a *bad* end in store for America, as he did for the Babylonians. A *bad* end.'

He looked at the sky for some time, as if drawing on its azure serenity to calm himself down. He stood up, said *bon*, shook my hand, and walked off.

Ahmad never came, so, noticing the policemen were asleep, I slipped out and returned to Jus de Fruits and showed the proprietor my stamped passport.

Later that morning Ahmad came knocking at the inn's steel gates. He was in his early thirties, skinny, with a rictus of rotten, caved-in teeth. His ruined mouth gave him a speech defect that made him bashful and garbled his paltry French and Arabic. However, he was painfully modest and would certainly make a pleasant companion. He told me he was related to the police chief and would be with me during my time in his town; he proclaimed himself a Fulani, a member of the ethnic group of animal herders originally from Senegal and now spread all over the Sahel. We shook on his daily rate and set off to see Abéché.

I told him that I needed to find Mahamat's former boss and showed him the letter. I was out of luck: the man had left Abéché years ago. But Mahamat's relative in the ministry had also given me, with a knowing grin, another person to look up, a certain Madame X. Could we find her?

'Madame X? Ah ha . . . she's known here for her . . . lifestyle,' he said with a sly smile, in a way that seemed to place quotation marks around the final word. 'I'd be *happy* to find her.'

In a neighborhood of blocky houses, with occasional palms adding splashes of green to a relentless dun and tan tableau, we found her house. I knocked on the steel door and paused to wait for an answer, but Ahmad just flung it open, walked in, and pulled me in too.

Madame was sitting on the ground of her courtyard, obese and morose, her legs spread in a wide V under a circus-tent boubou. She was shouting in an unfamiliar language at a brood of howling, naked toddlers and pounding mash with a pestle. Between pestle blows I explained to her in French who I was and showed her the letter from Mahamat's relative, which she tossed on the ground without reading.

'You're here for . . .?' she queried.

'Yes,' said Ahmad, stepping forward.

She waved us back into another courtyard – this one partly hidden by a wall – and went back to her pestling. This area was strewn with plastic tables and chairs and stacked with plastic cases of Castel beer. *That* was it! Her home was an informal, perhaps even illegal, bar.

We took seats. A tall young woman in a tight blouse and long wraparound skirt shuffled over to us, looking scarcely less grumpy than her mother. Speaking Arabic, I ordered beers for Ahmad and myself, but he demurred, saying he was on the job, and asked for a Maltina soft drink, restating the order in a language unknown to me. 'She may not speak Arabic,' he said.

I became aware of two young men in Western dress sitting in the shade a few yards away, sipping beers and looking sullen. I said hello to them in Arabic and French, and both glumly returned my greetings in French. One, named Ali, told me that he was a satellite technician, but Chad's location made reception difficult; an almost complete lack of electricity didn't help his business either. He asked me what I was doing in Chad. I told him I was a tourist.

'Tourist, right. All you whites say you're tourists, but you really come to scout out our riches. You're here for money. I'm not faulting you. This makes sense. You see, we have riches here, but we don't know how to extract them.'

I found his blunt suspicion disorienting and could respond only by saying I hadn't expected to find a bar in Abéché, much less one run by a woman.

'Oh, we're Muslim here, but not thoroughly so, though Islam killed a lot of our local traditions. You know, we see Osama bin Laden on television, and since September 11 we've been more Islamic, what with the U.S. attacking Afghanistan, but really, we're afraid of our government, so our support for him, if you could call it that, amounts to watching television, which is where I would come in if we had more electricity. Anyway, we have enough problems without Osama. God provides for all. We have no complaints, and no reason to follow Osama.'

'Are you Arab?'

'No.'

His answer sounded oddly final. We both looked at our drinks.

'If I might ask, what's your people, then?'

'I'm a Gorani,' he said. This evoked frowns on the faces of Muhammad, the other young man, and Ahmad. Ahmad said he was a Fulani.

'Don't tell him that,' interrupted Muhammad. 'You've got Hausa blood.'

'No I *don't*.'

'You *do*.'

It turned out that all present knew one another, but I had

spoiled the atmosphere by bringing up ethnicity. When Ahmad left to go to the bathroom, Muhammad was blunt.

'Ahmad tells you he's a Fulani. Well, he's no Fulani. He's just a Hausa. Hausas are really Nigerians.' Hausa, along with Fulani, dominate northern Nigeria and much of Niger too. Fulani consider themselves, thanks to their history of jihadist warring, high caste and above Hausa; and a Fulani-based elite rules northern Nigeria. 'Don't let him lie to you. We don't let our girls marry the Hausa, because they're not really Chadians.'

'It doesn't matter to me,' I said. 'Why shouldn't you marry one another here?'

'We want to keep our languages to ourselves, so we can preserve our secrets.'

Ali concurred. 'Languages ought to be kept secret. You won't hear us speaking our languages on the street. We speak them at home, so no outsiders can learn them. On the street we use Arabic.'

Ahmad returned. Their suspicion and sullenness made me feel unwelcome, and I asked Ahmad if he wouldn't mind leaving.

The sultanate of Wadai began as a dependency of the now-defunct sultanate of Darfur in what is today Sudan. The Wadai sultanate eventually came to dominate trade routes north to Benghazi and east to the Chari River. Sometime during the Middle Ages, Islam, probably introduced by Arab merchants, began to take root in Wadai among the lower classes. In the mid-1600s, an Arab named 'Abd al-Karim arrived in the region intent on furthering the spread of his religion. With support from Muslim Wadai, 'Abd al-Karim conquered the sultanate, overthrew its pagan rulers, established the present dynasty, and propagated Islam among all social classes, thereby earning himself the title by which he is known today: *Mujaddid al-Islam* (the Renewer of Islam). The Wadai's fervent faith impelled them to fight the French infidels hard during the colonial years.

My time with Mahamat in N'Djamena had left me troubled about Islam in Chad: with him, at least, the faith seemed as much a force for discipline and pride as a cause for disdain and prejudice. So, I decided I wanted to find out how relations stood between Muslims and Christians in Abéché now. I asked Ahmad if he could introduce me to the incumbent sultan, Ibrahim Mohammed Ourada, who has been on the throne since 1978. We paid a visit to the sultanate, a simple brick building off one of Abéché's sandy streets. There, we found a traditional Islamic court in session (such courts adjudicate matters relating to births, marriages, and deaths), but we learned that the sultan was away on business and were directed to his brother and deputy, the mayor of Abéché, Sanoussi Mohammed Ourada.

Ourada was a handsome middle-aged man with a kempt white beard and warm brown eyes peering out from under a billowing kadmul. He received me graciously at his office – a small, concrete one-story building strewn with the bundles of yellowed files that apparently signaled government activity everywhere in Chad. He spoke fluent classical Arabic, and, seated behind his desk between reams of Arabic-language documents, told me the history of his town and Wadai. The capital of Wadai was originally Ouara, some forty miles to the north of Abéché. Abéché didn't exist until a hundred years ago when Ouara's wells ran dry and the reigning sultan ordered 'all who carry the Qur'an' to pack their belongings and herd their livestock to the aquiferous abode of 'Abu Bishsha' – 'Father of Bishsha,' in Arabic – which became corrupted into *Abéché*. Who Bishsha was exactly, Ourada didn't know.

Ourada talked proudly of the *mujaddid* and told me about how his renewal of Islam eventually ensured the future of Wadai as a Muslim district within the secular Republic of Chad. A modified and softened version of shari'a was in force here. 'We don't cut off hands,' he said. 'We have secular courts for criminal cases like theft.'

I wondered aloud how Muslims got along with Christians, and how Christians reacted to living under shari'a.

'But all the native people of Wadai are Muslims,' he answered before closing our meeting. 'The state courts are for Christians from the south.'

'All?'

'Of course.'

Was this so? I had heard rumors that missionaries from the West operated in town. Had they enjoyed no success? And the previous night, I had seen Chadian Christians drinking at the Christmas celebrations in the Fania Bar. Were they all migrants? Perhaps Ourada simply chose not to acknowledge them to me, but neither had others in town; when I asked if there were any Muslims here who had converted to Christianity, they scoffed at the notion with one word: *mamnu'!* (It's forbidden!) This wasn't so surprising: apostasy in Islam, at least according to shari'a law, is punishable by death.

I would soon have answers to my questions.

I sat on a mat in the courtyard, the guest of the Arabic-speaking white Westerner at my side. Behind the high concealing walls of the villa, in the furtive shade of neems dancing to breezes from the Sahara, the chanting in Chadian Arabic rang out in numbingly bland, flat verse:

*Rabbuna mukhallisna*
*Huwa ja fi al-dunya*
*Rabbuna mukhallisna*
*Huwa khalla majd Allah*

(Our Lord our Savior
He came to this world
Our Lord our Savior
He left behind the glory of God)

The chanters around us, fifty or sixty Chadians, many converts from Islam, joined by a dozen or so Westerners, finished their stanza, cleared their throats, and began another hymn, this one decidedly subversive to Muslim ears, if delivered in the same anodyne manner:

*Ya al-hadi al-Masih*
*Yatu ja min as-sama?*
*Al-Masih!*

*Yatu ba'th min al-mayyiteen?*
*Al-Masih!*


(Oh [our] guide, the Messiah!
Who descended from heaven?
The Messiah!
Who arose from the dead?
The Messiah!)


While at the police station, I had run into the Westerner, who lived in Abéché – a trim, articulate, and polite middle-aged man about whom I will divulge no more details to avoid compromising him. Happy to meet a foreigner, he invited me home for a belated Christmas meal, though with an apology: 'If I had known you were here yesterday' – on Christmas Day – 'I would have invited you to our expat dinner. The one today is for the Chadians.' Who were these expats, and what were they doing in far-flung Abéché? His fluent Chadian Arabic led me to suspect he was a missionary; often missionaries and Peace Corps volunteers are the only foreigners to learn local languages in Africa. I accepted his offer: it seemed like a pleasant way to spend a day in Abéché before facing the rigors and uncertainties of the Sahara and the trip north.

He was a missionary, if a clandestine one. After the subversive hymn, a Chadian dressed in a baby blue caftan addressed the assembled (who sat segregated by sex on bast mats), opening his mouth overly wide and speaking with exaggerated precision in Arabic, with a Chadian interpreter at his side translating his words into French. His sermon touched on basic Christian notions: the prophet Isaiah foretold the birth of Jesus seven hundred years before the event; Jesus came not for the rich, not for the few, but for the poor, for the many, for all mankind, and salvation lay in Jesus and Jesus alone.

The translator's voice cracked and drew my attention: its owner was a mopish fellow in a drab gray suit that was wrinkled and two sizes too large. A tight, bulky brown polyester tie crinkled the blackened collar on his once-white shirt. (Though a few wore caftans, most of the Chadian men present were dressed and groomed like he was. *Why?*) He sat cross-legged and shoeless, the soiled soles on his formerly white socks pointing in opposite directions. The more animated the preacher grew, the harder the interpreter tried to match his oratory zeal, but he failed: with his voice cracking, his collar bunching, bone thin in his big shabby suit, he resembled a charlatan preacher in a Flannery O'Connor novel. His lips seemed covered in a white film, as though he had just woken up; I had the impression that his breath stank.

The preacher halted his homily and asked for questions. There was no response: the drawn faces around me showed boredom, and all eyes were downcast. It was as though someone had made them come here.

An uncomfortable moment of silence ended when a corpulent pink European, his hands on his knees, huffed and hoisted himself up out of the cross-legged position in which the mats prompted us all to sit. His paunch bulged through a synthetic yellow golf shirt. He smoothed his sparse red mustache and adjusted the bottle-glass spectacles posed on the bridge of his greasy, wide-pored nose. He ordered the interpreter to render his French into Arabic, and, his fleshy lips flapping, his clamlike tongue writhing as if trying to escape his mouth, he started haranguing the audience like an overfed, Gallic Jim Baker. Sweat popped out on his brow. Christians are a strange but wondrous lot, he said: they are forever sacrificing themselves and *never* tire of giving their *very last* coin for the sake of the Savior. Suffering was *good*, it was an *honor* to suffer for *le bon Dieu*; one should do nothing less than *seek* to suffer for *le bon Dieu*. 'Now let us open our hymn books to *'Seigneur, Prends Tout'!*' (Lord, Take Everything!) The assembled fumbled with their booklets and flatly hummed the words he crooned out in an affected, stentorian bass.

The preacher then calmed down to perform French versions of 'Silent Night,' 'O Come All Ye Faithful,' and other carols. The Chadians tried to sing along, but most soon gave up on the unfamiliar lyrics. Above the cracking tenors and faltering falsettos of those who persisted rose the increasingly fruity bass of the preacher, and sweat poured down his reddening cheeks.

Though they were in French, and despite the horrible preacher, I found the carols familiar and touching. They transported me back home to Washington, D.C., to when I was ten years old and eagerly awaiting Christmas Day, the lit tree, the stuffed stocking. My parents weren't religious, but before going to bed I said my prayers, not knowing what they really meant. My world then was a closed, *American* world, and I had no reason to imagine it was anything but a *good* world. That my world ran mostly on cheap oil from Muslim countries; that hundreds of millions of Arabs and other Muslims were watching as Western governments, led by my own, rewarded tyrannical puppet leaders in Muslim countries for the privilege of taking that oil; and that in fact the very faith of the Savior whose praises I sung in carols was alien, even heresy, to huge numbers of people on the planet, I had no idea. I was unaware then that Christianity could stand for anything other than holiday cheer and presents and candy canes and Santa and peace on earth.

Did the Chadians present understand any of that? If they had originally been Muslim, I was sure they did: throughout the Qur'an, Christianity and Judaism are evoked and refuted (though respectfully: Islam enjoins Muslims to tolerate 'People of the Book'), and, since the 1970s especially, revolutionary Islamic doctrines have flourished, if underground, almost everywhere in the Muslim world. But these Chadians had chosen to renounce their faith, and this troubled me. I sat there trying to figure out exactly why.

A Chadian man sitting across from me broke my reverie after the third French carol. 'Enough French songs! Let's go back to Arabic!'

A French teenage boy replied to him, in French, 'But these *aren't* French songs. They're translated from *English!*' On the Chadian the English-French rivalry was lost: both cultures were alien to him.

It was time to eat anyway, so hymn books were set aside. Servants brought out stainless-steel trays piled with steaming rice and gooey chunks of lamb. All, including the missionaries, ate with their hands, scooping out the rice and meat and gobbling it off their palms. I had often eaten with my hands, but in Arab style, using bread as a sort of scoop – a more sanitary procedure. The barehanded Chadian way left grease streaming down my forearms and much food on the bast mat.

I looked at the Westerners slurping grease off their palms. Though it was unhygienic and alien to them, they ate with their hands 'to assimilate and win the trust of the locals' – as one Westerner had put it to me that day – 'because you have to do this. You can't spread the message if they don't feel comfortable with you.' Among the Western women Chadian dress predomi- nated for the same reason – to win the trust of, and thus more easily convert, female adherents of the enemy faith. The mis- sionaries dressed to look like the enemy, penetrated the enemy's ranks, subverted them, and then aided them in renouncing their religion, culture, and identity. Indeed, the converts sitting around me *looked* like vanquished people; nowhere else in Chad had I heard flatter voices or seen duller eyes, not to mention worse clothes – Western clothes unsuitable for the heat and dust, for a dearth of laundries and irons.

But why were they here, then, if they weren't happy? Had anyone made them come? Yes and no. In Chad, and all across sub- Saharan Africa, most traditional (that is, pre-Islamic, pre-Christian) religions long ago had given way, first to Islam and later to Christianity, even though both new faiths were brought by outsiders – invaders, that is – motivated by the conquest of terri- tory and the acquisition of booty. Old African religions failed to retain their devotees because they couldn't provide the temporal benefits of the invaders' faiths: literacy, social order, science, and unity, where medieval Islam was concerned; or the superior arma- ments, technology, medicine, education, and, in recent decades, promise of a better life abroad, that Christianity could offer.

So what made the spectacle of Chadian converts to Christianity objectionable to me? The missionaries sitting around me were the soldiers of an unofficial army, chanting the battle hymns of their faith on the front lines of the conflict under way between the West and the Islamic world; they were recruiting future com- batants. Broadly speaking, they and their brethren have been succeeding: in the past hundred years, the number of Christians (mostly of charismatic sects) in Africa has risen from 10 million to 360 million, which is almost half the continent's population. One may foresee that, as this war intensifies, and long after the inevitable strife breaks out and drives the missionaries back to their countries, the Chadian converts will suffer charges of treason in their trenches.

The missionaries were propounding their culture, spreading their beliefs, and doing just as the Muslims had done. The introduction of Islam in the region had delivered a seismic shock to Sahelian history. Islamicized black Africans, smarting from Arab racism, began concocting genealogies, in Arabic, that asserted the consanguinity of Sahelians with Arabs or even the prophet Muhammad himself (e.g., the Mujaddid, and Mahamat's denial of his blackness and assertion of Iraqi blood). After the arrival of Islam, never again would Africans of the Sahel be comfortable as Africans. Christianity in Abéché might now be just the latest lunge of a defeated, deracinated people.

Yet if I had long reviled missionaries for their efforts in Africa, now I saw their success as historically inevitable. I could not defend African identity when Africans themselves were surrendering to the West's dominant religion, as, so many centuries before, they had surrendered to the Arabs and Islam. But here, where conflict between Muslim and Christian had so decimated the country since independence, the *last* thing Africans needed was more justification for strife, more reason for division.

If some conversion to Christianity in Africa is inevitable, the West nevertheless has more to give Chad than religion – much more. After all, on Enlightenment principles stand the U.S. Constitution and Bill of Rights; from Enlightenment principles came the French Revolution and democracy in the rest of western Europe. Would not notions of religious tolerance and equality among men help Chadians overcome their animosities and reconcile their divisions better than another doctrine positing a saved few enjoined to convert the misguided many?

I found myself asking, Where are the 'missionaries' of the secular culture of democracy and human rights and science, of free and responsible choice – in short, of the very civilization that developed from the writings of the Enlightenment philosophers who ushered in the modern age and who were thus responsible in large measure for the ascendancy of the West, the same technological prowess that helped the West to conquer Africa and other continents? Only after the Renaissance and Reformation did the West advance. Had it not been for these events, the West might be suffering the stagnation afflicting the Muslim world today. But the answer to my question was simple: reason, science, freedom, and democracy cannot be preached or imposed. If Africans would benefit more from the message of the humankind-centered Enlightenment than from beliefs that they should give when they had nothing, submit to Caesar when Caesar was corrupt, and reject science and evolution when they had cures, there could be no preachers of Voltaire, no haranguers of Rousseau, or what these and other philosophers taught would not be worth learning.

Such were my thoughts as I licked the greasy rice from my palms.

Late that afternoon, as I returned from the Christmas meal, the Harmattan hit. It drowned the sun in brown dust, and, after night fell, turned cooking fires on the corners into opaque yellow blurs and the headlights of mopeds into bouncing orbs of weak white light roving through the hazy brownish dark. I retreated to my room at the Jus de Fruits, closed all the windows, shut the door. The wind howled. It was as if I were languishing at the bottom of a great sand sea.

# 5

# DESERT OF DAGGERS

There had been a rebel attack near Adré, to the east of Abéché, and everyone was on edge.

A gale was howling in from the desert. Brandishing their automatic rifles, four soldiers, gaunt with hunger, their kadmuls tied bandit-style around their faces so only their eyes showed, jumped out into the piste and blocked our truck's way. By their boots lay a charred, six-foot-long acacia branch – the *barrière* marking the northern limits of Abéché. We slowed and waved, lest they suspect we were armed, and came to a stop. The officer among them pounded on the hood of our dented Toyota pickup and stabbed his finger at me.

I grabbed my passport and permit and leaned out of the window. '*As-salam 'alaykum!*' I shouted over the wind. 'I have a permit to reach Fada and Faya Largeau. I'm traveling with the brother of the *commissaire* [police chief] of Abéché.'

The officer stepped up and fixed me with unblinking eyes sunk deep in sand-encrusted sockets. He snatched my papers and stomped off into the mud hut just off the road. The other soldiers took up positions around our truck.

We waited. The sun showered searing light over the dust devils that spun across the tawny flats of sand and cracked clay around us, now and then blotting out the buttes on the horizon, obscuring the columns of skeletal cattle and spear-wielding herders trudging north along the piste. Dust was even blowing in through a hole in the floor of the truck, by my feet, so I took my new kadmul out of my bag and wound it around my head, covering my mouth and nose; it quickly alleviated the itchy dryness in my throat.

Ten minutes passed, and the officer did not return. I looked at Ibrahim. 'Well? Doesn't it mean anything that you're the *commissaire*'s brother? Why don't you show them who you are?' I had hired this Gorani youth precisely for the protection his status should afford, and I was distressed to detect fear in his eyes. He hesitated. 'Please, go talk to them.'

Reluctantly, he wrenched open the door and jumped out. He looked at me again, and I nodded that he should continue, so he shrugged and walked over to the hut and leaned in the doorway. He said something to the officer inside, and the soldiers started shouting and shoving him around – apparently out here name and status meant nothing.

I opened the door and jumped down myself. At that moment the officer emerged from the hut, waving my papers as though he might just toss them to the wind. He yelled something to me in Arabic, his words muffled by his kadmul and unintelligible.

'Excuse me?' I asked.

He pulled his kadmul away from his mouth. 'Money, I said! Give me two thousand francs or you don't get your papers back! I get good money for a foreign passport!'

'I'm traveling with the brother of the police chief.'

'Two thousand francs!'

I handed him a thousand. He looked at the crinkled bills and hesitated, but then he shoved my documents into my hand. The soldiers released Ibrahim and gave him a parting shove in the back, which he accepted passively. We jumped back aboard the truck, the soldiers removed the branch, and we roared ahead into the thrashing clouds of dust. Petit, our nimble-limbed mechanic assistant, balanced on his feet in the back, just behind me. Ahead was the wind-battered, sun-scorched vastness of the Sahara – and, for all we knew, rebels and land mines.

*

Two evenings earlier, as the Harmattan rattled the shutters on my room's windows at Jus de Fruits, I had sat down by guttering candlelight and taken out my map to plot my route into the Sahara. I sought to reach the oasis settlement of Faya Largeau, 550 miles to the northwest of Abéché, at the foothills of the Tibesti Mountains – the range of scorched escarpments and jagged peaks that run across northern Chad into Libya. To get to Faya I would have to cross terrain with a daunting barrenness and fierce inhabitants that have long made northern Chad one of the most isolated and ungovernable parts of Africa, and one the French never managed to pacify. No road led to Faya, but my map showed a piste winding there across the treacherously shifting dunes of Erg (sea of sand dunes) du Djourab, which began just west of Fada, an oasis village 350 miles due north.

To my distress, no one in Abéché could provide me with reliable information about what was going on up there, though the missionaries (who had never been to either place) did warn me that rebels and land mines posed a risk. No one was immune from the latter danger: in 2002 a mine killed Youssouf Togoïmi, the leader of the northern guerillas. Thus it seemed that the travel permit I had gone through so much hassle to obtain in N'Djamena gave me leave to enter territory over which the Chadian government had little control and about which it knew less.

For more than forty years this has been so. Until 1965 the French military tried to establish order in Chad's anarchic north and failed. Five years after independence, the troubles intensified. Arabic-speaking northerners, angered by (Christian) President Tombalbaye's repression of Muslims and by the Christian monopoly on power in Chad, took up arms against N'Djamena, with the support of Libya and Sudan. Tombalbaye's army proved too corrupt and incompetent to suppress them. Soon the entire country slipped into civil war; Muslim-Christian massacres ensued; the southerners were driven from power and the northerners took over.

That solved nothing, as it turned out, because no one could secure the north. In 1972, Libya, taking advantage of the turmoil, claimed part of northern Chad and invaded the potentially mineral-rich Aozou strip. (In 1935, Italy, which ruled Libya at the time, had awarded the strip to French-governed Chad, thereby moving the border between the two colonial territories sixty miles to the south.) In 1987 the French military drove out Gaddafi's troops, and three years later French secret services helped install Idriss Déby, a Zaghawa northerner. This appeared to stabilize the country, but not for long. In 1998 northern guerillas from ethnic groups antagonistic to the Zaghawa raised the banner of revolt against Déby, and the truce the rebels signed with N'Djamena in 2002 has been violated repeatedly. The north, in short, remains as wild as ever.

So, there is no regular transport to Faya or Fada. To find a driver and vehicle, I turned to the police station for help. After urging me to think carefully about whether I wanted to make the trip, and hearing that I certainly did, the chief's adjutant put me in touch with one of his relations, Ibrahim, who drove a Toyota pickup for the chief and who might be willing to take me at least as far as Fada. A well-connected driver, I thought, might prove useful in dealing with unruly soldiers along the way.

Ibrahim turned out to be a lanky fellow in his twenties who wore a navy blue safari suit and spit-polished black platform-heeled boots. His cheeks bore the fierce vertical tribal slashes of the Gorani, his people; nevertheless, his expression was always benevolent. His Arabic was minimal: frequently when he smiled and grinned the most, he understood me the least, but his pride as a Gorani prevented him from admitting it. He had, however, lived in Libya and driven the desert between Abéché and Fada many times, and this was what counted for me. His pickup, an ancient bone-colored Toyota, was the usual four-by-four rolling African menace, with no arrows on its dashboard dials, no glass in its side windows, a cracked windshield, and rusted wires for handles on its doors, which required repeated slamming to close. We settled on a price for his services, and I paid him half the amount in advance so he could buy fuel.

To handle the inevitable breakdowns, Ibrahim would bring along his sidekick, Salah ad-Din, a.k.a. Saladin (after the Kurdish sultan-hero of the Middle Ages who recaptured Jerusalem from the Crusaders). Ibrahim must have found it disconcerting to address this knock-kneed yet sly-eyed adolescent by one of the most redoubtable names in Islam, so he just called him Petit, or 'little one.' Petit was from an Arab village just outside Abéché. He was ambitious: he carried an Arabic language textbook with him and consulted it in his free moments, mumbling out words and puzzling over grammar.

On the day of departure, just after a Harmattan-blurred dawn, Ibrahim came rattling up to Jus de Fruits in his Toyota and lurched to a dust-squall stop. An orange oil drum filled with diesel fuel stood in the back, roped to the cab just behind my seat. Ibrahim and Petit jumped out and unfurled on the sand a twenty-square-yard green tarp. Atop it they placed our bedding and luggage, and then they rolled the ensemble into a bulky cylinder, which they stowed behind the drum. Inside the cabin we placed essentials for the trip: extra-thick Meccan blankets to keep warm in icy desert nights; a jerry can of water; and sacks of groundnuts and dates for food. I also had bought a kadmul to protect me against the cold and dust.

I said a hurried goodbye to the proprietor, and amid a rising wind we drove out of Abéché for the *barrière* and its crew of jumpy soldiers.

By midday the wind stopped, the blowing sand settled, and the sky arched above us in a canopy of deep, invigorating azure. We sped ahead into the desert. The herds of cattle dwindled and the buttes flattened into a stony tableland called *naqa'a* where acacias grew, bent and twisted as if tortured by the heat and sun. We tired of trying to shout over the truck's rattle and the engine's roar, so we talked little. Anyway, I found it consoling to stare off into the sweeping *naqa'a*, where nothing indicated the presence of man, nothing signaled the current century. Out there, it was easy to imagine eons past, when there was no London, no New York, no buildings or electricity; when men and women hunted and gathered, few and afraid and short-lived, naked and probably hot or cold most of the time. How long had *Homo sapiens* lived this way? Half a million years. In this desert, the last four or five thousand years of civilization seemed unreal, fear in the wilderness the natural state to which we would return if ever nuclear blasts bring our modern world to an end.

As the hours passed, the sun softened into a discus of brilliant amber and slanted toward the razor edge of the earth. Late in the afternoon we reached Arada, a silent settlement of colonial-era buildings, mud-block houses, and stately neems, where goats and donkeys foraged on sparse chartreuse grass patchily covering the white sand, and naked, dusty-faced stick-children with big bellies gathered around us and stared, the despair of orphans in their yellowed eyes. Soon after Arada, the cold of dusk set in, pouring into our cabin through the hole at my feet.

'*Al-saka*,' said Ibrahim, eliding the laryngeal gag in the Arabic *saq'a* (severe cold).

'*Wallah*. I hope this truck can make it to Fada. It seems to be rusting to pieces.'

'No, no! This car is *miya-miya! Miya-miya!* [mangled Arabic for 'one hundred percent'] I can drive it all the way to Libya!'

'Fada will be far enough.'

We started to talk, but soon we came upon a sight that frightened us into silence: ahead of us, atop an ashen bulge, a length of tree trunk lay across the piste. The *barrière* for Arada. Sure enough, a half-dozen soldiers tumbled out of a nearby hut and, waving their guns, came running up to the piste, mostly dressed in robes and rags and multicolored kadmuls. They shouted and motioned us to halt.

We did. To present our documents, Ibrahim got out and walked over to the hut, casting a long purple shadow on the golden-lit sands. The soldiers gathered around the truck and peered at me.

I greeted them with '*As-salam 'alaykum*.'

'*Salut!*' answered the officer. He grinned and stepped up to my window. Unlike the others, he wasn't wearing a kadmul or a caftan but khaki fatigues. His face was round and frank, with a flat nose; he reminded me of Mai. '*Salut, mon ami!*'

'*Salut! Ça va un peu?*'

'*Un peu, oui, oui.*'

We grinned at each other awkwardly, and I sensed he wanted something.

'Ah, say,' he continued in French, 'do you have a little book for me?'

'Little book' must be a euphemism for a bribe, I thought. I stiffened up. 'I'm traveling with the brother of the Abéché police chief. I have a permit to reach Faya. All my papers are in order.'

'Ah,' he said. 'You think I'm asking for a *formalité* – the customary dash of a thousand francs. 'You're a preacher, right? I need a new prayer book. I'm just going crazy out here. I'm a *sudiste* [southerner], you see, from Moundou. I'm a Christian.' He reached in and shook my hand again, taking me for a coreligionist. 'I've spent *two years* here in this post, and *eight months* before that in Fada, without going home even once. Imagine! With nothing to read! And all around only Muslims and sand! *C'est l'enfer!*'

That I was American (from the 'Christian United States' as he put it) pleased him, and I regretted not having a prayer book to leave him.

He understood, and we chatted about the loneliness of Arada, the emptiness of the surrounding *naqa'a*, and the beauty of the verdant, remote south – impossible to imagine out here.

Ibrahim came loping back to the truck, looking grim and exasperated. 'Go see the commandant. He's upset.'

Inside the mud hut sat a small man in his fifties with intense eyes and tribal-scarred cheeks. Above him, tacked to the wall, was a poster of President Déby, who was shown standing, his eyes raised to the heavens, his arms outstretched as if ready to embrace the long-suffering Chadian nation. LE BÂTISSEUR! (The Builder!) read the caption.

The commandant hugged himself against the cold, clutching a green down jacket over his caftan. He didn't look up at me. 'You should have come in to see me right away,' he said in French. 'Why didn't you?'

'I'm sorry, I didn't know I had to.'

He kept his eyes on the floor and wrinkled his brow. 'You should be more careful. You should be *respectful*. We're here for your safety. Do you know where you're going?'

'Yes, we hope to make Fada tomorrow.'

He raised his eyes to mine; this wasn't the answer he wanted. He looked down again and stuck out his hand. I gave him my passport.

'No. No,' he said gravely. 'Where's your photocopy?'

'*Photocopy?* Of what?'

He sighed and closed his eyes, and rocked back and forth as if the cold were getting to him. 'Of your *permit*. What else? What do you think I'm doing out here? We keep records here, and I have to know who's passing through my zone. I *must* have a copy. Remember where you're going.'

He wanted money, I was sure, not copies: there wasn't a Xerox machine from here to N'Djamena. I couldn't fault him, really: just above his head the *Bâtisseur* was mocking us all: his outstretched arms *really* seemed to mean, 'Give me! Give me!' What and whom did the Builder represent? His ethnic group and fellow Muslims and the power they seized to enrich themselves in a country foisted on them by departing colonialists, a sham country that could deserve no loyalty. And what was this officer's *real* job? Stuffing his pockets, aggrandizement. The president doled out key posts to his supporters, who in turn hired their relatives and other fellow tribals, ensuring loyalty. Salaries were rarely paid, but officials like this officer exploited their fiefdoms in any way they could. Bribes were their pay.

Without explanation, still looking down, he handed me back my passport. I ran back to the truck.

The sun set. We raced clanking and rattling alone across the desert, leaving a drifting wake of dust, beneath a grand cupolaed sky that was lucent robin's-egg blue in the west, pale violet in the east. Soon we overtook a camel caravan led by Gorani tribesmen, white-robed staff-bearing nomads with tar black skin showing through the eye slits of their kadmuls. Where were they going out here? Did they know anything of the world beyond the Sahara? I took out my blanket and huddled beneath it, feeling, as darkness fell, pangs of despair and alienation.

But not for long. Headlights glinted in our rearview mirror. I turned around to look, as did Petit, who stood up in the back. The lights were gaining on us; the vehicle was moving at great speed, bouncing over the piste, casting yellow beams in our wake.

'Who could that be?' I asked, recalling warnings I had heard in Abéché about bandits.

Ibrahim glanced back and jammed the accelerator to the floor; Petit was now bouncing from side to side in the back, clutching his textbook. But it was no use: within minutes they were gaining on us, and then all at once, flying at full speed through the dark desert, we were suffocating in their churning wake of twigs and dust and stones: it was another Toyota pickup, and its bed was filled with masked men.

They shouted at us to stop. Soon they cut in front of us and we turned to avoid slamming into them, skidding through the sand, crashing through bushes, and coming to a jolting halt.

We waited.

The driver of the truck cried 'Ibrahim! Ibrahim!'

'Moussa?' Ibrahim stuck his head out the window. 'Moussa, is that you?'

The two drivers, friends since childhood, jumped out and embraced. Moussa had heard from the commandant that we were ahead, and just wanted to say hello.

Toward midnight, that touching reunion behind us, we rolled on across the frigid sands, under a moonless sky. I tried talking to Ibrahim but found conversation exhausting because of his poor Arabic and the need to shout. This gave me an idea of just how tough it would be to rule Chad, where so many people spoke mutually unintelligible dialects; an Arab like Mahamat from N'Djamena, for instance, might have just as much trouble communicating with a Gorani out here as I did. And who, besides the Gorani, knew Gorani, the unwritten language of one of the remotest and most xenophobic peoples on earth?

The cold deepened. Ibrahim threw on a navy blue trench coat, Petit, an old down jacket. I began dozing off, wrapped in my kadmul and blanket.

The motor died and we rumbled to a halt in utter blackness.

Several times already the fuel tank had run dry, and the truck had stopped. Then, Petit had hopped down with a length of hose, inserted it in the drum's top aperture, sucked its free end until it spurted fragrant fluid, and then hurriedly shoved the hose in the gas tank. I expected him to do the same this time, but I was wrong.

'Out of gas?' I asked.

'No. Technical problem. Petit! Petit!' shouted Ibrahim as he got out.

Petit jumped down from the rear, grumpy with the cold and entirely covered in dust. He wrenched open the hood, and Ibrahim shone his flashlight on a mess of wires and tubes.

'What's wrong?' I asked.

Ibrahim poked around in the engine. He opened his coat and from his waist pulled out a foot-long dagger with an engraved blade and leather handle.

'You carry a dagger?' I asked, a bit startled.

'Oh, every Gorani does. Many enemies.'

He peered judiciously at the motor and massaged his chin, and he and Petit exchanged knowing glances. Ibrahim then plunged the dagger into the wires around the battery and made a series of precise hacking motions, resulting in a flurry of sparks and a few wisps of smoke.

'Fixed,' he said.

We reboarded the truck. He turned the key and the motor started.

We didn't go far. Somewhere just south of mountains on the horizon, perceptible only as low black hulks blocking the stars, Ibrahim pulled off the piste and drove deep into a grove of acacias. He twisted the key, and the dying engine's coughs echoed against invisible stony bluffs.

'We camp here for the night, hidden like this, just in case. Bandits. Anyway, Fada is closed at sunset. Bad idea to approach the *barrière* in the dark. The soldiers might be nervous.'

We climbed out. I took my mat, pillow, and blankets and walked away into the grove, and spread out everything on the hard, untrammeled sand. A few minutes later, in silence

unmarred by a single buzzing bug or hooting owl, hearing not
even the breathing of my companions (they were twenty yards
away), I fell asleep bathed in the ghostly blue luminescence
washing down from the stars.

From the east, a tint of translucent yellow invaded the sky, and
soon my frosty breath puffs were suffused with light. Finches
and warblers flitted about in the thorny branches above; my eyes
focused on a plethora of birds' nests. A thrush piped out a three-
barred query, and from somewhere in an adjacent acacia came a
matching, three-barred response. By the time the sun edged over
the horizon, doves were cooing and gurgling.

I sat up and looked around. Camels had marched through here;
there was dung in places; there were black beetles. Ahead of us
stood the Ennedi Mountains, red Martian eruptions of stone
announcing the outer limits of Chad and the start of the wildest
expanse of Sahara in Africa – a sight that brought on a chilling,
almost overwhelming emptiness within me. Entering the desert
is always this way: one thinks of it as scenery, perhaps romantic
and even inspiring. But the desert is really about alienation and
parting and death.

Our breath puffing white, we packed up the truck in silence.
Ibrahim let air out of the tires to better handle the sands to come.
We piled aboard and set out for the last hour's drive into Fada,
passing, on the way, just before the oasis, a derelict Libyan tank,
its hatch open, its toothed tracks sunk into the sand, its gun pointing south.

In front of a battlemented clay fortress, neems stood over cream-
colored sand, palm fronds hung motionless and white with the
morning sun's reflected glare. Fada was a clay village, and all
around its northern perimeter rose the granite peaks of the
Ennedi; to the west were barrens, somewhere beyond which the
wastes of Erg du Djourab spread rolling and lifeless to Faya
Largeau.

We pulled up to the fortress and soldiers poured out of the gate
to surround us. A few had guns but others were armed with

shortwave radios; and they frowned urgently as they fiddled with the knobs, trying to catch the latest news on Radio France International's shortwave service.

One lowered his radio and smiled. '*Salut.* Who are you?'

I pulled out my permit and passport. He took them. 'Ah ha! Welcome! Come inside!'

Inside the gates we found the fortress to be in excellent repair, except for its northern quarters, which appeared to have been hit by a shell. In front of them soldiers lazed about on the sand, talking in twos and threes, enjoying the warm sun and sipping tea from tiny glasses.

Inside the dark main room, a high-ceilinged cave, really, sat the adjutant commander behind an old wooden desk. He wore a Hawaiian shirt and sunglasses. By his Western dress and facial features I judged him to be a southerner; and he was friendly in a way that implied we shared something (religion, perhaps); I felt at ease with him. With a stutter and something like a nervous tic in his cheeks, he asked me to have a seat on the chair in front of him.

The officer handed him my papers. 'He just got here.'

'I came from Abéché,' I said. 'I'm with the police chief's brother, and as you see, my papers are in order.'

'Well, you're in luck. The battle just ended. It's best if you return today with the prisoners.'

'The battle? The who?'

'We just fought the rebels and captured fifty of them. We're sending them to Kalait by truck under guard. From there you can catch a truck to Abéché. I advise you to go with them. The soldiers will keep you safe.'

'It's taken us two days to get here. I'd like to see Fada. Anyway, I'm not heading south but onward to Faya Largeau.'

He took another look at the permit and sighed. 'There's no road to Faya from here, and no transport.'

'But there's a piste. Isn't it passable?' I was willing to take risks: for too long I had dreamed of seeing these oasis settlements to turn back so quickly.

'Look, there was shooting right here. I'm afraid I'm going to

have to take you to the prefect. He'll decide if you can stay.
Maybe you can even stay at his house. It's not safe here otherwise. So let's go.'

We set out for the prefect's house, walking down vacant sandy
lanes between stone walls shaded by palms and neems. It was too
early for people to be out and about. Now and then we heard a
donkey bray or a goat bleat, but the impression was of pristine
tranquillity, and it energized me to be there.

The adjutant looked both ways and lowered his voice. 'Say,
you have any *eeskee* with you?'

'Any what?'

'Any *eeskee*? We want to celebrate New Year's. It's only a few
days away.'

'Ah. No, I'm sorry. I don't have any whiskey. I take it you're
not Muslim.'

'Oh, I *am* Muslim. I'm from the south, so I chose my religion
deliberately. To advance. But I still like my *eeskee*. Could you
spare me a *formalité* for cigarettes?'

I handed him a couple of thousand francs.


The prefect permitted me to stay, and he quartered us in the
vice prefect's residence – a three-room single-story house of
stone arranged around a sand courtyard, with space to park the
truck under the neems. It was not immediately clear who the
vice prefect was: several taciturn northerners seemed to live
there, and showed up on the hour to turn on a radio and listen to
RFI's Africa bulletins. It occurred to me that without French
radio they would have no news at all. After so many decades of
independence, the government had still not managed to broadcast across much of its territory, and Chadians relied on the
former colonial power for news of their own events and the
world.


I invited Ibrahim and Petit to eat lunch in the town's sole *jizara*,
a wicker hut across from the fort, in the mud-walled area that
served as the village souk. Chunks of mutton and guts sizzled on
sheets of metal heated by palm-wood fires; the smiling Gorani

proprietor named the prices and, after we ordered, asked us to have a seat in the hut.

The breeze filtered through the straw walls and chased away the flies; light from the sky poured through the slats and ribbed us with shadows. The proprietor brought us a steel tray piled with mutton already stripped off the bones. He served the meat with fresh fiery *shatta*, plus halves of lime and a bowl of chunky-grained Saharan salt, and threw in loaves of bread still hot from the oven behind the hut.

Petit showed me the simple gastronomic routine: you first squeezed the juice from the lime onto your part of the tray. Then, using your fingers, you took the meat and slopped it around in the juice, after which you plopped it into the salt, and from there into your mouth. I did this. The meat dispatched me into ecstatic, shut-eyed reverie, and not just because after two days of dates and groundnuts my palate was ready for a change. I couldn't help thinking that this was how we were meant to eat: the sheep had grazed free, never knowing hormones or antibiotics; the salt came straight from the Saharan earth, uniodized, never purified or packaged; the limes were small, but they, like the plant used to make *shatta*, were grown in Chad's south. I wondered if the freshness of the food here contributed to the clear skin and lean builds of the Chadians, who here in Fada, at least, resembled Ethiopians and Somalis, with long noses and high cheeks.

We ordered a second helping.

During our walk around Fada, a village of five thousand people, we had seen camels wandering in and out of town, men riding donkeys, and goats scavenging. But aside from an army Toyota pickup with a machine gun mounted in the rear, there were no vehicles. Over the meal, I queried Ibrahim about driving me to Faya and expected him to demand a huge amount. (Whom else would I find?) But he stated a fair price, and only after we had reached an agreement did he speak of the difficulties of the route.

'The piste is hard to follow. One wrong turn and you go off into the desert or hit a mine. How many people have died out there after a single wrong turn! Then there are the rebels . . .'

He was willing to risk all this for a couple of days' more pay.

Why? Honor, he said. The Gorani sense of honor, plus the com-
mitment he made to the chief in Abéché to keep me safe, forbade
him from abandoning me.

Ibrahim began talking of Faya, which he was eager to see
again. 'Faya is big city of the desert, a city of trade and life. It has
a huge palm grove. It's the most beautiful place I've ever been.
You should see the hotel there! It has electricity and water, and
televisions in the rooms show Libyan programs. You see, Libyans
are the main guests. They bring everything from Tripoli! Food!
Pepsi! Clothes! Libya is very rich, you see.'

'You make it sound like paradise. What about the rebels?'

'I think the fighting is over around Faya. One thing, though.
Before we go I must buy a *girba*' – a goatskin water bag. 'We
must take a lot of water to cross Erg du Djourab.'

Later that afternoon, as Petit dismantled our truck engine into
a spread of bolts, widgets, and metal doodads on our tarp to make
certain unspecified repairs, Ibrahim and I toured the ramshackle
souk and its *girba* merchants – old women whose wares hung on
bent nails in mud huts. *Girbas* were headless goatskins on which
the holes for the legs, necks, and penises had been bound with
string to form watertight bags. Ibrahim preferred girbas to jerry
cans: 'A *girba* keeps water cool and gives it a pure taste.' He soon
found one, and we would be ready to move on the next morning.

As the sun fell over Fada's sandy labyrinth, we ran into Ibrahim's
uncle, a pensive old man named Suwi whose white goatee sharply
triangulated the chin on his coal black face. Suwi fiddled with his
daggers as we strolled along, pulling one now from a sheath on his
wrist, now from a holster on his waist; perhaps, like many here, he
also had a hidden blade strapped to one of his calves. He and
Ibrahim talked at length in Gorani, of which I could understand
nothing; this freed me to enjoy the sight of Fada as it dissolved in
amber twilight. We walked out past the palms, down the walled
lanes into the oasis, and out into the desert, toward the cliffs
rising at the edge of town.

'A Gorani who doesn't know his camel dung loses his camel,'
Suwi said to me, with Ibrahim translating. 'This dung belongs to

my old camel, that dung to his son. We track our camels by their dung.'

We reached the base of the mountain, a colossus of striated red granite, and stopped on the sand under a ruined clay lookout tower. Suwi massaged his knee.

'You are limping,' I noted.

'During the war with the Libyans I was hit by a shell in the knee. It's healed now.' He picked up what looked like a foot-long chunk of rusty pipe. 'A piece of a stinger missile. Ever since I was a little boy I've seen war, I've seen people dying. It's never stopped. All we know is war.' He smiled. 'All I'll ever know is war.'

'Is it better now, with the truce?'

He smiled again. 'There will be more attacks.' There was no sorrow in his voice.

I tried contemplating fighting in terrain that could kill you even if bullets did not. Three times in the past forty years, coup leaders had declared a period of 'national reconciliation' in Chad, and three times it failed. To be sure, as Suwi said, there will be more attacks.

We turned and looked out over the land: to the north, in darkness now, were stony chasms and massifs. To the west, the sunset bathed the nearby *naqa'a* and the distant sands of Erg du Djourab in delicate pink. The white kadmuls and caftans of my companions glowed, as if phosphorescent. For now, at least, there was peace.

# 6

# THE GUNS OF FAYA LARGEAU

Powered by the midday sun, a gale was tearing off Erg du Djourab, pummeling Fada with rolling waves of hot sand, blinding us with glaring grit. Clutching our kadmuls to our chapped faces, Ibrahim and I made a final, hectic supply run around the wind-ravaged village as we prepared to depart for Faya. We filled our oil drum with diesel fuel; topped off the *girba* with water from the *jizara*'s well; and bought more dates and nuts in the souk. But when we arrived back at the vice prefect's, we discovered that Petit was elsewhere, our tarp was gone, and an apparently vital item in our truck's stock of spare parts was missing – a curious wire-covered widget that resembled a spark plug. ('*Une bobine*' – a bobbin or electrical coil – Ibrahim called it. His Arabic failed him and he could not elaborate, but he said the engine might not work without it.)

Coming just before a trip on which we would need all our luck, these losses boded ill. Ibrahim ducked inside the vice prefect's den and told him about the disappearances, which turned out to be a mistake, for he construed the report as an accusation. Thitherto an unflappable man whose sole activities during our sojourn had been praying, performing ablutions, and listening to RFI, the vice prefect came stomping outside and, standing arms akimbo, declaimed to me, 'We have *never* had a thief in Fada! *Never!*'

'With your permission,' Ibrahim answered, 'it must have been

Petit, that Arab boy of mine, who robbed us! I'm sure of it!' He turned to me. 'Petit was the only person alone with the truck when we were out!'

'But if we need that *bobine* to reach Faya,' I asked, 'why would he steal it? After all, he'll be with us, and he'll suffer too if we have trouble.'

'He's a *thief*, that's why! He must be in the souk selling our things right now! That, that *Arab!*'

Later I would learn from Ibrahim that he believed, as would Petit, that God would decide whether we made it to Faya; hence Petit could steal whatever he liked without affecting our chances of survival. I didn't share their confidence, but, dependent on the two of them as I was, I had no choice but to put my life in their hands, as they put theirs in the hands of God.

It was time to go. I didn't want to leave Fada with the vice prefect cursing at us, so I handed him some francs and apologized, which soothed his rancor. We thanked him profusely for his hospitality and jumped in the truck. We would not wait for Petit to show up; we would head out now to find him along the way.

Fighting the wind, the vice prefect grimly wrestled with the metal gates and threw them open with a clang and a bang. Our engine coughed and ignited, and we lurched out into the sandy gales, heading toward the fortress so that Ibrahim could retrieve his driver's license (which the adjutant had seized on our arrival). We passed the army Toyota pickup on patrol, bouncing down the cratered alleys beneath thrashing palms, scattering villagers, the turbaned soldiers in its rear manning the machine gun and shouldering Soviet-made rocket-propelled grenade launchers.

Just as we rolled out of the souk we came upon Petit and slowed so he could leap aboard. I expected a confrontation, but Ibrahim put his trust in God and said nothing about his suspicions. This I later judged prudent: in the desert, discord could spoil the cooperation on which our survival might depend.

We skidded through the sand to a halt by the fort, and soldiers set upon us. Their red eyes and slurred speech told us New Year's celebrations had started a day early: it seemed someone had found a sizable stash of *eeskee*.

Ibrahim shouted that he would be right back and jumped out.

The soldiers leaned in through our windows, their eyes spider-veined. 'Nasrani, give me a magazine! Nasrani, give me a book to read! We need reading material!'

'I'm sorry, I don't have anything to give you. I'm very sorry.'

One strapping belligerent clearly in no need of more *eeskee* grabbed my collar. 'Look, Nasrani, you don't know who you're talking to. I want you to give me a *magazine* to read, and now.'

Thugs pestering me for magazines seemed odd at first, but then again, both alcohol and reading offer escape – the only thing a rational being could yearn for in this torrid wilderness. Presently a sergeant pushed him aside and put his hand on my shoulder. 'Please, come immediately to the adjutant's office. There's a problem.'

I jumped out and, slanting myself into the wind, ran through the mud portals of the fortress. Ibrahim stood looking panicked outside the adjutant's office. 'He won't give me my papers back until you give him the *formalité*!'

I ran inside. 'He hasn't given me the *formalité*!' said the adjutant, like a petulant child, arising from his desk.

'I've already given it to you, don't you remember? For cigarettes!'

He handed me Ibrahim's papers and looked ready to say something. Before he did, I grabbed Ibrahim's arm and pulled him away. I suffered an urgent presentiment – we had to leave now or we might not get out at all.

We ran back to the truck and found it surrounded by more soldiers, their loose kadmuls whipping vertically in the gale, their boots untied, their rifles flopping on straps from their shoulders. Two of them hoisted their rifles to their backs and were clambering aboard the truck bed, and more were readying themselves to do the same.

'You're taking us to Faya!' the two already aboard shouted to me.

Their weapons disinclined me to argue, and besides, they looked sober and might come in handy should rebels or bandits attack. But four other soldiers pounded on the hood, drunk, and demanded we take them too.

Ibrahim gave me a questioning look.

'No way,' I shouted. 'Let's get going!'

Ibrahim hit the horn and restarted the motor. A blast of wind struck, buffeting us with a blinding billow of sand, and we rocketed ahead, the soldiers at our hood jumping aside.

We swung around and headed west, toward the sun, and out onto descending desert tableland littered with black chunks of basalt and dead scrub, swerving to avoid abandoned Libyan tanks sunk crooked in the sand, veering to miss shell fragments and shrapnel. There was no *barrière*, for few traveled this way. Ahead the Ennedi Mountains cut ridged silhouettes of black against the flaming white haze of the sky.

At a puzzling sign saying HELP DEMINAGE ALLEMAGNE (Demining Germany) we picked up the piste and passed camel skeletons strewn in the sand. Had they been killed stepping on mines?

I turned to Ibrahim. 'What does that sign mean? That they've de-mined this piste, or that they want help in doing so?'

He couldn't read and didn't know, and may not have even understood my question, but in response he swerved off the piste, which could have been mined; or perhaps the miners would assume one would avoid the piste and so would have laid their charges in the surrounding land – who knew? We were, as Ibrahim liked to say, in God's hands now.

'I married for love,' said Ibrahim an hour later, wrestling with the wheel as we hurtled from crater to rut. 'You should know your wife before marrying her, or at least meet her. I'm modern in my thinking, even though I only managed to get a couple of years of schooling.'

This admission fit with what I knew of his character. Although his weak Arabic hindered conversation between us, he was of a sunny disposition and always sincere. No matter how much of a beating his truck took, no matter how outlandish the prices quoted him by merchants in the markets, he never lost his temper. In fact, it seemed that no one in Chad, apart from soldiers, even *had* a temper: patience and stoicism were prevalent (and necessary) personality traits here. Often I felt afraid or frustrated or nervous, but voicing my emotions won me no sympathy: Chadians lived beyond fear and despair, trained by their faith to accept in silence the lot God apportioned them. They would make stalwart friends and redoubtable enemies.

Or such were my impressions. With Ibrahim in particular, the language barrier proved frustrating, and it kept me from really getting to know him. Before coming to Chad I thought Arabic and French would allow me to communicate with everyone; I was wrong. How many peoples here spoke languages that were, as my sullen bar companions in Abéché had informed me, secrets, unknowable, the treasured codes of those craving isolation from even their own compatriots? And as Mahamat had warned me, Chadian Arabic could be tough to understand for speakers of other dialects. Spoken with flamboyant African rhythms, its guttural and glottal consonants and vowels elided, Chadian Arabic sounded like a second language learned imperfectly, which for many, including Ibrahim, it was.

We had been bouncing along the bases of the bread-loaf granite Ennedi ridges, but then reemerged into the open desert. The sun was now sinking into a roiled, apocalyptic sky, infusing the dust clouds churning ahead with hot orange and infernal red before dying in a purple-crimson nova. We then entered upon dunes that, for hundreds of yards at a stretch, covered the piste; we rocked and yawed over their bulges and into their troughs. My fears of hitting a mine had given way to concern that we would get lost, and I noticed Ibrahim had stopped talking and was squinting at the sands.

'There! There it is!' he shouted. A black oil drum protruded, lopsided, through the sand.

The eastern boundary of Erg du Djourab!

Darkness soon descended and hid the Erg's immensity, leaving us blacked-out on an undulant sand sea, waiting for oil drums to pop up dark against the pale sand as we sailed farther from shore, from the *naqa'a* that, if nothing else, afforded us with landmarks of stubble-brush and stone. The cold set in, and Ibrahim rewrapped his kadmul in a bulky way that retained heat, as did I. Warmed, I dozed off.

I opened my eyes to silence. We had stopped. Above us stars coruscated like shattered ice in a black velvet sky. We were deep in Erg du Djourab.

'Is everything okay?' I asked with a cough, finding my throat caked with dust.

'I don't know the way in the dark. If we go on now I may get lost. We should stop here.'

Fine by me. We disembarked, sore from the violent ride, covered in dust, and went around back. We now had five soldiers with us. In the mined zone we had picked up three more – hapless fellows who had finished a long stint of 'guarding the piste' (sitting by an acacia for days with only bread to eat and water to drink) and whom I pitied too much to refuse a lift. Ibrahim and I found them all in the back, covered with dust, huddling in their parkas and kadmuls next to Petit. He roused them, and they groggily grabbed their bedrolls and jumped down. After staggering about a bit, all of them phantoms of dust with dusty rifles, they marched off to camp by a sandy hillock. Petit and Ibrahim joined them, which left me alone by the truck.

I turned and looked out over Erg du Djourab. Bosomy swells of silvered sand stretched away under a waxing moon, pumpkin-hued and giant. Few regions in the Sahara required more expertise to navigate than this, even in daylight, and I felt grateful for Ibrahim's prudence.

I assembled a windbreak out of my travel bag and the jerry can, behind which I spread my mat and blankets. With my head wrapped in my kadmul, I settled in to watch the stars shoot and the moon brighten. From my companions I heard nothing: they were either too cold to talk or already asleep.

The wind soon expired and a primordial peace settled over the sands. As my eyelids grew heavy, I drifted into ruminations. This desert hardened the people inhabiting it, and, by turning daily life into a feat of survival demanding discipline and skill, bred among them a sense of superiority over the easygoing forest-dwellers to the south, a superiority entrenched further by the sacred sureties of Islam. Though it was open, the desert fostered a closed world of faith and rigor and harsh judgment: almost every decision here could have lethal consequences, and the scarcity of water, food, and shelter instilled a fear of the stranger as a rival; banding together to protect one's own was as natural and necessary as preying upon those outside the clan.

I awoke to the peach-colored sky of a translucent dawn. Fearful of moving and admitting the near-freezing air into my bedding, I spent a long time motionless and supine, watching the day break. From my spot on the sand in the beatifying auroral pallor, Erg du Djourab spread vaster and more mysterious than I had imagined in the dark: from horizon to rolling horizon, rippled dunes in voluptuous mounds of the finest golden sand, offering, however, to my suddenly alarmed eye, no hint of a piste, neither a marking barrel nor a tire track.

Soon the others assembled by the truck's rear, stiff with cold and grumpy, and Ibrahim and I climbed into its frozen innards. Chance contact with its metal surfaces produced a nearly cryogenic burn. I thought of how the greater cold that I had experienced in Siberia had produced less discomfort, probably because there were no extremes of temperature there. Here in the Sahara one could not adjust to the thermometer's daily descents and climbs.

But the engine wouldn't start.

'*Al-saka!*' said Ibrahim.

After a twenty-minute hood-up examination, Ibrahim decided that it wasn't the cold that kept the motor from turning over; we needed that *bobine* that Petit might or might not have stolen. All Chadians present drew their knives and commenced poking at the engine; sparks flickered out from the battery, but to no avail. Nevertheless, half an hour later, after much more daggered fiddling and the cleaning of a plastic tube, the motor chugged to life. From then on, every hour or so, the truck would die and we had to repeat the daggering procedure. These delays upset me: it was New Year's Eve, and I was set on reaching Faya, with its promise of hotels and *réveillon* celebrations, before dusk and the lowering of the *barrière*.

We charged on across the Erg. Frequently we found that sand had buried the oil drums, but they now had ten-foot black and white poles attached, and these poked crookedly through the sands at hundred-yard intervals, marking the way across dunes that grew so mountainous, we had to detour around them, leading us off course and into trackless terrain. The engine roared and gagged, and Ibrahim muttered about that blasted *bobine* and the perfidy of Petit; the near-vertical sun washed all color away, turning, by noon, our gilt sand sea into a hilly domain of steely glare overarched by the incandescent sky. Repeatedly we floundered ascending the dunes, slipping backwards into troughs, and had to dig our way out.

Two hours after noon, we were cutting through choppy dunes streaked with cement gray limestone. We lost the oil drums altogether. The ashen ground melded with the pewter sky, and I closed my sun-fatigued eyes and wished for arrival, trusting in Ibrahim's mastery of the terrain.

In the last hour of daylight, we halted atop the crest of a giant dune. Ahead, beneath the failing sun, limestone terraces ten or fifteen feet wide descended to a boundless palm grove in whose distant reaches rose a minaret and stone houses. Faya Largeau! It looked to be what it was: the largest oasis town on earth.

Ibrahim was excited. 'We'll just make it before they close the *barrière!*'

He gunned the motor and it died.

After another repair session with the knives, we bounced down the terraces toward the oasis and pulled up to the *barrière* – a wire strung across the piste between two barrels, marked with strips of paper.

Kadmuled soldiers bounded out of nearby mud huts to level their rifles at us.

'Halt!' they shouted in Arabic. 'Who are you? Where are you going? What are you doing here?'

Ibrahim explained. We were too late, they answered: they had just closed the *barrière*.

Ibrahim switched to Gorani and pleaded with them, telling of the 'Nasrani' and the *'commissaire'* (those words I recognized), but got for an answer an indignant head-shaking diatribe peppered with Arabic words like 'rebels thirty kilometers away!' and 'attack!' and 'no way!' The eyes showing through slits in kadmul masks betrayed no sympathy, only fatigue. One of the men was soon pointing his gun barrel at a sand patch where we could park and pass New Year's Eve.

But the exchange dragged on, and Ibrahim began calling on God and asking for mercy. To my astonishment, just as the sun slipped away and the sky turned violet, an officer unhooked the wire and raised the *barrière*. Ibrahim hit the gas, but the officer called to stop us again. He warned us to slow when passing the sentries on hillocks amid the palms ahead so that the soldiers could get a good look at us, otherwise they might open fire. After enjoining us to register immediately with the police, he stepped aside.

We rolled along the winding piste into the palm grove. Now every fifteen yards turbaned soldiers atop the hillocks waved at us to halt; they came loping down, their caftans tangling between their legs, their guns swinging, and listened to Ibrahim's pleas and explanations. *'Imshee!'* (Go!), they said, relenting.

We careened past a final row of palms and entered the town – a maze of whitewashed stone walls and sandy alleys. All around us stone and sand and palm and sky glowed with the immaculate light of a rising moon: the world luminesced in silver-blue, and I felt arrived and delivered. But up trundled a khaki Toyota bristling with machine guns and grenade launchers. The masked soldiers in its back shouted something to Ibrahim in Gorani, and he shouted something about the hotel. They shook their heads.

'The hotel's been closed,' Ibrahim said. 'They say we have to go now to the police chief and present ourselves, or we'll be in trouble. It's right over there.'

There was a pounding on our cabin roof, and Ibrahim stopped. Our soldiers dismounted and waved goodbye to us; I never saw their faces, owing to their kadmuls. The engine would not restart for us to drive the last twenty yards. We got out to walk, carrying my bags.

A dozen soldiers jogged by us in loose formation, their weapons bouncing at their waists. Just up ahead, a helmeted sergeant wearing a camouflage jacket over his caftan waved his rifle at us.

'You! Come here!'

We both took out our papers. He snatched my passport and examined it. A smile creased his face. He addressed me in French. 'You go inside here, please' – he pointed to a blue steel door in a cement wall – 'and see the police chief.' He then occupied himself with Ibrahim's papers and his vehicle permit and wanted to know where Petit was from.

Behind the steel door, high walls surrounded a hilly lot of sand with what looked like a bomb crater in its midst, next to which stood a white stone bunker. In the back of the compound beneath shaggy palms was a three-room stone house fronted by an overhanging roof. Under a bright bare bulb, a soldier slumped on a chair beneath the light, his head and face wrapped in a khaki kadmul, his eyes behind dark sunglasses.

'*As-salam 'alaykum!*' I said, hoping he was a Muslim. He didn't answer but cocked his head to one side. Seconds later, a man whose stern countenance and disciplined gait signaled high rank came out of one of the rooms. He was about forty years old; his Caucasian features gave him the look of an Ethiopian, though he was very black.

'*As-salam 'alaykum!*' I said to him.

'*Salam*,' he replied in a clipped way. 'Papers.'

He took my passport and my travel permit.

'*Amriki?*' he noted with surprise, even alarm, and studied my face, and took my passport over to the light for a closer look. The soldier got up and leaned over his shoulder and, taking off his glasses, peered at my passport, and then at me. The guard who had directed me here walked in, smiled, and nodded approval at the terse description of me: *Amriki*.

The chief, however, was unmoved, and asked in Arabic how I had reached Faya, and who had authorized my trip here. The piste was mined – did I not know that? I explained that the brother of the police chief of Abéché had driven me, and pointed to Ibrahim, who was loitering by the front door, nervous of entering. This failed to legitimize me.

'Look,' the chief said in annoyance, 'this is a war zone. We're fighting off rebel attacks every night. I don't understand what you're doing here.'

'I always wanted to see Chad, and heard that Faya Largeau was the largest oasis town in the Sahara. That's all.'

He raised his eyebrows. 'You'll remain here under guard, as my guest. This is for your own good. We have a curfew here that starts at ten-thirty in the evening. Only the military patrols are out after that. So you're not going anywhere until tomorrow.'

The guard introduced himself as Hussein. He eyed me with unabashed curiosity. 'You'll hear the shooting at night, really!' He smiled broadly. 'Very dangerous!' He could not have looked happier.

Ibrahim and Petit left to look for a *bobine*, saying they would be by in the morning. The chief finished his document check, saying, 'I'm keeping your passport until you go, which should be very soon. *Very* soon.'

It was New Year's Eve. What does one do for fun in a Saharan oasis town under rebel attack? After the soldiers and I finished off a tray of gluey rice and pungent lamb, Hussein hoisted his automatic rifle to his shoulder. 'There's a *pari-vente* I was thinking of going to . . .' The *commissaire* had gone home, so we were free to sneak out and party.

A half-hour's hike down unlit, moon-dusted lanes deep into the middle of Faya brought Hussein, the soldier in sunglasses, whose name was Isa, and me to the outdoor bar Chez Elyse, where plastic chairs and wobbly wooden benches stood half-sunk in silken white sand, beneath palms with fronds drooping dark against the star-washed sky. Scarved women stepped lively, bringing giant bottles of beer to their customers – frank and friendly-looking soldiers from the south chatting up women from the north veiled in milhafas. A boom box blasted out Congolese pop, and couples shimmied on the cement dance floor. Now and then the gusting breeze prompted all present to hug their camouflage jackets and milhafas tight and turn away from the blowing sand.

Hussein pulled me to the back of the bar, where lopsided tables were set up behind a ragged straw partition. 'The official government section,' he said. 'No informers here. Besides, we can't fraternize with the privates. It would be bad for our image.'

We took seats on the wobbly government bench. From behind his dark sunglasses Isa said that he had come on 'special assignment' from N'Djamena to 'finish off these rebels,' although no one had managed to accomplish this task in the past forty years, or eighty years, or hundred years. He spoke in a belabored way that suggested he was drunk or stoned, but he wasn't.

Hussein smiled and told me he had graduated from a military academy in N'Djamena and was a relative of the (Gorani) ex-president Hissène Habré, who had been deposed in 1990 and was now exiled in Senegal. His job here in Faya was to guard the police chief.

I ordered us a round of beers.

'It's rough out here,' Hussein said, winking at the plump mama across from us.

'The rebels just shot down our air force. Our whole air force,' Isa added.

'Your whole air force?'

'Yes, all two helicopters. But we'll get them for it. They're only thirty kilometers from here, out in the mountains you see to the north.'

'What're they fighting for?'

'What do you think?'

'I don't know.'

'Chad is rich. They want our riches.'

In fact, the uranium deposits in the Aozou strip over which Chad and Libya had fought for seventeen years had proved non-existent, so 'riches' hardly sufficed as a casus belli. Northern Chad was what it looked to be: thousands of square miles of barren, useless terrain.

Encouraged by inviting glances from Hussein, another large woman sat down on the bench in front of us. She was dressed in a yellow-green milhafa and wore a scarf tied in a bow atop her broad forehead, and she had scars on her pockmarked cheeks. She drained her beer and stared at me, and her cheeks puffed out with a burp.

She smiled at me. 'You a Christian?'

'After a fashion.'

'Then you can come pray with us tomorrow at the church. We're very faithful here. Would you buy me another beer, one Christian to another?'

'Sure.'

Hussein leaned over to my ear and whispered, 'You know what "Christian" means, don't you?'

'What?'

He chuckled at my obtuseness. 'It means she's a whore. She's available for you, here and now. All the women here are.'

'Thanks very much, but I think I'll pass.'

'But it's New Year's!'

'You've got to party, young man!' the large woman said to me in a hectoring tone. 'We don't have New Year's here very often. It's not like in Europe, where every weekend is New Year's. So buy us another round of beers!'

A little while later, when it was nearing ten o'clock, I suggested we might head back to the chief's compound. I didn't want to violate the curfew. We said goodbye to the Christian woman and walked out into the lane now glowing with moonlight. We got halfway down the street when shouts rang out in Arabic behind us.

'Hey you! You're stealing our women!'

Two drunk soldiers were dragging their guns in the sand and staggering along behind us, their faces half-hidden behind loose kadmuls, their boot laces untied. Between us and them were two petite and giggling women who clutched their black shawls to their faces with their teeth.

'There must be a misunderstanding,' I said to Hussein.

'No, there isn't.'

The girls passed me, and one tried to tickle me, which doubt-less the soldiers found incriminating, for they erupted into more shouts.

'You see,' Hussein explained, 'Isa and I have made arrange-ments . . . It's New Year's. We'll take you back and then go with them.'

Hussein shouted something at the soldiers and went back to challenge them. A cursing match broke out, and he began push-ing and shoving them. The girls, waiting just up ahead, laughed and ducked around the corner palm. One stuck her hand around the wall and made a beckoning motion to me, and there was more giggling. Then I noticed that the street around me was alive with veiled, beckoning women and boozy-eyed, love-struck soldiers. Islamic or not, Faya Largeau was a brothel town and probably had always been one, given its location on prime trade routes.

Hussein trotted back up to us, having pulled rank on the sol-diers and extracted an apology from them. With the two women now keeping ten yards ahead of us, we resumed our hike to the chief's, stumbling across more giggling women and their armed paramours in the moonlit lanes.

In the morning, the chief stuck his head in my doorway. 'It's New Year's Day, so come eat camel with us.'

I had spent months riding camels in the Moroccan Sahara and was dearly fond of them; the last thing I wanted to do was to eat one. The thought of those blubbery-lipped, noble-hearted beasts having their throats slit in the Islamic way, tumbling to the sand, choking on their own blood, and then being hacked into pieces set my stomach turning. But I couldn't refuse my host. Camel meat turned out to be succulent and sweet, perhaps the tenderest flesh I have ever eaten. I couldn't stop myself from devouring a bowlful of it.

The chief wiped camel juice from his lips and loaded rounds into his pistol, which he packed in the breast of his caftan. He stood over me. 'Come with me. I now will show you Faya.'

Hussein rose to the challenge, grabbing his automatic rifle, and we all jumped aboard the chief's Land Cruiser.

Under a whiteout sun, lashed by gales driving sand, we hurtled around Faya. It turned out there was really little to see. Thanks to a history of warfare and traditional Islamic privacy, Faya was hidden behind high walls, save the center: a flyblown hodgepodge of tin and mud huts with skittish goats and mean-eyed donkeys foraging in rubbish heaps, all covered in dust and wincing from the wind. Only the florid hues of fluttering milhafas provided relief to the eye from stark sand and sun.

We broke free of the lanes and bounced out into the oasis, passing Arab nomads leading camels and army Toyotas on patrol, on which gunmen swung machine guns, kadmuls fluttering behind them like the ragged standards of advancing armies. Farther on, in the lime-whitened desert, camels were lined up by men digging in ditches: they were mining salt, and the caravans would carry much of it throughout the Tibesti region. This region's economy owed almost nothing to the outside world and took little from it.

The chief nudged me. 'Look!'

Under the shifting shade of nearby palms, water was spouting out of the earth into yard-wide cement troughs, which directed the currents to nearby plots of tomatoes and onions. 'We never get a drop of rain! All our water comes gushing up out of the earth by natural pressure. It lets us grow all this food for ourselves, if we never have enough to sell to anyone else. We're self-sufficient up here, which is good in case of attack. So we have fertile land without a drop of rain. Have you ever seen such land?'

I told him I hadn't. We crashed on through the oasis trails, and twenty minutes later we were riding into a village half-buried in sand and harried by winds. There were no men, but women were about. On seeing us, they scampered into their huts and peered at us from the doorways. The chief drove in weird evasive zigzags, and a broad, excited smile creased Hussein's face.

'We're in Dozanga, a rebel village,' said the chief. 'It's most dangerous to be here now, but they know I'm the police chief, so they're scared.'

At that he jerked the wheel and made as if heading for some

women, sending them running, sandals flapping, down an alley. He laughed.

'Where are the men?' I asked.

'In the mountains. We can't stop them from coming down at night for provisions. It's always been this way. We Chadians are unfortunate. We haven't been able to develop because we're always fighting, and our people are always starving as a result.'

We turned back into town and passed by one of its few schools. It had a fitting name – the High School of the Martyrs.

There seemed to be more drama in the chief's statements than there was in the conflict itself. The fight-by-day, visit-by-night schedule the rebels of Dozanga kept indicated complacency on both sides. I wondered how much these rebels and their war resembled the Bedouin of old Arabia and their raids, which they carried out as much for sport as for booty, often with minimal loss of life. Since there were no riches under the sand here, and no hated Christians in power now, maybe the rebels up here fought because, being young men, they liked to fight; maybe their conflict was, ultimately, as pregnant with meaning as a riot between fans of rival teams at a European soccer match. Maybe it would never stop, and maybe it made no difference.

'We always liked the Americans before,' said the chief as we ate a camel dinner later that day. He was frowning, and his eyes were hardening. 'Because blacks in the U.S. are advanced and have their rights. So we liked you. Before Bush, that is. Not now. I see that you Americans don't respect human rights. You are Ariel Sharon's puppets, and you destroy the world's faith in you by supporting that state terrorist. You don't care about the poor. You aren't true to your ideals. When Bush stole the elections, you didn't even demonstrate. Some democrats you Americans are. You lecture the world about free elections but do nothing yourself when your elections are stolen. And to stop one man, Osama, you destroyed an entire country, Afghanistan – a country of the poorest people on earth. Is that manly – picking on those poor Afghans? Bush doesn't think about his place in history. *I* think about my place. With my job I could take bribes and be corrupt, but that would be bad for me in the eyes of history. But Bush . . . what *man* launches a war against an entire country of poor people to kill one person?'

'I think you have to understand that after September 11, the United States felt it had to do something.'

'Even worse than Bush is Tony Blair. By God, I swear it, Blair's a billy goat.'

'A billy goat?'

'Yes. Like a billy goat, he'd hump a cow or a camel or a dog on Bush's orders. He would do whatever the U.S. asked of him. He's worse than a traitor. He's not a *man*. Now Mullah Omar, there's a *man*: no matter how much Bush screamed and yelled, Omar wouldn't hand over his friend Osama. Friendship and honor come above all. For *men*, that is.'

The chief's diction was clipped, his Arabic precise. He was not some radical who had memorized the Qur'an in a mud madrassah; he was educated, and he followed the news broadcast on the BBC's Arabic radio service. He was stating grievances with the United States that one might hear anywhere in the Islamic world, but contrary to what he said, I was sure those grievances existed before Bush and the war in Afghanistan, before September 11, and before Sharon came to power. They derived from the general impression that the West is anti-Islamic: it supports Israel over the Palestinians, exercises hegemony in the Gulf to protect the oil supplies on which it depends, and props up tyrannical regimes that cater to its interests. These truths have incited discontent among Muslims across the world for decades. But Bush (and Blair) angered Muslims in a newly and uniquely personal way, and evoked a disgust whose likes I had never before seen in twenty-one years of overseas travel.

My attempts to engage Ibrahim in talks about politics had failed, both on account of the language barrier and because he was illiterate. The conclusions one might draw are obvious: the more education spreads in the Islamic world, the more hostility toward the West will increase and the more Muslims will perceive (and find infuriating) the discrepancies between ideals the West proclaims and the realpolitik deals and policies by which it survives. If democracy takes root in the Islamic world, educated Muslim voters will choose candidates opposing the West and regimes will change, but to the detriment of the West.

The French colonel's sweaty, shaved cranium and wire-rimmed spectacles sparked sunlight as he jerked the steering wheel right and left, piloting his jeep over the pitted lanes through advancing clouds of pillaging sand, with me bouncing about helplessly on the front seat. Toggle-eared and barrel-chested, he carried himself with the swashbuckling aplomb one hopes to find in military men but rarely does.

A Chadian patrol Toyota was heading toward us down the alley, bouncing over the ruts. The colonel swerved playfully into its way and out again, provoking the Chadians to frantic evasive maneuvers and a near collision with a mud wall.

He laughed. 'They can't drive! They're like children with their cars!'

Pretty young women strolling along unveiled he warned, with a shake of the forefinger, 'I'm jealous, you hear! Don't you flirt with men now! Behave yourselves!' He turned to me, adding, 'Their men whip them if they flirt, you see!'

From the chief I had learned that once in a while a French military aircraft flew in from N'Djamena bringing supplies. Since I had to return to N'Djamena and was tired of the desert, I thought I might approach the French and see if they would give me a ride.

The planes came because the French still maintained a small military base at the edge of town – a small but significant base. No one in Faya forgets that French air force raids drove the Libyans out of Faya, prompting them to abandon their tanks with less than Gaddafian revolutionary zeal and hightail it back home on foot. The French also operate a much larger base in N'Djamena. Both installations support France's postcolonial policy in Africa (France has troops stationed in five African countries), which, no matter what Paris says about American *hyperpuissance* and unilateralism, remains colonial and aims unabashedly to protect French interests (mostly economic) in its former fiefdoms by propping up *présidents amis* or engineering the overthrow of disobedient rulers. Amid all the discourse in France about human rights, one rarely hears about this, though President Jacques Chirac pledged to change his government's Africa policy after coming to power. Neither is the idea of France's colonial-era *mission civilisatrice* dead. The French provide their former colonies with aircraft, arms, medicines, doctors for their hospitals, and French university education for their young.

The colonel deposited me at the Faya base (an adjunct to a Chadian military facility of some sort), where I spoke to the *chef d'escale*, the hulking and gallant Captain Philippe Fouquet, whose swarthy complexion suggested Caribbean ancestry. Captain Fouquet had a manner both authoritative and affable that allowed him to keep on good terms with the Chadians yet manage the most valuable service one could provide in Faya: escape. When the supply flight touched down, Fouquet found himself besieged by desperate Chadians for whom the flight was, as it would be for me, the only safe and easy way out of Faya. He told me that he would have to request permission to take me aboard from the ministry of defense in Paris, but that this should be no problem.

Shortly after dawn the next day, when I was supposed to depart, another gale arose in the desert, melding sky and earth in a maelstrom of burning sand that made me wonder if any plane could possibly land or take off. Ibrahim and Petit, who were readying themselves for the drive back to Abéché, showed up at the chief's door to say goodbye.

How many people in my life had helped me, at considerable risk to themselves, using all their knowledge and talent, to travel from one dangerous point on this planet to another – people to whom I owed my life but could pay only a modest daily wage? Beyond almost every foreign correspondent's reportage in the Third World there stands a driver, a translator, a fixer, and yet where are they credited? They are rarely mentioned, and for a good reason: to do so would detract from the glory of the correspondent, who would rather remain, to readers at least, the lone civilized buccaneer using his or her battle-sharpened acumen to interpret turbulent events among troubled natives. In reality, the correspondent, like me, relies on locals to get around, understand what is going on, find food to eat and a safe place to sleep, and frequently to deal with obstreperous officials, even criminals. In the end, the correspondent flies out and the fixer stays, possibly to face those same officials alone but without the protective presence of the foreign press agent.

I embraced Ibrahim and Petit, made them gifts of my desert bedding and a few other things I would no longer need, and said goodbye.

At eight in the morning, Captain Fouquet's jeep careened up to the compound's door, on schedule, and braked with a squeal. I was ready, bags packed. The chief was bathing in the pit-toilet enclosure. We shouted our valedictions over its cement wall, and I ran outside and tossed my bag in the jeep.

The wind battered a ragged procession of men, women, and children trudging out to the airport, satchels atop their heads like refugees. We drove alongside them, moving slowly in case a child should skip out into the road, as often happened.

'They're going to try to get aboard that plane, you see,' said Fouquet. 'All hell breaks loose when that plane arrives. But I tell them they need to be cleared by the Chadian authorities, who usually just reserve seats for themselves and their families. It's always the same.' Forty-three years after independence, the Chadians were not only still listening to French radio for their news, but relying on the French to get them around their own country.

We wheeled through dust devils and pulled up to a single white concrete structure the size of a provincial railway station, with broken windows and a smashed-up control tower. The airport. Behind it was the runway, and beyond that, dunes and the open Sahara. Fouquet honked to disperse the crowd, and we drove through gates to park next to the runway. Lying in charred ruins at the runway's head was the Chadian air force: two burned wrecks of helicopters shot down by rebels.

We alighted. Soldiers, women with children, and elders and turbaned young men jammed around us, demanding seats.

Fouquet waved his clipboard. 'Back! Back! Please! I have only eleven free places. The Chadian officer will assign them to you, not me!' He clearly enjoyed exercising his authority and having an audience. He turned to me. 'There's nothing I can do. Come on, let's check the runway – there could be a dead camel or goat out there, and I've got to give the pilot the all-clear signal. In this sandstorm he won't be able to see anything.'

We rode up and down the runway with exaggerated slowness. We found nothing. Fouquet then climbed down from the jeep and ran back out to the middle of the runway. There he stood, putting on his headset and wiping the dust off his red and white signal batons.

I stood and waited with the crowd. We all stared into the glare-infused sand swirling above the dunes at the runway's end, shielding our eyes and searching for the plane. How could any plane land in this sandstorm? Fouquet had told me that since the dunes were always on the move, the pilot's *point de repère* would be a rock outcropping on the other side of the runway.

Fouquet started waving his batons at the sandstorm. We squinted but discerned nothing, heard nothing; we were on the wrong side of the wind. Finally, a faint iron gray blur limned into the gaseous brown sky – a Transall C-160 troop transport plane. It hung suspended, tilting its wings as if balancing, but in fact rocking on gusts as it descended at high speed, zeroing in on our runway. All at once the roar of propeller engines hit us, and we covered our ears. The huge craft bounced onto the runway and taxied to a rapid halt.

There was no tarrying. The rear trapdoor opened. Soldiers in full combat gear jumped out, wielding submachine guns, and took up guard positions fore and aft. Soldiers from the base hurried to wheel containers of fresh provisions off the plane and down tracks on the trapdoor, and then rolled empty containers aboard. Fouquet jogged back to us and gave us passengers numbered tags and lined us up. On his shout and at the flourish of his baton, we jogged into the blowing sand and boarded the Transall through the trapdoor, to settle into red canvas seats beside containers netted and bolted to the floor. Fifteen minutes later we were airborne, with the fierce desert light filtering into the cavernous hold through porthole windows.

Six hours later, after a stop in Abéché, we touched down in N'Djamena.

# 7

# THE SULTAN OF KANEM

Against an evening sky of ethereal azure, atop arching, sugary white limestone portals, a block-lettered, hand-painted sign announced in French, SULTANATE OF KANEM. Just beyond the portals, inside the courtyard, stood a turquoise-shuttered limestone house marked SULTAN'S PALACE – POST BOX 13. There was something fantastic and fablish about the comic-strip designations and birthday-cake colors. Even the inhabitants of the surrounding village of Mao looked like extras from a made-for-TV adaptation of *Arabian Nights*: astride picturesque black stallions, dressed in flamboyant turbans and shimmering robes of maroon and royal blue, the Maoans might have been on their way to commit debaucheries with the queen at the palace of King Shahriyar. Yet again Chad astonished me: How had such people made it into the twenty-first century untouched by the modern world?

The isolation imposed by the desert (Mao is two hundred miles north of N'Djamena) partly explained how. The horses of Mao reminded me of a historical fact of continental significance: the tsetse fly helped halt at the Sahel the southward advance of Islam in West and Central Africa. In the jungles nearer the Equator, tsetse flies carry and transmit the lethal nagana virus to ungulates and thus, by killing livestock, hindered the equestrian and camel-riding Arabs in their penetration of sub-Saharan Africa.

Had it not been for the tsetse, Islam might have spread as far as the Cape of Good Hope, and the 360 million Africans who bear the Bible today might be chanting suras from the Qur'an.

The Arabs did, however, make it to Mao, as the presence of horses still attests, and so the legend goes. The people of Kanem, the Kanuri, trace their lineage back to ninth-century Yemeni migrants who allegedly introduced Islam and established the Sayfawa dynasty that was to last a thousand years. At its zenith, what history books refer to as the 'empire of Kanem' spread from Tripoli in the north to the edge of the Wadai sultanate in the east and to Lake Chad in the west. This was one immense, if perilously barren, swath of Africa – barren but strategically vital, thanks to the intersection of Saharan trade routes there. When trade was at its peak, during the Middle Ages, the sultan of Kanem controlled the caravan routes from Libya, Egypt, and Sudan south across the Sahel to black Africa. But Kanem's glory days are over now. The current sultan, Alifa Ali Zerzeti, who is said to be more than a hundred years old, reigns over a palace and a P.O. box. He also functions as an intermediary between the Kanuri people and the government in N'Djamena.

After returning to N'Djamena from Faya Largeau, I found Mahamat at the taxi stand outside my hotel. I asked him to drive me out to see Mao, Kanem's capital. He said he would be delighted to oblige and expounded on the prospect of journeying into such storied demesnes. 'You'll see new Mao and of course ancient Mao,' he said, 'which is one of the splendors of Chad . . . and that sultan they've got there is *truly* noble!' However, he warned of the dangers. Getting to Mao involved crossing bandit-prowled terrain, and friends of his had recently been attacked in their Land Rover, robbed of all their money and possessions, and locked in the trunk. (They escaped after jimmying the trunk's lock.) He also warned me that under no circumstances must we arrive unannounced; we would have to seek permission beforehand for the visit from the sultan's son, the prince, or we could be considered intruders. (The Kanuri are suspicious of outsiders, Mahamat said.) Once there, for safety's sake we should spend the night under guard in the sultan's palace.

The sultan's power might have been greatly reduced from what it was during the days of empire, but apparently he still held enough sway to help find his son a job at Esso, the oil company, which had an office in N'Djamena. A quick visit to his well-mannered heir ended with the prince's promising to call ahead to the sultan and introduce us so there would be no misunderstanding. Then we switched the Peugeot for a Land Cruiser belonging to Mahamat's uncle – ordinary cars, Mahamat said, could never handle the rugged piste to Mao – and set out.

After passing Massaguet, we bounced off the paved road onto powdery *naqa'a* and headed north, soon cresting dunes and crashing through scrub, winding up wadis, traversing desert considerably more contoured and rugged than the terrain stretching east to Abéché. Eight hours after setting out, in late afternoon, we spotted the limestone houses of new Mao atop a sandy eminence rising from a palm oasis. I found the palace soft on the eye, small but harmonic. Mahamat told me he found the palace disappointing: it could never compare to the castellated grandeur of ancient Mao, which it would be his pleasure to show me the next morning. But first we had to pay our respects to the sultan.

We drove into the courtyard. An old man clad entirely in immaculate white, from pointy-toed slippers to peaked kadmul, minced out from behind a wall. He did look suspicious, or so Mahamat's description of the Kanuri disposed me to regard him. He introduced himself as the *wazir* (vizier, or minister) of the sultan and, skipping the elaborate greeting ritual, asked what exactly we were doing there, and who I was.

Mahamat cast me an I-told-you-so glance as he explained our mission. 'Our brother Jelal has come all the way from the United States to see the sultan. Would His Excellency find a few minutes to grant him an audience?'

The vizier glanced at me and frowned with alarm. He took Mahamat aside and murmured something to him, shooting more incriminating looks my way. He then minced away behind the wall again.

Mahamat strolled back to me, his eyes shifting from side to side. He spoke out of the corner of his mouth. 'Ah, hmm. The prince, it seems, never called here to announce us. We've broken the protocol.'

'What are the consequences?'

'We are at the mercy of His Excellency.'

'Well, we're already here, and it's too late to go back. So what do we do?'

'Please, do just as I say, or you could give offense. For starters, take off your shoes before entering His Excellency's presence, and speak only when His Excellency addresses you.'

I would later understand that the sultan's Arab ancestry elicited such respect from Mahamat.

The vizier stepped out from behind the wall again. 'The sultan will see you now! Come!'

Mahamat lowered his head and fell in behind the retreating vizier, as did I. We followed him into a limestone-walled maze of white sand alleys to the 'court' – yet another sandy lot – and were requested to remove our shoes. Two plastic garden chairs stood in front of a rickety K-Mart aluminum chaise longue with an avocado green plastic cushion on it. To one side was a room with a doorway draped with a ratty batik cloth. The evening sky bathed us in a glow that gave the crude surroundings an almost Grecian, still-life elegance.

'Be seated!' ordered the vizier, pointing to the chairs.

Our plastic seats squeaked and cut their way crookedly into the sand as we sat down; my legs shot up and I nearly toppled over backwards. No one cracked a smile, though, or even acknowledged my contretemps, although the vizier peered at my chair to see if I had damaged it. Here in hardscrabble Chad, such furniture was hard to come by and exuded an inviolable solemnity. The vizier slipped behind the batik cloth, and Mahamat kept his eyes down.

We waited.

The voice of the vizier sounded through the batik. 'All rise for the sultan of Kanem!'

We struggled to stand, with further creaky remonstrations from our chairs and more leg follies. Once afoot, Mahamat bowed his head and opened his hands in a gesture of supplication, and glanced at me from the corner of his eye; I did the same.

Apparently to honor the sultan, Mahamat recited the Fatiha (the opening sura, or chapter, of the Qur'an). An old man in a lop-sided and towering white kadmul and plush aquamarine robes doddered out of the side room and, prodding the sand with his cane, made for his K-Mart throne. He sat down on it and pulled his legs up, one at a time, and stretched out. He turned and, tilt-ing his head in a regal way, regarded us with friendly eyes. His café au lait skin, long nose, and thin lips did hint at Arab ancestry. He looked remarkably fit for a man who, supposedly, had lived more than a century.

The vizier barked, 'Explain your mission to the sultan!'

I repeated the supplicatory gesture with my hands and looked down. 'Your Highness,' I said in Arabic, trying to recall suitably royal locutions from my readings of *Arabian Nights*, 'I am a humble visitor from the United States. I have heard much about the glo-rious history of your sultanate and wanted to gaze upon its riches for myself, and especially upon the ancient seat of your empire, Old Mao, which I understand has no counterpart in glory either east or west across the Sahel.'

Silence. The sultan's amiable features soured, and he furrowed his brows. Mahamat squirmed, his eyes shifting right and left.

The vizier cleared his throat. 'You must not speak Arabic, but French, so that His Excellency may understand you.' (I later learned that his native tongue was Kanuri, a Nilo-Saharan lan-guage unrelated to Arabic.)

I made the hand gesture again and repeated myself in French, which didn't sound right at all here in this Arabian-style palace. But the sultan's glower softened into something like, well, senility.

'I've been on . . . on the throne since 1947,' he said in French, stuttering slightly. 'We have ruled this land since . . . since long before the French came. We are guided by the law of Islam, shari'a, in our customary affairs. We . . . ah.'

He seemed to lose his breath and his train of thought. I nodded gratitude for his address, fearful of speaking until given permis-sion. He turned and muttered a few words in Kanuri to the vizier, and then, without explanation, rose from his K-Mart throne and prodded his way back behind the batik. Our audience was over.

The vizier pointed behind us to a strapping young man with tribal slashes on his high cheeks. He came over, his magenta robes richly contrasting with the limestone white around us.

'I am the son of the sultan. Follow me.'

He led us back out through the maze and around the front of the palace, through the gates of another courtyard in the rear. He explained we would be the guests of the sultan that night and then excused himself to prepare our meal.

We were to dwell in another Grecian, still-life scene. A limestone chamber strewn with red carpets would serve as our quarters. In a corner of the courtyard, above a well, stood a majestic neem, forest green against the now lavender firmament. I began to relax, relishing the thought of sleeping under the stars here. Nowhere outside Africa can one find such colors at dusk and dawn.

Once we were settled in, Mahamat's forehead wrinkled.

'What's wrong?' I asked.

'Oh, nothing. I, I, well, I never sleep well away from my wife.'

An hour later the son returned with an engraved silver tray topped with two platters of roasted, crispy-skinned chicken, a pot filled with chunks of mutton braised in pepper and onion sauce, and hot loaves of bread. The food's aroma mingled with the fresh desert breeze. Again I thought, Is there any place else in the world where food smells so good, where one enjoys more the cool of the deepening night after the heat of midday? He took the tray into our chamber, set it on a mat, and lit a candle.

'Please.'

He walked out. We sat down to eat in the flickering yellow light. The chicken was tart, the mutton spicy, and our appetites seemed to grow the more we devoured. The bread savored of a stone oven and Saharan salt.

'So,' I asked, 'what could have happened to me for violating protocol?'

'I don't think there would have been any danger, really. You're American. Americans are a valuable race.'

'A valuable race?'

'I mean, no one would dare touch you. If you hurt one

American, you hurt all Americans, and your government could respond with bombs and bullets. We know this well. So, wherever you go as an American you're above the law.'

'I don't think that's quite true.'

'Of course it is. Look, our African presidents, they're *puppets* in the hands of the Americans. They're not really independent at all. Americans are clever and they know how to control other people. They never act without thinking about what's in their own best interest. You're the world's most valuable race.'

Sated, we readied ourselves for sleep. I spread my blankets out on the sand and wrapped myself in them, then watched the stars in the blackening sky turn from specks of glitter to burning points of light. Mahamat bedded down in the stone chamber, but he slept little: all night he sniffled and shifted about on his mat. He missed his wife.

The next morning, after we breakfasted on rice and more chicken, the vizier came for us.

'Before we visit Old Mao, the sultan would like you to enjoy the treasures of our *Salle d'Histoire*.'

I had no idea what these treasures might be and was eager to find out. But the *Salle* turned out to be a small, dusty room stocked with dusty artifacts in dusty, cracked glass cases. The vizier spoke flatly as he pointed to the various items.

'This is a bowl used to drink water.'

'Is it ancient?' I asked. 'It looks like the bowl we used at dinner last night.'

'We have always eaten from this sort of bowl. Follow me.'

He pointed to another bowl similar to one we had just seen at breakfast.

'And this, this is a bowl we use to drink soup from.'

'How old is it?'

He ignored my question. 'This is a drum. Over here is a what we call a big drum – we use it at weddings. To pound on.'

'Excuse me – are these things old or new?'

He gave me a puzzled look. 'Yes . . . and this is a leather wallet. We keep our money in wallets . . . These are spears . . . and these are sandals made from soap wood' – more everyday items from everyday life past and present in the sultanate, and everywhere else I had been in rural Chad, for that matter.

The vizier then led me to the central exhibit: yellowed black-and-white photographs of bygone sultans, with the dates of their reigns marked at the bottom. A text typed on a grimy sheet of paper offered an abbreviated version of each sultanate's history: the determined efforts of King Dounama II to stamp out animism and spread Islam in the thirteenth century; the eventual transfer of the seat of the 'empire' to the west, to Gaga, in Bornu; King Alouma's purchase, in the sixteenth century, of muskets from the Turks, an acquisition that changed the regional balance of power and allowed him to expand Kanem to include Hausaland and Yorubaland in what is now Nigeria, as well as Tibesti and Aïr in present-day Niger. Finally, the Fulani mujahid and *mujaddid* Usuman dan Fodio besieged the Kanuri and the empire crumbled.

But what did 'empire' mean here, and what was its legacy? Kanem's desert expanses had always been open to invasion and settlement by other nomadic Saharan tribes, which ensured a degree of harmful instability. Hence, no substantial Kanuri merchant class could develop; palace revenues came from booty and slaving raids conducted against peoples to the south. The Kanuri people's talents had amounted to the bric-a-brac piled in these dusty glass cases. The empire of Kanem was, and then it was no more, and who would now know the difference?

A twenty-minute drive north by Land Cruiser brought us to dunes speckled with wisps of chartreuse grass. The vizier and Mahamat got out, looking grave.

'Why are we stopping here?' I asked.

'Why?' Mahamat whispered. 'Why, we're in Old Mao!'

The vizier spread his arms. 'Until a hundred years ago this was the seat of empire. Then they moved to New Mao.' He pointed to one dune. 'That's the jewelers' quarter.' He gestured at another. 'Over there, to the left, you see the metalworkers' quarter.'

Mahamat nodded.

'I don't see anything but sand,' I said.

'That of course is the prefecture, and to the right, the Qur'anic school.'

'My, my!' exclaimed Mahamat. 'Your empire was glorious! Such history! Standing here, I feel I'm traveling back in time a thousand years! And to think, in a few years the desert will cover everything.'

I felt like the straight man in a Monty Python skit. 'What are you talking about? The desert *has* covered everything!'

'No,' the vizier said. 'That's the jewelers' quarter, and over there —'

'I heard all that, but why do you keep talking as if you see things? You can't see a *thing* here except hills of sand.'

Mahamat's stern eyes told me I was giving offense. I might have been, but I was genuinely perplexed.

The vizier continued. 'You saw the wealth of the kingdom in the *Salle d'Histoire*. It *was* a *grand* empire, and it was founded by Arabs. Here you see the actual city itself.'

Mahamat concurred, and with much flourish described quarters and palaces and arches and doorways he could never have seen, or perhaps were identical to the ones on the palace in which we had just spent the night, minus the P.O. number. Eventually he fell silent, lost in reflection about the glory that was Kanem.

*Sultanate* and *empire* were weighty words conjuring up images of wealth and sophistication, legacy and history. The museum, with its exiguous exhibits, belied the bombast and showed that this 'empire' had been a patch of desert under the control of a particular ethnic group at a particular time – nothing more.

That was my judgment. But my companions' reaction told me something else. For them Old Mao was as real as New Mao, and it certainly *meant* more. As in the Middle East and North Africa, here, history – or legend – is everything, providing spiritual sustenance and identity when reality is sterile and violent. History dignified the dithering sultan and cast ennobling light on the spare bowls and rusty spears in the museum. History told them that once they had been great, and great they will be again, after the current interlude of decline has passed. This amounts to self-deception, I concluded, but then I reconsidered: the sultan here ruled over desert, stone houses, and poor people, but thanks to legend his office commands respect that the screeching soldiers and pseudo-European pomp of the presidency and government in N'Djamena would never enjoy.

# 8

## NIGERIA AGONISTES

'I believe that Nigeria is a nation favoured by Providence, [and has been] commandeered by history to facilitate mankind's advancement. The vast human and material wealth with which she is endowed bestows on her a role in Africa and the world which no one else can assume or fulfill.'

— CHINUA ACHEBE,
Nigerian writer and dissident

At my hotel back in N'Djamena, the waitress, a Sara woman with sad eyes and a droopy mouth, brought the goateed man seated next to me at the bar a cup of tea. He looked to be in his thirties. His bountiful beige robes and peaked white tarboosh suggested he was a Nigerian, as did his aplomb and language. The bar's ambiance was pacific, and the sunset over the Chari River just outside, magnificent, but he berated the waitress in Hausa-accented English.

'My sister, what is this tea, costing a thousand francs [$1.50]? In my country, this tea is costing ten naira, not *even*!' He stuck his forefinger in the brew. 'Oh, a thousand francs, and what is this water! Not hot! My sister, heat this tea!'

She looked intimidated and puzzled, so I translated for him. He was not grateful.

'So, you're American?' he said, narrowing his eyes, pushing back his tarboosh, and straightening up. He introduced himself as a native of Maiduguri (where I was about to go) and an official of Borno State, the 'home of peace,' visiting Chad for the weekend. After that, his voice began rising. 'Since Bush came, the *whole* world hates America . . . You Americans, you turn the whole world against you now, not just Arab countries. Saddam, if you attack him, will *bloody* the United States! The entire Arab world will rise up! . . . Iraq has weapons that can reach the United States, weapons nobody knows about!' He squirmed in his seat, as if foreseeing a Scud-born chemical attack on New York City. 'Saddam's soldiers don't fear death, but U.S. soldiers *fear* death!'

He was now expectorating with his words, and I leaned back to avoid the airborne spittle. To change the subject, I mentioned the aborted Nigerian Miss World pageant and the accompanying Muslim-Christian riots over the journalist's remark that the prophet Muhammad would have chosen a wife from among the contestants. I asked him what he thought of all the killing. Didn't he find it excessive?

His reply came in hissing verbiage, without irony.

'We are Muslims and men of peace. I would *kill* the journalist who wrote Muhammad would be happy with this contest – an *insult* to Islam. And I would *kill* the editor of the newspaper too.'

He kept his eyes riveted on mine; he looked capable, even desirous, of killing me as well. A question posed itself in my mind: Given that the British had drawn Nigeria's borders, tossing together so many different peoples who hated one another, wouldn't the country be better off splitting, say, into two zones, one northern and Islamic, the other southern and Christian? I put the question to him.

'Nigeria must be one country,' he replied, in a steady, analytical tone. 'The north produces all the meat, but the south has all the oil.' He added, of his own volition, 'I make my money by misusing my position. This is of course Nigeria's problem, but I am rich. I have a nice residence and an AC car from this, but my salary is *not* important.' He had said it: the north needed the south for oil, and the corruption stemming naturally from his country's unworkable structure granted him a birthright to booty he felt no shame in claiming. His solution to the dissidence and protest that inevitably result? 'Any Nigerian who criticizes Nigeria must go out from Nigeria.'

He concluded with a diatribe against (Christian) President Olusegun Obasanjo and by showing me the tribal scars on his belly: ethnic Hausa slashes, he said, that the defunct dictator Sani Abacha had carried as well. 'A man with such scars can't be defeated. He will leave power only when dead!' (In fact, Viagra may have defeated Abacha: he is rumored to have succumbed to a Viagra-related heart attack while rutting on a pair of Indian prostitutes.)

These were his last words to me – an odd valediction. Saying nothing more, he turned back to his tea, and I excused myself to pack for my trip. He had shown his rage to be four-faceted: religious, anti-Western, tribal, and greed-driven. Were a bandit or a convict to talk this way, one might feel no surprise, but this man's English bespoke a sound education; his income should have lifted him above the anger of slum-dwellers; and his awareness of world events indicated a degree of sophistication. He was, in short, the hope for Nigeria's future – and yet he was filled with rage.

After talking to this man, I felt a strange rush of excitement about going to Nigeria, for his ravings and vehemence owed much to his country's unique status in Africa as a potential great power. For millennia Nigeria's territory – a patchwork of Sahel, rain forest, and fertile plateau larger than Germany and France combined – has supported some of Africa's most advanced civilizations. Its writers have produced an English-language literature of world renown. Its musicians have created entire genres of modern African music. Its land abounds in oil and natural gas. With a population of 130 million (almost one out of six Africans is Nigerian), 45 percent of which is younger than fourteen, and a growth rate of more than 3 percent a year, Nigeria is Africa's most populous country, and it well deserves the epithet 'the Giant of Africa.'

What happens in Nigeria *matters*, which prompted me to include the country in my Sahel trip even though I had already been there and despite what every seasoned traveler to Africa knows: Nigeria is one of the most dangerous countries on a dangerous continent. The State Department Web site for Nigeria cites the 'considerable risks' posed by 'violent crime, committed by ordinary criminals as well as by persons in police and military uniforms . . . kidnapping for ransom . . . fraudulent or criminal' taxi operators, and dangers caused by 'business, charity, and other scams.' It warns that 'visitors and resident Americans have experienced armed muggings, assaults, burglary, kidnappings and extortion, often involving violence. Carjackings, roadblock robberies, and armed break-ins are common in many parts of Nigeria . . . Law enforcement authorities usually respond to crimes slowly and provide little or no investigative support to victims. U.S. citizens have experienced harassment and shakedowns at checkpoints and during encounters with Nigerian officials.' For travelers to Nigeria, fear is the beginning of knowledge.

The next day, sunlight showered desolating glare over the dead plains across the border in Cameroon, the northernmost tip of which I would have to traverse to reach Nigeria. Separating Chad and Cameroon was the Chari River, meandering, muddy yellow and drought-depleted, between ragged shoals. On the Chadian side, where Mahamat and I stood waiting at the head of the two-lane border bridge, heat-stricken teens hawked sugar cane and Cokes in feeble voices; caftaned beggars circulated listlessly, led by bony-kneed children, intoning plaintive verses from the Qur'an; giant trucks with ALLAHU AKBAR! (God Is Most Great!) painted at the top of their cracked windshields lumbered past, the pointy horns of their panting cargo – cattle from Nigeria – spiking the white-hot sky. These torpid comings and goings raised a cloud of dust that hung in the air and gave the glare a gritty palpability.

Inside the cement shack, a Chadian border officer, dressed in a stained khaki shirt and frayed blue jeans, struggled with his bare feet to suppress the flops of his dying dinner – a yard-long catfish caked in slime and mud – on the floor. Shaking his pen to get the ink flowing, he asked for my name and profession and opened his ledger. I told him. Mahamat stood next to me, his head cocked and his face frozen, as ever, with contempt. *This Christian dog!* his look seemed to say. I felt scarcely more charitable toward this man myself: he had kept us waiting for a half-hour while he sipped his tea.

The delay made a bad situation worse. It was now one in the afternoon. I had hoped to leave N'Djamena early in the morning and arrive in Maiduguri, some 150 miles east, early in the afternoon, but the Cameroon embassy had taken a long time to issue me a transit visa, and as a result we had set out late. Now, thanks to this official and others, it seemed certain that I would violate Rule Number One when visiting Nigeria: never arrive after dark.

The catfish flopped, and the officer handed me my passport. We walked back out into the glare, done with an hour's worth of nervous dawdling under the greedy eyes of five separate customs and border officials, three of whom had asked Mahamat for a *formalité*; they were for some reason too shy to address me directly. He refused.

'I detest these people,' Mahamat said as we opened the doors and climbed onto the sticky-hot front seat of his Peugeot. 'A man so ignorant he can't sign his name looks at you as if you were a worm and searches your things, and examines your passport, and makes you wait for his stamp, and then wants *you* to pay *him!*'

We drove across the bridge into Cameroon and jumped out. There, in contrast, matters at customs were quick and simple: one stamp from one official in a spiffy navy blue uniform, a '*Bienvenu!*' and I was legally in country. Mahamat was pleased and newly voluble. 'Ah, Cameroon! Here I can breathe freely! This is a state of law, unlike Chad, where you have no freedom of expression, where they can execute you for anything, and there're mass killings and no one cares. Here you're free and no one kills you.' His gruff demeanor softened into mere regality. Gruffness must be, I decided, a defensive shield in a land where one either fears or is feared.

We got back into his Peugeot. As we motored down the (now impressively) smooth tarmac toward Kousseri, the town where taxis departed for Nigeria, Mahamat grew glum. I thought I knew why: we would soon be saying goodbye. I felt sorry about this too,

and even oddly apprehensive: since my arrival in Chad, he had
helped me at every turn. He had taken me under his wing and
never asked for anything beyond his driver's fee; in fact, he had
frequently paid (or tried to pay) for my meals. Now, with our
time running out, I told him how much I appreciated his help and
companionship. He brushed off my thanks and said that by helping me, a stranger, he was only doing his Muslim duty.

We drove into Kousseri through its outer shack-neighborhoods,
rumbled down neem-shaded streets, and pulled up to a melee of
shouting drivers and hooting station wagon taxis and pickups
chugging out exhaust – the road station. The sun had passed
its zenith and was now gilding the floating skeins of dust and
smog.

Mahamat turned off the motor, and we sat quietly for a
moment. He had spent four years working in Maiduguri and
knew it well. 'Look,' he said at last. 'Don't take any risks over
there. We're afraid of Nigerians; they're scheming and violent.
Don't go out at night, and keep your wits about you in the day.
There are just too many things happening there. It will be worse
for you than it was for me because of your skin color. You can't be
too careful. Wait here.'

He got out and strode over to a taxi whose owner had been
shouting 'Fotokol! Fotokol!' – the last town in Cameroon before
the Nigerian frontier. He grabbed the driver's sleeve and ordered,
in Arabic, 'Take my brother Jelal to the Nigerian border. See that
he arrives safely.'

The driver was a timid, wiry man in a blue caftan. He glanced
over at me with dubious eyes. 'Are all his papers in order? Does
he have a Nigerian visa?'

'He has all the papers he needs. I'm trusting you to see no
harm comes to him.'

The driver nodded assent. I would be the last of six passengers, so we would leave immediately. I jumped out and grabbed
my bag. Again I thanked Mahamat. We embraced and promised
to write, and I squeezed into the cab.

Our driver was of a philosophical bent. On the dashboard he
had pasted a sticker reading, QUI VIT SANS DEFAUT? (Who lives

without a fault?). He urged me to relax and said he would see me safely to the border.

Only fifty-six miles separate Kousseri from Fotokol, but as soon as we left town, the paved road turned into piste, which degenerated into a track so cratered we had to abandon it for the adjacent fields, and six or seven police checkpoints further slowed what should have been a high-speed if bouncy trip across Cameroon. Each police stop lasted fifteen or twenty minutes, and many resulted in the forcible extraction of passengers who presented the wrong documents or no documents at all. 'You are a thief, not a worker!' or 'You are a vagabond, not a student!' the police would say to the unlucky ones, approaching anyone heading to Nigeria with suspicion. My driver told me that thieves and other crooks took taxis to get as close as they could to the border, and then crossed into Nigeria on foot.

I was worrying about my certain after-dark arrival in Maiduguri, but I tried consoling myself by thinking fatalistically that whatever happened to me in Nigeria would happen and I could do little now to influence it. But I reconsidered: fatalism cannot replace a plan of action for dealing with bribe-hungry soldiers or armed robbers. Travel in Third World countries demands the cleverest, most practical kind of engagement, not contemplative detachment. Nothing returns you to the here and now more quickly than the threat of assault. The knot returned to my stomach.

Three hours later, the driver and I were the only ones left in the cab. Just west of Fotokol, we pulled off the tarmac (the road near the border was paved) onto an ashen lot, near a bridgehead by the Yedseram River, which was winding along the border under the dusky sky, dust-clouded and oxblood red. The dark was deepening beneath the heavy boughs of eucalyptus trees and primeval baobabs across the river in Nigeria. The landscape itself appeared to become more menacing.

Even before we stopped we were besieged: thirty or forty teenagers on mopeds, barefoot and in rags, raced their motors and skidded and swerved through the dirt into a circle around us, churning up more dust and exhaust and shouting, 'Taxi to

Nigeria! Taxi to Nigeria!' Walking across the border bridge was forbidden; for some reason, one had to take a moped (a 'taxi') or drive a car.

I paid and thanked my driver. I opened the door, and it was wrenched from me by the youths. I stood up and the crowd crushed me against the taxi; the dust choked me and stung my eyes; moped riders groped at my pockets and yanked at me. I covered my wallet with my bag and forced my way free of the cab, but a youth on foot tore my bag from my grasp and set off jogging with it toward a moped at the lot's edge. Knocking over a couple of kids and nearly falling down myself, I ran after him and yanked it back. The roaring mob of mopeds wobbled and lurched around after me. '*Masta!* Taxi! Take me, *Masta! Masta!*'

My driver shouted to me, 'Wait, wait, no! Come back! Alhajji will take you to Nigeria! Alhajji! He's my friend!'

He pointed to a frail young man in a silvery caftan waiting perched on his moped at the side of the road by the bridge, away from the fracas. Alhajji means 'one who has made the pilgrimage to Mecca' and inspired confidence, at least if names were to be believed. I pushed my way free of the toughs and ran over to him. '*B'sur'a!*' (Quickly!), Alhajji said in Arabic, gesturing that I first hand him my bag, which he ensconced on his lap between his arms and the handlebars. I jumped on the rear. We peeled out and circled round, passing the cursing mopeders, and bounced across the tarmac onto a dirt road leading away from the bridge.

'First you must change money,' Alhajji shouted in broken Arabic over his shoulder. 'No money change in Nigeria.'

We pounded down the dirt road, swerving in the dust, and pulled up to an open-sided straw hut amid abandoned merchant stalls. There, another crowd sitting in the dirt jumped up and surrounded us. One tall man, whom I took for a Hausa because of his tarboosh and emerald robes, reigned among them. He held out a brick of filthy, disintegrating bills with pictures and numbering so faded and abraded as to be nearly unreadable. 'What you got?' he demanded in French. 'Dollars? Euros?'

'Dollars. What's your rate?'

'One hundred dollars – thirteen thousand naira.'

As far as I knew, this was a reasonable rate. But I feared a ruse – unofficial moneychangers at borders are often crooks.

'I'll change fifty dollars. Show me the money!' I demanded.

'Give me the dollars first!'

'No way.'

He counted out naira from his brick and handed them to me. With the crowd pressing in, I started recounting, having trouble making out the numbers. The bills were limp; they were twenties and fifties and hundreds, all mixed up. This hindered an accurate count – which had to be his ruse, I thought. I counted twice and both times came up five hundred naira short.

'Give me five hundred more!'

He rolled his eyes and smiled. He handed me a five hundred note. I gave him fifty dollars. Alhajji honked maniacally, the crowd dived out of our way, and we jerked ahead. We spun around and rolled back onto the tarmac and over the bridge toward Nigeria. The Yedseram was now palely aflame with the dying sun.

On the Nigerian side a man in a hooded blue cape and high black boots stomped out of a tiny brick booth.

'Stop! Passport!'

I showed him my document. 'Go get your stamp!' he said in a barrel voice. 'Not advisable to travel *faada* tonight. It is *daaan*gerous.'

Beneath giant spreading trees, we pulled up by a one-story cement building with a porch. In the front yard, off-duty officers were kicking around a soccer ball. I noticed no one else was crossing the border with me. I got down and walked to the door. Inside a large, mostly empty room I found a dwarfish middle-aged man in a tan uniform sitting with his arms crossed, watching CNN on a television in the corner.

'Ah ha!' he said, jumping up. 'Welcome! You are welcome! Right this way!' He pronounced 'welcome' as if it were two words.

He took my passport. 'Welcome! Ah ha . . . Welcome.' He flicked through the pages repeatedly and finally looked up.

'This doesn't say your profession. What are you?'

'A travel writer.'

'A triter?' He pronounced it 'try-taa.'

'A travel writer.'

'What's a triter?'

'Travel *writer*,' I said. 'I write about' – here I needed to watch my words – 'about trips for tourists and the like. Holidays.'

'Ah. I see. So I see. Welcome.' He sat back and looked at the passport, and then up at me with something akin to regret in his eyes. He slapped the passport against his palm and arose slowly, gravely, portentously even. 'Come.'

He led me to an office in the back, where a batik cloth served as a door. Was this a booth in which I would be strip-searched, my hidden bundle of dollars discovered, the extent of my relative wealth exposed? Why did every border crossing in Africa have to involve so many uncertainties, so many fears?

He paused and glanced at me again, and flung open the batik. A huge man in a kingly green caftan stood up, jutting out his chest as though confronting an intruder: he looked like the Jolly Green Giant. Above him hung a lopsided portrait of President Obasanjo, a reminder, I consoled myself, of recent democratic change. (In 1999 Nigeria returned to civil rule.) Maybe something had changed for the better, and maybe officials in this out-of-the-way border post would have received orders to welcome foreigners instead of harassing and threatening them as they so notoriously did in the past. But then again, the elections that brought Obasanjo to power had been rigged and a riot had broken out at his inauguration.

The small man announced with fatigued gravity to the big man, 'A freelance journalist.'

The giant strode over and yanked the passport from him. He shouted at me. 'What you here for? State your purpose!' 'Purpose' he pronounced 'poor-pose.'

'I'm a travel writer. I'm on vacation.'

'Who sponsor you? How you get to Africa?'

'I flew to Chad.'

'Why? Why Chad?'

'Why Chad? I had to arrive somewhere.'

'But why you pick Chad?'

'Well, I —'

'What you going to write about Nigeria?' He stepped up and loomed over me; I took his size and proximity as a threat.

'I'm on vacation. I'm not planning to —'

'Who pay you to come here? What you investigating?' As though he might find clues in my passport, he rifled through its pages. 'Wait! Ah ha! You have Nigerian visa!' he shouted, as though discovering evidence that disproved everything I had said.

'Yes, I do.'

'It expired!'

'Pardon me, but it's still valid.'

'No! It expired! You got this last year!'

I pointed out the dates. There was nothing mysterious about them. The visa was plainly valid for two more months.

Why the hostility? Why the shouted, erroneous declarations? Did he hope to scare me into offering a bribe? To be fair, tourists are rare in Nigeria, and the country has a reputation as a hideout for drug dealers and swindlers, so some suspicion on his part was inevitable. He kept peering at the visa and flipping through my passport and returning to the visa. Finally he shouted something in Hausa and turned away from me. The small man came over and took my passport from him, and then led me back to his desk in the main room.

He stamped my passport. 'I advise you to go no farther now. Armed robbers are on the highway. Stay in Ngala tonight at the Borno State Hotel. Good luck to you.'

Outside, the silhouettes of great trees rose through the humid dark into a star-spangled sky. Alhajji was waiting on his moped, still embracing my bag in his lap. I jumped aboard. We drove down the deserted bumpy road toward the hotel, just west of Ngala, our feeble yellow headlamp illuminating gnats and moths streaking upward to strike our faces and sting our eyes.

The hotel turned out to be a smattering of bungalows overseen by a kind Hausa manager whose face I would never see, owing to the dark.

He led me to my abode saying, 'Wel*come!* You are wel*come*. Wel*come* in Nig*ee*ri*aaa*.' He shone his light around my new home for the night, a bungalow under eucalyptus trees. The bungalow had once been well appointed, that was sure, with heavy chairs and desks with writing blotters, a broad bed, and a plush if dirty carpet. A thick layer of dust covered these furnishings, as if they were historical artifacts from Nigeria's prosperous first decades. Maybe back then government men had stopped here and passed the night before heading over the border to other young and promising African countries.

'Do the lights and water work?' I asked.

'Of course.' He handed me a candle and a packet of matches and walked into the bathroom. There he thumped on a barrel filled with well water and showed me the bucket I could use to flush the toilet. 'One thing,' he said. 'I advise you to arrange with your friend now about chop. We got no food out here, and no moto, so ask him to take you to Ngala for chop.'

'I'll do that. Thank you.'

I paid him for the room, and he wished me good night.

An hour later, to the angry rumbling of generators and the theme music of a James Bond movie playing on TV, Alhajji and I sat in the patio of a restaurant in Ngala, a village of straw storefronts lit by kerosene lanterns. We 'chopped' meat and chili and rice, washing down our meal with Coke chilled under blocks of ice. The sounds of explosions and gunfire from the television blared over a sermon from a Christian faith healer in the next yard. The meat was rubbery, the sauce from a jar, but I was safely in Nigeria, having again been helped by a Samaritan who had serendipitously materialized and who had asked for nothing, not even fare for the moped ride. How could he know that I would pay him for his service, treat him to a meal? Why had I found such hospitality so often in Nigeria and other parts of Africa? I felt gloriously safe and lucky.

The proprietor, a roly-poly man with gray hair and a toothy smile, approached our table. Looking at his short-sleeved shirt and his squat southern features, I decided he was a Christian.

We chatted a bit. I paid him, and he said, glancing at Alhajji, 'God sent this man to help you cross the border tonight and avoid the rogues. You are in God's hands. Welcome to Nigeria! You are wel*come!*'

'Thank you.'

'Say, do you fear *God?*'

'Ah . . . why?'

'I belong to the Church of the Deeper Life. Do you know it?' His voice and eyes were fervid.

'No, I'm afraid not.'

'Well, let me tell you . . .'

Someone turned up the volume on the sermon next door, and it drowned out his words – a minor miracle, at least for me. He gave up trying to talk and shook my hand. Alhajji and I left him for the ride back to the hotel.

At the hotel the manager had waited up for me, wanting to be sure I returned safely. I tried to explain to Alhajji that I wanted him to come back in the morning to take me to the motor park for Maiduguri, but neither his Arabic nor his English sufficed for him to understand me. The manager translated. When I tried to pay Alhajji, he just smiled, said '*Bukra*' (Tomorrow), and drove off.

'Don't worry. He is your friend now,' said the manager. 'He trusts you to pay in the morning. Give him whatever you like. Good night!'

I walked back to my bungalow, finding my way among the eucalyptus trees with my flashlight. Rather than sleep on the sagging bed, I set up my mosquito net on the floor and padded it with my Chadian blanket. All night I listened to the plangent screeches of birds in the trees, the thumpy, panicked clambering of monkeys on the roof, the timid scampering of lizards on my porch. I was almost afraid to believe my good fortune.

Then I thought of something. I turned my flashlight on my wad of nairas, bills emblazoned with the august portraits of Nigeria's many statesmen and scholars. I counted them out again and found that I was still five hundred naira short: the moneychanger had ripped me off somehow. But no matter: as Chinua Achebe had said, in so many words, Nigeria is a country of promise, a fateful land, 'a nation favoured by Providence.' I fell asleep thinking that Nigeria was more than the sum of its huts and inhabitants; the grand notions it evoked created, for me, romance and a thrill. There were risks here, but Nigeria was worth running them.

# 9

# FEAR AND FAITH IN
# MAIDUGURI

Arriving in maiduguri, straightaway I sensed the vitality and bygone oil wealth that set Nigeria apart from Chad. The beat-up roads were paved and marked with lanes. Under long-dark traffic lights, women sporting trim black uniforms and trig brown berets directed a madcap cavalcade of vehicles, a few of which even had intact windshields and attached bumpers. There were sidewalks and curbs and grassy roundabout isles with statues and well-tended neems to provide shade for man and goat. Shops without bullet holes sold clothes, cutlery, hardware, and videos; there were Internet cafés and a plethora of business centers offering, at least outside the daily twelve-hour power blackouts, fax and printing services. Cheesy billboards advertised Mr. Bigg's burger joints, ointments for the happy family, skin-lightening cream (is there an African city where these are not in demand?), and dozens of candidates for upcoming gubernatorial and presidential elections. Yet besides all these amenities were signs of Nigeria's distress: polio victims with pretzel legs, seated on skateboards, scooted perilously through traffic to panhandle at intersections; children led teetering, glaucoma-stricken elders in search of alms; and a foul bluish exhaust haze blighted the air, rasping the throat and burning the eyes, mingling with the stench of the iridescent flux clogging the open-air sewers by the sidewalks.

The taxi ride in from Ngala had passed without incident. After settling into a hotel, I walked out to do some sightseeing, joining surging crowds of men in elegant caftans (invariably of green or purple or blue, but almost never plain white, as in Chad) and peaked *hula* fezlike hats, passing rows of children seated and rocking autistically back and forth beneath the neems, chanting verses from the Qur'an under the raised canes of their imams. (Memorizing the Qur'an is still the only education many children get in the north.) Stately women robed in boubous, their hair hidden under elaborate floral wraps, commanded attention at every turn. How was this display of beauty possible if shari'a was in force? And why were women in a shari'a state directing traffic?

I set aside these questions in favor of more practical concerns. I needed a moneychanger, and, wanting to ask directions of an English speaker, I stopped a young man in Western dress. (I had learned during my last visit to the north that men in caftans often knew only Hausa.) He responded in correct English, not the pidgin commonly spoken in Nigeria, 'Why don't I take you there? It's hard to locate.'

'That would be kind of you.'

Dodging cars and sweating in the worsening heat, we started walking. He introduced himself as Ezekiel, a Christian from the south working as a clerk in Maiduguri because there were no jobs in his village. He was married and his wife was pregnant; her pregnancy would soon interrupt her engineering studies at the local university. He had two children and was putting them through private school ('Education is the best thing we can give our children'). He was in his late twenties, or some fifteen years younger than I; out of respect for the difference in our ages he called me 'sir.' This made me uncomfortable, but Ezekiel possessed an unshakable sense of decorum.

He was happy to meet an American. 'You Americans did good work in Afghanistan, sir. You freed people from Muslim tyranny. You should do the same in Iraq, sir.'

'You're the first person I've heard talk this way since I arrived in Africa.'

'Of course, sir. I'm a Christian. You see, here we mix politics with religion. We vote according to a candidate's religion. That's our problem.'

'So how is it living as a Christian under shari'a?'

He glanced around as if making sure no one could hear, and lowered his voice. 'Shari'a is *too* bad, *too, too* bad. I'm a *faithful* Christian. I *hate* shari'a but I must obey or they take me to jail. And it is hypocrisy. They drink anyway, even if shari'a forbids it. They just do it secretly.'

Ezekiel added that although in Maiduguri the authorities had acted quickly to discourage rioters after the Miss World contest, sending troops into the streets, tensions still ran high between Muslims and Christians, mostly on account of the coming war between the United States and Iraq. As we walked he kept an eye out to make sure no one overheard us.

'I must speak quietly about the United States. It is dangerous for a Christian to support the U.S. Muslims get angry. But I *am* a Christian and I *won't* desert my religion. You see, I believe God made the world in six days and rested the seventh. I am faithful, sir.'

'You don't believe in evolution?' I asked.

'Science only confirms the Bible, sir. You go to the forest and see army ants all marching in one direction. This is evidence of God, of a creator and the purpose of every beast. It is the mystery of Jesus. I am a *faithful* Christian, sir.'

I asked if by chance he knew of the Deeper Life Church to which the restaurateur in Ngala belonged.

'Oh, them. They're extremists. They're fanatics! Have *nothing* to do with Deeper Life people. Extremists, sir!'

After I changed money at his friend's, Ezekiel walked me back to my hotel. It was getting dark, but as we arrived the lights flickered out across the neighborhood.

'Ah, Nigeria! Don't worry, your hotel will send a man to bribe NEPA and the lights will come back.'

'NEPA?'

'Nigerian Electric Power Authority. If you don't bribe them, they cut your power. We are a rich country, sir, but our leaders are rogues.'

Ezekiel told me he wasn't working the next day, so I asked him if he might like to show me around town, and he agreed.

The morning sun burned through the exhaust fumes hanging above the rush-hour traffic, making sightseeing even early in the day a sweaty, choking endeavor. Ezekiel and I stuck to the neem shade as we walked down clamorous Banks Road, above which, on brick portals just ahead, blocky white letters read, WELCOME TO THE SHEHU'S PALACE.

The current shehu (Hausa for 'sheikh') of the emirate of Bornu, Al Hadji Dr. Mustapha Umar el Kanemi, descends from the former rulers of the empire of Kanem who remained on their thrones even during colonial times. (Kanem became known as Kanem-Bornu after the capital, in the thirteenth century, had moved west from Mao into present-day Nigeria. The British made Maiduguri the capital of their version of the emirate in 1907.) The British governed through the shehus rather than rule directly and risk provoking nationalist, anti-Christian sentiment. The federal government of Nigeria chose to continue the policy, thereby minimizing ethnic and regional tensions, for before independence the north had never belonged to a political union with the Christian south. Imagining that a visit to the palace might be interesting, and that, given the inviting sign, it would pose no problem, I asked Ezekiel if we might see about taking a tour.

'Why, ah, yes. If you like, sir,' he said.

The palace was unromantic and functional, a two-story brick structure built around a pebbly courtyard, with many balconies. Out front, children played soccer on a sandy field. Ezekiel, speaking Hausa, asked a passerby how one visited the palace; the man pointed to a small side door.

We walked through the door and climbed a stairway crowded with men in traditional dress – supplicants, apparently, judging by their bowed heads and meek faces. At the top of the stairs a muscled soldier in fatigues stood guard next to a doorway jammed with more meek people waiting their turn to enter an office. Ezekiel said something to the soldier about 'the American' and pointed to me. The soldier in turn pointed to a small man in a high blue *dara* cap and silky blue caftan, sitting behind a desk under a portrait of the shehu, a fleshy older man with broad nostrils who looked somnolent, even bored. The small man was reading a newspaper in English, slowly sounding out the words.

The room was crowded, and we edged our way in. The soldier went over and bent down to say something in the small man's ear. I gathered he was the shehu's secretary.

He started and looked up at me, slapping down his paper. 'Who are you? What do you want?'

Ezekiel stepped up to his desk. He clasped his hands behind his back, and, lowering his head, began nodding toward me and explaining in Hausa something about the 'Amareekan wri-*taa*,' the shehu, and the palace.

The small man listened, his brow wrinkling in alarm. When Ezekiel finished, he extended his hand and blurted out, 'Show me your passport. Right away.'

I handed it to him.

'What you do here?'

'I'm a tourist.'

'Where is your card stating such?'

'Card?'

'Have you seen the SS? You should have presented yourself to the SS.'

'The SS?'

'The state secretary! At the governor's office! Have you presented yourself or not?'

'Why, no. I had no idea —'

'No idea? You should have presented yourself *immediately*. What are you doing in our palace?'

Ezekiel interceded in Hausa. But the man's brows narrowed further and he stiffened in his seat and shook his head. What was Ezekiel saying? I felt helpless not understanding Hausa, but repeatedly I heard the word 'writaa' and I wondered if my profession didn't alarm him – in so many parts of the world, writers and journalists are considered spies. Then I noticed Ezekiel's hands were glistening with sweat, and sweat was dribbling down his forehead and soaking through the back of his shirt.

The man blurted out more harsh-sounding words in Hausa and again addressed me. 'How did you get in here? Who authorized you to come to Maiduguri? Who let you into our palace?'

'I'm sorry, I didn't mean to upset you. I thought the palace was open to the public. I'm just a tourist. The sign outside says 'Welcome,' so I thought I might —'

'I am asking you *who* authorized you to come here, and *why* you haven't presented yourself to the SS!'

'I'm sorry, sir, but I have a visa, and no one told me anything about the state secretary. Had I known, I —'

'Give me your passport again.'

I did. He rifled through the pages until he got to my visa.

'There's nothing here – nothing! – authorizing you to visit Maiduguri.'

'There doesn't have to be, with all due respect. The visa is enough.'

'No, I *said* you have no permission in this visa to be here in Maiduguri.'

Ezekiel objected meekly in English, saying something about a visa sufficing, but the angry little man cut him off and demanded to know his name. On hearing it, and, I believe, understanding Ezekiel to be a Christian, he demanded to see his papers too. With trembling and sweaty hands Ezekiel showed him an ID.

He pointed to Ezekiel and spoke to me. 'This man brought you here?'

'No, I asked him to come here. He had nothing to do with —'

'This is very complicated, *very* complicated! I must now inform the shehu.' He got up and exited through a side door, which he slammed.

The guard set hard eyes on me; the supplicants regarded me with frank alarm. Ezekiel was drenched in sweat and shuffling from foot to foot, looking down, beads of perspiration dripping from his chin and splattering on his dusty shoes. I thought maybe we should just leave while we could, but then the man had our papers, and what would that soldier do, and what had I done wrong?

The small man flung open the door. 'Follow me. In here. Both of you.'

He led us into a broad chamber carpeted in plush maroon where light seeped in through closed white curtains. On a leather easy chair sat the shehu, thick-jowled and middle-aged, wearing blue robes and a blue *dara*, sniffling and contorting his mouth and nose as if he had a sinus problem.

The small man pointed to a chair in front of the shehu. 'Sit! Explain yourself to the shehu.'

The shehu wriggled his nose and made a slight but tortured snorting sound. He appeared ready to doze off.

'I'm very, very sorry, Shehu, sir,' I said in English. 'I meant no harm and certainly didn't want to bother you. Thank you for receiving me. I've heard much about how beautiful your palace is, and I just thought if it wasn't a problem, I might ask your permission to see it. But I —'

'Oh, of course,' he said. He sniffled; fluids gurgled in his sinuses. 'Of course. Yes. Welcome to my palace. I'm the shehu here, and I can allow a visit. We've been ruling this land since, well, for a long time, since before the British. You see, I rule traditionally, the governor rules . . . politically. I' – he snorted again, and yawned – 'I do what I can for my people.'

I thought to ask him a question, but his eyelids grew heavy and he motioned to the small man, who opened the door for us. Our audience was over.

The small man led us down the stairs to a reception room, where marble tables stood on ornate gilded legs, surrounded with ornate gilded chairs; in the corner sat a throne. The room opened onto the courtyard, where children were playing.

The aide shut the door to the stairs and marched up to me.

'You whites! You whites fear *nothing*! You just don't get it.'

'I'm sorry? Get what?'

'You think you can just walk into the shehu's palace and start making demands. If it were up to me, I'd *never* have allowed you in here.'

'But the shehu didn't seem to mind.'

'You just don't get it. You do not *fear*.'

'But the palace is open to the public. What about the sign? All those people in line, weren't they waiting to see him?'

'Yes. But they are *his* people.'

I glanced over at Ezekiel. He was still sweating and looking at the floor, his hands clasped behind his back.

I wanted to change the subject. I was rattled and suffered a foreboding presentiment about what this could mean for Ezekiel. I could only think of remarking on the obvious. 'The shehu's reception room is beautiful. He doesn't mind it being so open to the street? In the U.S. there would be security concerns.'

'Look, in the U.S. everyone is educated. Your Western education, everyone there has it. Everyone thinks he has rights, so people become dangerous and you have all these problems, and your president has to be afraid of his own people. Well, we don't have Western education here, and we don't need any of your Western ideas. We are traditional and peaceful. Understand?'

'Yes.'

'Good.'

He led us back to the palace door and held it open for us. 'Your tour ends here.'

I said goodbye to him but he didn't answer, and I walked out. He stopped Ezekiel and delivered another angry lecture to him in Hausa. Ezekiel kept his head low until he finished, saying 'sorry, sorry' in English.

Finally the small man shut the door, leaving us on the street in the heat and fumes.

I hardly knew what to say. 'I'm really, really sorry, Ezekiel. I had no idea. What happened?'

'That man is illiterate and stupid and *ignorant*. He's going to have me fired, sir, I know it. He demanded to know why I brought a white to the palace and asked the name of my boss and where I work. He thinks you're spying and have come to hurt the shehu.'

'What would give him that idea?'

'*What?* Sir, he knows we're both *Christians*. After all, I told him my name. He knows the United States is fighting the Arabs. He's a Muslim, so he's ignorant. They're fanatics, the people in the palace. Islam is a cult. If you had been an Arab they would have welcomed you as a king and given you a meal. But you're a *Christian*, sir.' He paused. 'If I criticize Islam, they'll cut off my head and hang it high! What sort of religion is that? It's a religion of killing, killing like the Twin Towers. Don't you see?'

I felt helpless and vulnerable and careless. 'Well, I . . . I won't let him do anything to you. I'll go to that SS if he tries.'

'Look, my boss is a Muslim too, and he'll say, "*What* were you doing taking a white to the palace?" They stick together. Sir, just think about September 11. What kind of religion could justify such an attack? You can't reason with these people. Once a Muslim, *always* a Muslim.' He patted the sweat on his forehead with a soiled handkerchief and added, with some calm, 'But I'm a Christian. Whatever God prepares for me I accept. Job suffered and so can I. I'm ready. Job didn't lose faith and neither will I.'

God smote Job with boils and killed his family on a faith-testing whim; his fate hardly inspired optimism. I felt almost ill with guilt and fear for Ezekiel. I looked at his pressed white shirt and black trousers; I noted his sweaty nervousness and prim manners. How they contrasted with the oriental dress and supreme confidence of men streaming past us, men certain, I thought I divined, of their faith, of their place in Paradise, of their superiority over hell-bound infidels like us. Here in the Muslim north of his own country, Ezekiel the Christian was almost as foreign as I was. How could he live every day fearing the people around him, all the while suffering the strictures of shari'a law?

But I also thought what could happen to me here. To whom could I turn for help? The men in caftans now seemed alien and threatening – to me. They shared *nothing* with me – not faith, not language, not customs or worldview or education. The aide's words about 'whites' rang true, in a way – I never thought to fear. His suspicions seemed, in the abstract, well grounded, for my skin color was that of the historical oppressors of his people and the current enemies of radical Islam. Why *should* he believe me? My very willingness to travel to his land could be construed as arrogance, as deriving from a conviction that as an American I should be able to move freely throughout the world, even into his palace and office. In fact, that was almost what I *had* thought.

I told Ezekiel of my fears. He had a different take. 'About me, sir, I don't know . . . but if anything happened to an American here, the whole town would flee back to their villages, fearing the bombing that would come from your government. After all, the U.S. is the world's policeman . . .' He wiped his brow and said, in a cracking voice, 'Should we go to church?'

'Of course, of course. Anything you like.'

We hailed a cab. It took us through the leafy and hectic center, way out into a slum of dusty streets and tin shacks, near where the arid expanses of the Sahel began. Here and there skinny children played, chickens clucked around trash heaps. The ride calmed me down. We stopped at the end of an alley. I paid the driver and we got out. The taxi drove off.

I looked up. A hand-painted sign above a steel gate said, DEEPER LIFE BIBLE CHURCH.

Deeper Life? Deeper Life! 'They're extremists!' Ezekiel had said. 'Fanatics!'

'Wait, Ezekiel, is this your church? This *can't* be your church.' I had no desire to go from Muslim extremists to Christian extremists. 'You don't like these people. You said —'

'No, it's not my church,' he cut in, sweating anew. 'I thought you said it was *your* church.'

Just then two men stepped out of the gate and slowly marched our way, their shadows menacing silhouettes on the sun-bleached dust. One of them was coal-skinned, in a dull gray suit, and he had the harsh bony skull and searing manic eyes of a martyr; the other was a brawny thug wearing a short-sleeved shirt that showed his biceps.

They halted, and the dust they kicked up floated our way. 'You there!' commanded the martyr, his voice hollow and deep. 'What you want?'

'Hello,' said Ezekiel. 'This is an American and he wants to see your church.'

'Why?'

'He's a Christian. He has no one to pray with because he's a foreigner here.'

The two men looked me over from head to toe. The martyr spoke, his lips moving in an exaggerated way: 'What is your *poorpose*? Who told you about us?'

'A man in Ngala. He helped me and said he was from your church.'

'What was his name?'

'I don't know. He owns a restaurant. I don't mean to bother you, really. We can leave if —'

He cocked his head and fixed his eyes on mine. 'Come inside. We can't talk on the street. Not safe.'

His office was furnished with a scratched-up desk and thread-bare sofa and sheaves of Bible tracts, plus a spindly chair that looked as if it belonged in a police interrogation room. Thin white curtains let in the glare from the street, accentuating the place's ascetic feel. The sole luxury item lay on the desk: a fat Bible, gilt-edged and leather-bound. God's word was enough décor.

The martyr, directing me to the Inquisitional chair, sat ramrod straight behind the Holy Book, and the window light from behind his head brought into skeletal relief the bones in his cheeks, the grooves of his shaved cranium. The brawny man stood next to the wall and folded his thick arms, ready, it seemed, to stop us should we try to escape. Ezekiel eased himself onto the sofa behind me. Adopting a penitent posture, he lowered his head and clasped his hands.

The martyr raised his eyes and looked down his nose at me. 'I wonder if you've heard how *Jeees*as died.'

'I think I have.'

'Where do you fellowship?'

'Fellowship?'

I 'fellowshiped' nowhere, of course, although twenty years ago I had attended a few Bible study sessions in Virginia, so I recognized the term and the evangelical brand of Christianity it signaled. Now, after our distressing visit to the shehu's palace, I felt simultaneously as relieved to sit with this pastor (who was, at least in a roundabout way, of my culture – and how much Christianity seemed like my culture at that moment!) as I was intimidated by him. But I knew I shouldn't fear: at least doctrinally the preacher should be obliged to seek my salvation. I was not inclined to argue with him.

'Well, it's been a while since I —'

'Jesus died on the cross, for *you*. For *you* and your sins. *Areyougettinit?* Before, we sac-*ree*-ficed lambs to be saved, but now His blood cleanses you.' His speech, forced out by a large tongue through widely stretching lips, resounded with all the booming vowels and mellifluous consonants of Yoruba, the main language of the southwest. His words lilted and lingered in my ears like an incantation; they were hypnotizing. 'Are you born again?'

'No, I'm afraid not.'

'I get it. "Except ye see signs and wonders, ye will not believe"?'

'Well, I think faith is a gift. Either you have it or you don't. Isn't that in the Bible somewhere? Isn't there a doctrine about God electing only some people to be saved?'

'That is heresy you speakin' there. Heresy is the work of Satan. No, Jesus says, 'Verily, verily I say unto thee: Except a man be born again he cannot see the kingdom of God . . . He that believeth not is condemned already, because he hath not believed in the name of the only begotten Son of God . . . Ye must be born again.' The hour cometh. So what is stopping you from being born again? Perhaps you know Lazarus?'

'The one Jesus raised from the dead?'

'There are two Lazaruses in the Bible. I speak of the one who came to Jesus asking how he could get to heaven. Jesus told him to give away his wealth. Lazarus went off in despair; he couldn't do it. So you must have something preventing you from having faith. 'The hour cometh! The hour cometh!' *Areyougettinit?*

He went on for some time, quoting from the Bible, his lips opening wider and wider, his eyes blazing, his pupils dilating, beads of sweat forming on his bumpy brow and remaining suspended there. At any other time I might have found his homily tiresome, but now, I am almost ashamed to say, I found comfort in his dramatic Yoruba-inflected rendition of King James's English, in his desire to save me.

I glanced over at Ezekiel. He was still sitting with his head bowed, his hands clasped, and he was repeating the words of scripture; this was obviously relaxing him. I felt no desire to stop the preacher and interfere with Ezekiel's fellowshiping.

'*Areyougettinit?* Look at the world,' the pastor said. 'It is dilapidating all around us. There are wars and rumors of war. *Areyougettinit?*'

'Getting what?'

'Wars and rumors of war!' repeated Ezekiel, rocking back and forth with his eyes fast shut. 'Wars. The final days, the Tribulation.'

The preacher continued. 'Your decision RIGHT NOW is between HELL and HEAVEN. There is fighting and killing, war and rumors of war. Is it *not* clear? Can you not see! *Areyougettinit?* Wake *up*, before it is *too* late! 'In those days men shall seek death and shall not find it; and shall desire to die, and death shall flee from them'! The devil is working through those around you, believe *it!* You must decide and stick to *it!* Remember what Jesus said: 'I will come on thee as a *thief*, and thou shalt not know what hour I will come upon thee!' *Areyougettinit?*'

'Well, these might be the final days . . .'

He didn't care to debate. 'You *must* decide. Are ye ready to give your life to *CHRIST*, right here and NOW?'

His tone began alarming me. 'No. I'm sorry, I don't think I am.'

'You love *THIS LIFE*, then?'

'I need time to think.'

'Jesus tells you, "He that loveth his life shall lose it; and he that hateth his life in this world shall keep it unto life eternal." Do not *abide* in darkness! You now *abide* in darkness!'

'You abide in darkness!' echoed the thug, head down, deep in inner realms of prayer.

'You *abide* in darkness!' murmured Ezekiel.

The preacher glanced at his Bible and up again at me. 'You are born of woman, and all who are born of women will suffer. Thus it is said in Job. Pain and suffering – that is your lot. There is only one way out.' He leaned over the desk, his eyes burning into mine, his mouth opening wide, his teeth and tongue seeming to swell, his throat straining thick-veined over his collar. 'I want you to decide right *NOW*, and not delay, to be born again!'

'Right *now!*' boomed the thug. 'Come out of the dark!'

'I'm afraid I can't. I used to go to Bible sessions. But I —'

There was something threatening in their commands. Had

poverty bred such fervor? Were words and faith all they had here? Sometime over the past couple of centuries European missionaries had converted their ancestors to Christianity, but now these three were as confident of their divinely sanctioned superiority over me as were the Muslims: just as Muslims had, they had configured the world into two camps, the abode of peace and believers and the abode of war and infidels. I could see why religion sparked slaughter here.

In Europe, the Protestant-Catholic wars of the seventeenth century had lasted thirty years, decimated the continent, reshaped the political landscape, and left nation-states in place of religious empires – progress born of violence and disaster and exhaustion. Here in Africa, European invaders had initiated a perversely reverse variant of this process, setting up, in short, colonies-cum-countries that divided peaceable ethnic groups into new configurations in which they became hostile to one another, and introducing faiths that estranged them further. The outcome was slaughter. Dialogue between religious communities had not worked in Europe before the religious wars; there was no reason to expect better in Africa.

'The past is *past* and the hour is *nigh*. Let us pray for you. I want you to pray that Jesus come down right now. Will you do that?'

'I, well, look . . .'

The three of them closed their eyes and began praying aloud in a cacophony of *Gods* and *Jesuses* and *final hours*. I closed my eyes and pretended to pray too, but then opened them: the martyr and the thug were staring straight at me.

In this pastor's eyes smoldered a zeal that could turn to rage and lead to slaughter, here or anywhere. But maybe to survive in this country one needed to be thus blinded; zeal was better than despair. In contrast, I felt I could offer them only a sort of enlightened nihilism that would, if they ever accepted it, shred the belief they shared with Muslims in God and broaden the intercommunal divide, and offer no solace in this disaster-prone country where one needed every comfort to get through the day.

At the end of the session the martyr led us around to the back of the church compound to a bookstore and asked me to buy something as a donation. I took a King James Bible and resolved to read it, cover to cover. Then they released us.

The next day was Sunday. Ezekiel invited me to have lunch at his home – after we attended his church, the Victorious Jesus Christ Disciples Gospel Church, out in the neighborhood of London where he lived. London turned out to be a reeking, collapsing quarter of shacks and sewers, ashen roads and refuse heaps, and bony cattle and goats. Despite the filth, the church was in good repair. It was a one-story cement building with many windows that let in the light and breeze, and with, on the back wall, a painting showing a (white) Jesus descending from heaven accompanied by (white) angels. Next to the painting were the words 2003 – MY YEAR OF ACHIEVEMENT! A dozen or so comely young women, whose broad cheeks and straight noses indicated descent from one of Nigeria's northern peoples, stood prim in black dresses, their hair under black scarves, in front of what looked like a set of 1950s high school drums.

The church echoed with excited chatter and was almost full, and we were lucky to find seats. People quieted down when a man approached the podium wearing a red tie and blue oxford shirt and chinos; he resembled attendees at the fellowship meetings I had frequented in Virginia. Wide spaces separated all his front teeth.

He wasted no time. 'Praise the Lord!'

'Hallelujah!'

'What year is this?'

'2003! 2003!'

'Hallelujah!'

'Amen!'

'Praise the Lord!'

'Now, people, listen here! The year 2003 is your year of achievement, when you achieve your goals and all your dreams! Now, you people here, you talk too much to do this. Just as the boss calls the employee to account for his expenses, so Jesus will call you to account for your words. You blather all morning and all day, the more you blather, the more you lie. Be quiet, people! Take account of your words! To come to God, and to achieve your dreams, you must come broken and contrite. If you do this, you will excel, because God wants you to excel! God made you to walk in high *places!*'

'Hallelujah!'

'Amen!'

'Praise *the Lord!*'

At that the congregation stood up, and a young man in a blue blazer went up and sat down behind the drums. He brandished drumsticks and began banging away. The choir broke into a hymn – a staid hymn, I thought, not nearly as passionate as Gospel music in the States – sung in Hausa-accented English. Ezekiel urged me to sing along, but I didn't know the words.

Soon the pastor left the stage. Another pastor replaced him, and he had a comic look: he was dressed in a black suit, and his pinched and sweaty face was set beneath a Don King–like afro.

'Okay, people. A woman go to market and want to buy a dress. The dressmaker take out a dress and hand it to her. "Is it costly?" she ask. "Five thousand, Madame!" She look angry. "Oh, give me *jabu* [an inexpensive fake]! I no got money for the *reee*-al thing." Okay, she is wrong, that lady. God want you to have the *reee*-al article! The oreegeen*al!* But you must pay high price. Joseph spent *so* long in the desert, Jesus wandered *so* long in the desert. You don't want the wilderness experience, people, but the wilderness experience is the price you pay, see?

'Now, what are the three connections you need to achieve your goals? Because this is 2003. The Bible show us. The purity connection: Joseph was pure. The power connection: God was with Joseph. The people connection: Joseph associated with the right kind of people. These connections are the key to success!'

The more he preached, the more he gesticulated and jumped about. The sermon sounded like an evangelical infomercial, but then, these were poor people who had found a faith of action that they could put to the test in this world. How this sermon differed from the hellfire exhortations of the Deeper Life pastors.

Finally, the pastor concluded, shouting, 'I want you to say it, to *shout* it: I'll be an achiever in *Jesus*' name! I'll be achieving my goals in *Jesus*' name! Amen!'

'Amen!' Ezekiel shouted on command, with all the rest of the people.

This, hard work and faith and a hope of success here and now, was Christianity for Ezekiel. After church, as we walked to his home, Ezekiel told me of his plans: he would earn a second degree (in computer programming); he would find a job in an advertising company; and he would work till he had enough money to return to his village and open a shop. He wanted to do something for the people back home.

And Ezekiel had a long way to go. Buoyed by the sermon, ready for success, Ezekiel opened the rusted tin door of his home: a two-room shack with a tin roof broken in places so that the sun shone through, illuminating cement walls splotched with the blood of murdered mosquitoes; a door off its hinges covered the entrance to a pit toilet. A mattress and a broken sofa were his only furniture; a pole ran between the walls, on which hung his and his wife's scant wardrobe, but the shirts and dresses were ironed and clean, the shoes on the floor shined.

A decaying Bible was his only book, but unless you sat under the hole in the roof, it was too dark at home to read when the lights failed, as they did for most of the day. His wife, a stout woman with a convivial smile, squatted over a gas burner and stirred the stew and rice we would eat for lunch. Their two children played quietly in the adjacent room. For this hovel Ezekiel paid the equivalent of thirty dollars a month.

Yet all this sufficed, for now. 'What God has in store for me will be fine. I'll open my business in my village, and we'll move there. I'll make it – with God's help.'

The shehu's secretary never bothered Ezekiel. In the palace, either reason or, possibly, the charitable nature of the shehu himself had prevailed.

# 10

# RETURN TO KANO

Bucking the Harmattan's adobe-colored gusts, my station wagon taxi hurtled out of Maiduguri onto the highway for the two-hundred-mile trip west to Kano, weaving between giant cattle and grain trucks with bumpers and sides that were painted with declarations of their turbaned drivers' faith: BACK TO ISLAM! GLORY TO GOD! ALLAHU AKBAR! Now and then we halted for tree-branch checkpoints, where black-uniformed, jackbooted officers of Operation Fire for Fire (as the latest state paramilitary campaign against armed robbers was called) banged their rifles on our hood and demanded bribes; my driver always paid. At the outskirts of towns we slowed to pass long lines of cars waiting at gas stations. Though Nigeria produces two million barrels of oil a day, most of this is exported for dollar-earning sale abroad, and fuel shortages are endemic.

I was eager to see Kano again, a city that has always loomed large in Muslim West Africa's history. Since its founding a thousand years ago, Kano has served as one of the grandest emporia of the Sahel, a rival to Timbuktu and Gao, ever the meeting place of traders from the desert and merchants from the coast. In the seventeenth and eighteenth centuries, Kano was the capital of a Hausa kingdom thriving on trans-Saharan trade and on the production of leather and textiles, but in 1807 it fell to the fundamentalist Fulani mujahid Usuman dan Fodiyo, and, almost a hundred years later, the British took over. Kano now has two million people and is Nigeria's third-largest city. As such, it has suffered from the squalor and crime that afflict most of Nigeria's urban areas, to say nothing of devastating bouts of Christian-Muslim rioting.

As my taxi shot through the Harmattan's haze, I drifted into recollections of my first sojourn in town, in 1997. After parting with Sarki, I had met Mustafa, a Hausa in his late forties with an engaging countenance and open Western manners that distinguished him immediately from his more traditional northern compatriots. His clothes set him apart as well: blue jeans and a madras shirt. He was educated in a way unusual in the north, having studied engineering in England and Germany, and his articulate, British-sounding English bore no trace of pidgin.

Mustafa told me he was a former air force officer trying to start up a plant in Kano to process scrap metal. 'Look at all the wrecked cars around here,' he said. 'They're a danger to the environment. I'd buy them up and do a service to the nation, and make a profit besides.' Opening the plant was not going to be easy. He was from another town in the north and had yet to establish the high-level government connections in Kano that he would need to get his project approved.

We were staying in a hotel in Sabon Gari (Hausa for 'strangers' quarter,' where the city's Christians live). Mustafa invited me to join him on a walk to the nearby police station, where he had urgent business to take care of. On our way there we passed Christian bookshops and shacklike Igbo bars blaring Afro-beat, where smartly dressed Christian men and women sat at tables outside, drinking beers; Sabon Gari was alive with all Nigeria's diversity, and it was a vibrant, easygoing place.

He told me how he saw Nigeria. He spoke with a pained urgency. 'Our crisis is one of not belonging. We Nigerians don't feel we *belong* to our state, or that our state belongs to us. We still belong to our tribes, and exclude others on a tribal basis. We who have been outside the country know what a government should be, and how it should represent the citizens. But most people here don't even understand what citizenship and statehood mean.

Our constitution gives us citizenship, and we can live anywhere we want in Nigeria by law, but in practice people from other tribes may not accept us. They can frustrate you in business or even kill you. Unfortunately we are at heart tribal and religious more than Nigerian. *I* don't feel I *belong* here.'

'What could be done to change things?'

'The first question we must address is abolishing monarchy' – the rule of the shehus and emirs. 'The emirs are on government stipends, but they aren't clean and people resent them. People are divided in their loyalties and exploited by two governments, and so belong to neither. The press is for sale and is loyal to its financial backers. The common man is duped in elections. What we do to ourselves is worse than the slave trade, really, *worse*. The slave trade had a point: cheap labor. Our suffering has no point.'

We reached the police station, a mess of sooty buildings surrounded by a brick wall topped with barbed wire. As we entered, Mustafa told me why we had come: the night before a drunk had approached him in the hotel, saying, 'You owe me money. Give it!' and slapped him. Mustafa, using the influence of his military rank, went to the police and promptly had his assailant arrested. He didn't believe drunkenness had anything to do with the assault and suspected that someone, perhaps a competing businessman, might have ordered the attack to drive him out of town.

Lizards skittered around the compound's earthen yard, babies were crying, and a woman was pleading in pidgin with an officer to show mercy to her incarcerated husband. The officer yawned at her entreaty and played with a rope whip, slapping it lazily against his thigh.

We entered a white cement shack marked CRIME BRANCH – IF YOU DON'T LIKE THE POLICE, NEXT TIME CALL A THUG IF YOU ARE IN TROUBLE. A fluorescent bulb flickered across grimy walls; a female officer with Fulani tribal scars on her cheeks, wearing a Fulani head wrap, sat filling out forms. She motioned Mustafa over to the desk opposite, above which was scrawled in sloppy black letters, INSPECTOR'S CRIME CORNER – KEEP OFF AND BE COOPERATIVE! The sergeant there, his face slashed with

Hausa tribal scars, shook his Bic and took down Mustafa's personal details, beginning with tribe, in a red ledger.

Mustafa ordered the officer to give his attacker 'discipline.' The officer nodded and led us around to the jail, a concrete cell with one tiny window near the ceiling. Through its bars protruded a profusion of sweaty arms, knees, and noses – prisoners who lacked the money to buy their freedom or who, like Mustafa's assailant somewhere among them, had crossed someone powerful. Mustafa brushed off my question about a trial as irrelevant. Connections and rank would determine who punished whom and for how long. The man would be released when he saw fit, and only when he had paid him a lot of money as compensation.

As we walked back to the hotel, I asked Mustafa if his education abroad had alienated him from his countrymen. As he began to answer, a bare-backed and barefoot vagabond approached us, smeared with white ash and carrying a drum. He peered into our eyes, banged his drum, and quacked.

I told Mustafa that I had read that such almsmen were considered holy. Ignoring the beggar's outstretched hand, Mustafa stomped his foot with exasperation. 'That's *exactly* the problem. This man here is simply a lunatic – but my countrymen consider him holy. How can we educated ones feel we belong? An educated man here without connections will find no job. According to his character either he will become an alcoholic, an armed robber, or, if he is strong, he will hang himself.'

His desperate eyes told me he had considered all three options.

'Our society is split in two,' he went on to say, but he believed that things were not hopeless. 'With education and development people will become true citizens of their state and demand accountability from it.'

Mustafa talked about Nigeria's need for counsel from the West; he believed that with it, the country, availing itself of its natural resources and educated population, could help revive Africa. 'I would like an audience with President Clinton to explain something to him: what we need is *not* aid and not sanctions. They do no good. We need *guidance*, we need help in *educating* our people about what a state and citizenship are supposed to be, about democracy, about who belongs to whom. Only when we understand all this will things in Nigeria change.'

I never forgot Mustafa's analysis: it was free from dollar figures, aid jargon, shibboleths about free trade and development, and even compassion; he diagnosed Nigeria's problems and offered hope of a cure. Living in the West, he had absorbed the values of the Enlightenment – the most precious and distinctive legacy the West has to offer. If Nigeria had citizens as intelligent as he, there *was* hope.

We had not corresponded after I left Nigeria. Now, as my taxi dodged trucks and rolled toward Kano, I resolved to look him up in Sabon Gari.

In midafternoon, shrub and trees grew scarce on the Sahel and the desert crept in. Wicker-hut villages eventually disappeared, and the Harmattan haze began thickening with blue-gray exhaust fumes, an eye-burning miasma set aglow by the sun. Soon we entered the low cement suburbs of Kano and found ourselves navigating amid mopeds and minibuses and buses and overloaded carts and dilapidated taxis, heading for the center.

My taxi deposited me at the Central Hotel. Under a dribbling cold shower of rusty water, I scrubbed away the grit covering my face and hands from the eight-hour trip.

I later searched for Mustafa in Sabon Gari but learned that he had long ago left the hotel, leaving no forwarding address. The proprietor told me that he never opened his scrap metal factory.

The next morning, on the lumpy sandstone brow of Dala Hill, I stood with my guide, Ahmad, and observed an awesome panorama. The Harmattan was blowing off the Sahel in stifling gusts, driving wavering curtains of reddish dust over the crumbling walls of the old city, obscuring the minarets and emerald green dome of the Central Mosque, hiding the distant battlements of the emir's palace, all but concealing the stalls of Kurmi Market around the base of the hill and rendering sepulchrally vague the tomb-marking stone shards of the Muslim cemetery just beneath us.

Vertical tribal scars called *saagu* ran down Ahmad's temples and marked him as a Fulani, a member of the mujahids who became Nigeria's emirs and shehus. His dress – a pea green riga robe and a high white zanabukar cap – gave him an air of gravitas, and he took long, pensive strides, as if pondering weighty matters.

In such heat and wind, breathing was a chore and our eyes began drying out, so we decided not to linger. We descended into the twisting lanes of Kurmi Market. As in 1997, every shop was a shack of corrugated steel and crooked beams and mud, but now, able to relax more, I studied the wares for sale, which were more varied than the bleak terrain around Kano might lead one to expect. Peddlers presided over greasy slabs of *gurasa* (pancakes soaked in vinegar); piles of hot red peppers called *ataragu* stood next to hotter still green ones; boys pushed carts stacked with log-size yams; a man plunged his hands into slabs of stinking, gluey *dadawa* tree bark used for soup. Just when the fumes from all these delicacies were about to overcome me, we emerged into a quarter where kebab sellers tended lamb and chicken on spits, women lugged translucent plastic jugs of orange palm oil, and little girls circulated with trays of bananas or packets of ground-nuts on their scarved heads.

We emerged onto a road leading to the emir's palace. People held kerchiefs to their mouths to protect against the Harmattan, which here was stirring up refuse and twirling it around in tiny whirlwinds.

A little boy in a skullcap walked past, giving me an unpleasant, even harsh stare. He wore a bin Laden T-shirt. I asked Ahmad about it.

'Oh, most people here support bin Laden as a religious leader,' he said. 'We aren't so sure that he was behind the terrible accident of September 11.'

'Accident?'

'Of course. That was terrorism, and terrorism has nothing to do with religion, and bin Laden is a religious leader, therefore he couldn't have done September 11. By the way, it was a terror act against the world, not just America, so don't think you alone should grieve. Four Nigerians died that day, you know. We

Muslims separate terrorism from religion. The real terrorism comes from Bush: he invaded Afghanistan, and now, to get Iraq's oil he's going to invade Iraq. *That's* terrorism.'

'So why aren't people here hostile to me, since I'm American?'

'We separate Bush from the American people. Evil comes from Bush, not from the American people, who are honest. We know the Republican party is a party of power and big money.'

We were approaching the crenellated clay portals of Kofar Wamba, one of the gates to the old city. Nearby was a storefront from which echoed raucous chanting in Arabic – a Qur'anic school.

'I studied in a school like that,' said Ahmad. A wistful look came over his eyes, but a dirt-laden gust made him wince.

We stopped and looked inside. The school was a concrete storefront with navy blue shutters, a floor strewn with old green and red carpets, and grit-splotched walls hung with banners bearing quotes from the Qur'an, all gilt lettering on black. Some fifteen boys of various ages, sitting cross-legged, rocked back and forth, reciting suras from Qur'ans open in their laps. In front of them sat the imam, a white-bearded elder whose blue robes draped in shimmering profusion from his narrow shoulders. His chanting was low and rhythmic, soothing, and began with the three letters of the Arabic alphabet that open the Sura of the House of Imran:

'*Alif lam mim.*' He gave me an inscrutable glance – was he disturbed by an infidel's presence in his doorway? – and continued. '*Allahu. La illaha illa Huwa al-hayyu al-qayyumu, nazzala 'alayka alkitaba bilhaqqi musaddiqan lima bayna yadayhi wa anzala al-Tawrata wa al-Injila min qablu hudan lil-nasi . . .*' (God. There is no god but He, the living, the everlasting. He has sent down upon thee the Book with the truth, confirming what was before it, and He sent down the Torah and the Gospel aforetime, as guidance to the people . . .)

'He is Sharif [a descendent of the Prophet Muhammad] Hamad al-Mustafa, a respected imam,' said Ahmad. 'Would you like to meet him?'

I said I would. We took off our shoes and gingerly stepped

onto the carpets inside. The boys continued chanting, though they eyed me with curiosity, and a couple couldn't help giggling.

A little while later the lesson ended. The imam closed his Qur'an and dismissed his students. I approached him and introduced myself, speaking Arabic, and told him that his choice of verse much pleased me.

He asked us to sit down. 'You flew from America to Kano?' he asked in faltering Arabic.

'No, I flew from Paris to Chad, and from Chad I came here.'

'Ah, Chad! A wonderful land of Islam, with all the *tariqas* [Sufi sects]! They say *all* the daily prayers there – they're very religious.' At times he would turn to Ahmad and speak in Hausa, which Ahmad translated for me into English.

'You've been to Chad a lot?' I asked.

'Many times.' His face beamed; his eyes were a warm brown. 'I've made the hajj forty times, often crossing by land from here to Mecca. Ah, the deserts of Chad!'

Forty times! His wrinkles were well earned.

'I'm about to go on the '*Umra*' – the lesser hajj – 'but this time I'm flying. War has closed the routes. Do you know Chad?'

'A little.'

Urban Kano raged outside: a din of horns and backfiring mopeds and ancient Opel station wagon taxis crashing over potholes; the spirited arguing in Hausa of a turbulent stream of men in caftans and baggy *wando* trousers; and beggars and vendors and children everywhere. Yet all this ruckus fell away as I listened to the imam talk. My own travels in Chad now seemed unworthy of mention – for him the Sahara was a realm of purity and faith, and if he suffered there, he did so as a penitent – but I gave him what news I could of the places I had visited and he was happy to hear about them. In his eyes I saw compassion, the same compassion others had shown me since my arrival in the Sahel. I relaxed in his presence and realized how foolish I had been to interpret his surprised glance as some sort of anti-Western hostility. That I was an American made no difference to him.

A man came in and sat down with us and introduced himself as the imam's student. He wore a fluffy white turban, and his pure white caftan was embroidered with royal blue. His Arabic was fluent. (For the sharif Arabic was a language of liturgy, not communication.) He asked me if I was a Muslim but accepted my negative reply with a smile and said something that explained their tranquil demeanors: 'We are Sufis.'

Sufism is an Islamic sect that promotes a transcendental, mystic relationship with God. It once enjoyed much popularity in lands where Islam supplanted local religions, as it had across the Sahel and in North Africa. This much I knew, but I had never spoken to Sufis before, and I asked them how they, from the pacific standpoint of their faith, viewed the tensions between the West and the Muslim world today.

'I can't really say,' replied the imam in Hausa, with Ahmad translating. 'These are worldly affairs. We know nothing of them, of the wars going on between kaffir and kaffir, or between the kaffirs and Iraq.'

His student added, in Arabic, 'Actually, we *do* know of the war between Israel and Palestine, and how America supports Israel, and how the Muslims lose the war because they're weak. But God doesn't help the oppressor: this we know too. We love all our Muslim brothers, we are all part of the *Umma* [Islamic Nation], but God decides in the end. To God alone belongs the power.'

The imam added, 'We do not concern ourselves with *al-dunya* [the temporal world], but with God and *al-akhira* [the hereafter]. We know nothing of bin Laden. We're neutral.'

'Neutral?'

'Yes, neutral,' said the student, calmly. 'These wars are signs of the final days. We don't fear *al-dunya*. We fear God alone, and God alone will judge. Only the ill man understands illness; the poor man poverty; the wounded man the wound. Help comes from God and God alone, and the Unjust will not triumph. For us it suffices to know this.'

The imam and his student had to go, and they took their leave of us, walking us to the door of their school.

From the eighteenth-century rise of the first Muslim fundamentalist creed, Wahhabism, to our times and al-Qa'ida, Sufism has suffered the hatred of Islamic extremists, who have waged lengthy campaigns to extirpate it as heresy. In many parts of the Arab world, they have succeeded, and I had never expected to find it thriving in Kano.

The next day, the Harmattan swept across the late-afternoon sky, filtering through its ocherous dust the fiery orb of the falling sun and creating a sunset of awe and splendor befitting the Apocalypse. I retreated to the Ultra Modern Bar on the roof of the TYC Hotel, in the heart of Sabon Gari, wondering if I could enjoy a beer and perhaps a little of the free-and-easy Afro-beat dance scene I knew during my stay in 1997 – after all, Sabon Gari was the Christian quarter. But shari'a had since been imposed even there, and I found the bar deserted and derelict. A gutted television stood wrecked on a table above a ripped-up sofa sitting knock-kneed on snapped legs; rotting mattresses covered much of what was once an open-air dance floor; and to dampen whatever hint of kaffir spirit survived, a weathered sign proclaimed, NO DANCING ON THIS ROOF GARDEN. NO JUMPING UP AND DOWN WHATSOEVER UNDER PAIN OF STRICT PENALTIES. From below and all around, where pedestrians and vehicles and goats and donkeys teemed and seethed in a grid of wrecked pavement and dirt alleys, arose clouds of dust and exhaust that melded with the Harmattan haze.

I was the only guest. No alcohol was served, but a waitress from the snack bar brought me a Coke, and I sat down on the broken sofa by a rusty table to read more of the Bible I had bought in Maiduguri. Sitting above this befouled cityscape, I started to understand the book's appeal: it conjured up a pastoral world lost, a simple world, fictitious as I believed it to be, in which, I couldn't help thinking, we were meant to live. A principled world in which a 'man shall cleave unto his wife' and honor his parents; where wealth was measured in 'cattle and silver and gold'; where a jealous God whose wrath waxed hot demanded submission, but who could be appeased by the savor of burnt offerings; where it was recognized that 'the wicked walk on every side . . . the vilest men are exalted,' but where, in the end, the Redeemer, the Lamb of God, would come to bear away sin and promise whosoever believed in Him eternal life. The very language, Manichean and elegant (in the King James translation), soothed me; the universe it described made sense. No wonder Christianity was growing so quickly in Africa as Africa decayed, and no wonder Ezekiel and his fellow parishioners took such comfort in it.

I read from Revelation, the book of the Bible prophesying the Apocalypse, until darkness came on. Then I headed down the stairs to catch a taxi back to my hotel, the description of the world's end still vivid in my mind's eye – the day of wrath and thunder and lightning, when the earth would quake, the sun would blacken and the moon turn red, and smoke would pour forth from a bottomless pit; when hail and fire mingled with blood would fall to earth and multitudes would seek death and not find it; when noisome and grievous sores would cover men as the mark of the beast.

Now the sun was dying, casting streaks of scarlet into the clay-colored firmament of the Harmattan. Once on the street, which was little more than a cratered dirt track, I emerged into the press of beggars and peddlers and the din of traffic, into clouds of exhaust and dust stabbed by roving twin beams from multiple rows of taxis and minibuses and mopeds bouncing along without regard to lane. There was no sidewalk, and the traffic surged by the very wall, often pressing me to stand flat against it. Minibuses trundled along, their attendants shouting at pedestrians and mopeds to move aside, whipping them away with leather straps. Trucks blared their horns, asserting the right of the big over the little. Jalopies rattled through potholes, and now and then fenders broke off and clanked on the ground; drivers cried out, screaming like banshees and demanding passage. In the intersection, youths directed traffic freelance, taking handouts to escort cars through the melee. The moon shone red through the fumes.

# 11

# THE MUJAHID OF SOKOTO

*A*LLAH! *ALLAH! Karama! Karama! Sadaqa! Allah!'*
Crying for alms in keening Arabic, the crowd of gimping beggars, noseless lepers, clubfooted hags, and drooling, spindle-legged elders pressed around me on the sun-scorched lot, huffing fetid breath in my face, grabbing at my sleeves with gooey hands. Badamasi, my teenage guide, ignored the assembly: he was used to it, and expected me, a visitor to Sokoto (a small town 250 miles northwest of Kano) from an impossibly blessed and distant land, to show mercy. I tried to. I dropped what bills I had into their tin bowls, gently freed myself of their clutching hands, and followed Badamasi through the portals of the mausoleum of Shehu Usuman dan Fodio.

One of the first Sahelian fundamentalists in Islamic history, the Fulani *mujaddid* and mujahid Shehu Usuman dan Fodio waged a populist jihad that, in the early nineteenth century, led to the foundation of a Muslim empire that covered more than 180,000 square miles in West Africa, embraced some 10 million people, and included Kano and Maiduguri. His was an empire born of injustice and rage. Originally from Gobir, once a Hausa state in the desert north of Sokoto, dan Fodio in his youth secured a solid education in Islam and classical Arabic and spent his early adult years preaching against the profligate ways of the Hausa

elite, demanding justice for Hausa peasants angered at exploitative taxation and despotism. In 1804 he launched his jihad, which
galvanized the masses and triumphed. The victorious dan Fodio
assumed the titles of 'commander of the faithful' (*sarkin musulmi*
in Hausa) and 'caliph,' God's viceroy on earth, and Sokoto
became his capital, the seat of his caliphate, and home to his
mausoleum. (There were many caliphs in the Muslim world; dan
Fodio's authority held sway only in West Africa.) As a result of his
jihad, the Fulani replaced the Hausa as the region's elite, and,
though dan Fodio appears to have been an ascetic zealot wanting
nothing more than to establish the kingdom of God on earth, his
cohorts were less principled: they seized Hausa land holdings
and perpetuated the misery of the masses who had helped them
to power.

Like other emirs of the north, the emirs of Sokoto, desirous of
retaining their authority under the colonial system of indirect
rule, collaborated with the British, all the while dismissing their
foreign overlords as short-timers. They were right: the British
came and left, and the emir of Sokoto is still the spiritual leader of
Islam in Nigeria, presiding today over what is supposedly the
strictest of the shari'a states. The masses, however, are as miserable as ever – as the crowds of beggars at the mausoleum attest.

Badamasi and I walked through the mausoleum's sandy
grounds to a stark, plain stone structure with a main room that was
hung with banners from the Qur'an in Arabic praising holy war,
faith, and the value of good works. Beneath them the shehu's
tomb lay unmarked under a black shroud, as did the tombs of his
disciples. This simplicity accorded with the austere message dan
Fodio preached, which is essentially the message of all Islamic
fundamentalists: that Muslims must eschew mortal vanity and
Mammon and return to the pure, abstemious Islamic society that,
they say, existed during the early times of the faith. Dan Fodio's
ideal was the Baghdad-based Abbasid Caliphate that began
in the eighth century and lasted until the Mongols destroyed it in
the thirteenth.

There was little to see in the mausoleum, just as dan Fodio
would have wanted. We soon walked back outside. The

mausoleum, so plain, even crude, depressed me for more than
aesthetic reasons, though I could not say yet just why. Back on the
dusty lot in front, Badamasi introduced me to Nasiru Sidi, a delicate young man whose clear eyes and polished English bespoke
education; in fact, he was a mathematics student at a university in
town. Nasiru's family are descendants of dan Fodio and look after
his tomb. He was happy to talk about his ancestor, and I asked
what dan Fodio's legacy was.

'Dan Fodio saw that people here were worshiping idols,'
Nasiru said, 'so he called on them to accept Islam. They refused,
so he had the right to wage jihad against them; Islam gives
Muslims the right to conquer people when they refuse to accept
the faith. He did good work. So you see, his legacy is that even
today we're Muslims and have shari'a: we cut off the hand of a
thief if he has stolen more than a thousand naira; if people forni-
cate we cane them ninety-nine times or put them to death.'

'That's a bloody legacy. You're educated. Don't you think that's
pretty extreme?'

'Not at all; it is justice. Anyway, it's very difficult to prove for-
nication: you must have four witnesses who actually see the penis
in the vagina.'

'How many people have been executed here?'

'We've had no executions yet. Crime is very low.'

Was it? Or was shari'a not as strictly enforced as he led me to
think? Though floggings for drinking alcohol do occur frequently,
only one thief has lost his hand, and neither of the two death
sentences (by stoning) decreed against northern women for adultery has been carried out. No cinemas are allowed and bars have
been closed, but in Sokoto hotel clerks did a thriving if surrepti-
tious business bringing their patrons beer. Quite a few women
went about unveiled. This apparent leniency stems in part from
the absence of a legitimate enforcing authority: the police, who
still operate under a constitution mandating the separation of religion and state, cannot (or should not) arrest people for offenses
committed against Islamic law. The closest thing the northern
states have to an Islamic police force, zealous Muslim activists
called Hizba, has no legal authority.

A scholar at the Aminu Kano College of Islamic Legal Studies in Kano had justified to me the lax enforcement of shari'a in another way: 'The Qur'an says, "There is no compulsion in religion." Our [Islamic] principles are voluntary, and only for those who profess Islam. The Hizba can only persuade Muslims to follow their religion. Prosecution is a last resort after a man has been warned to change his ways.' Perhaps, I wondered, the pro-shari'a movement was more about reasserting Muslim political identity vis-à-vis the despised Christian southerners than really implementing the 'blood, stone, and cane' Law of God.

Something else was puzzling me. With war looking probable between the United States and Iraq, I had been expecting a cool, possibly hostile, reception in Sokoto. But I experienced nothing of the sort, even from the police officer who questioned me at my hotel about the motives of my stay. I asked Nasiru why.

'Muslims know every man's life is written to the end, so there's no reason for anyone to bother you. Islam, you see, doesn't allow us to harm you. What is written will be.'

'But I've read about widespread support for Osama bin Laden here. The people in al-Qa'ida aren't so passive.'

'Osama is our Muslim brother, and we pray for him because of that. By the way, Bush hasn't proved a hundred percent that he did September 11. Many here believe the Americans did the attacks themselves. But Bush we don't like: he's always disgracing and attacking Islam. We saw this in Afghanistan. Now, just because of his father, Bush wants to attack Iraq and disgrace Islam more. But this doesn't have anything to do with you, so you are safe with us.'

On that reassuring note, Badamasi and I said goodbye to Nasiru and left to take a walk around Sokoto, a town of multiple modern thoroughfares cutting through mud-hut suburbs peppered with signs in Arabic announcing, I FEAR GOD! I ASK GOD'S PARDON! and GOD IS MOST GREAT!

The Islamic window dressing aside, Sokoto seemed a pleasant enough place, though bland, and Badamasi had trouble thinking of sights to show me. Architecturally, dan Fodio left behind nothing besides an unmarked tomb. Sokoto boasts not a single spectacular mosque, not one magnificent palace, not even one historical market. In its dullness and austerity, his capital contrasted sharply with the capitals of the sultans and caliphs of Ottoman Turkey and the Middle East and North Africa, where mosques, palaces, markets, and Qur'anic schools rank among the greatest works of architecture anywhere, the images of which continually came to mind as I examined the mud-and-stone starkness of Sokoto.

Neither did dan Fodio seem to live on in letters. His writings were said to number more than a hundred and concern ritual and correct forms of Islamic worship. But I tried unsuccessfully to find them in the local library, and they were not sold on the street or in bookstores, though the works of other Muslim scholars from Arab countries were. If dan Fodio's rule spread literacy (mostly in Arabic but also in Fulani and Hausa, which were in his day written in the Arabic script), it did not spread respect for, or even a desire for, education beyond that obtainable in Qur'anic schools; to this day, Hausa and Fulani tend to see little value in scholarship, and literacy levels in the north remain the lowest in Nigeria. Thinking this through, I saw why the bare mausoleum had depressed me: it stood for ignorance and a spirit-crushing austerity unknown in most of the Islamic world. The last thing impoverished denizens of dry earth needed was leadership from a man advocating a sumptuary religion and urging them to eschew arts, letters, and progress and be content with adobe, rock, and the word of God.

The Harmattan abated three days after my visit to the *mujaddid*'s tomb. In crisp dawn light and a cool westerly breeze, I boarded a Toyota station wagon taxi at Sokoto's motor park for the five-hour ride back to Kano, from where I planned to head north the next day to Niger. My driver, a young Hausa with cat's-whisker tribal scars, sold me two of the three seats in the middle row, and I settled in for the journey.

A man who looked to be in his sixties, trimly bearded, with an Arab complexion and a Roman nose, occupied the third seat in my row. Instead of the usual Hausa zanabukar or *dara*, he wore an embroidered white skullcap, and over his shoulders hung a coarse brown woolen cape – apparel that gave him the look of an ascetic foreign to Nigeria. He cast me a quizzical glance and, addressing me as *batoure* ('white man' in Hausa), asked me something. I told him I didn't understand Hausa.

'Ah.' He switched to Arabic. *'Titkillim kalam al-'Arab?'* (You talk the talk of the Arabs?)

We began chatting. He told me he was a Kanuri from the desert near Chad, and part of his family hailed from Arabia – hence his Arabic and complexion. He was an inspector of schools. He spoke in a deferential tone, thanking me for my responses. After introducing himself as Abdulrahim, he asked my name.

'Jelal,' I said.

Most Muslim names in Arabic are either nouns or adjectives denoting religiously desirable attributes. *Abdulrahim* means 'slave of the Merciful One'; *Jelal,* 'loftiness' or 'sublimity.' I chose Jelal not for its sense but because people in Morocco, where I served in the Peace Corps, had morphed Jeff into Ja'far (a name whose retching letter *'ain* I disliked), while Jelal sounded similar to Jeff and was uncommon.

'Thank you. Jelal. Hmm . . .' He nodded and smiled. 'You mean *'Abd* al-Jalil.' (*'Slave* of the Sublime One' – that is, God. Jalil is the adjective of Jelal, and figures among the list of *al-asma' al-husna,* the ninety-nine attributes of God. I had intentionally chosen the less pious Jelal.)

'No, I mean Jelal.'

'You should call yourself *'abd.'*

'But I'm not Muslim, and I'm not a slave.'

He pondered my words, nodding. 'Even your leader, the president of your faith, called himself *'abd.* So you *should* be *'Abd* al-Jalil.'

'Really, I'm just Jelal.'

'Thank you. Where are you from, 'Abd al-Jalil?'

I told him.

'Ah, you're American! Thank you.'

'Why?'

'Well, thank you for talking to me. You must be a great man. Americans rule the world.'

'I don't think Americans rule the world.'

'But you *do* rule the world. However, your president . . . your president Bush is guilty of the sin of Cain. All men are brothers, but Bush has killed and is killing his brothers. Why does he kill when the president of the Christians forbids it?'

'The president?'

'What's his name now? The leader. Cristy or something like that.'

'You mean Christ.'

He wasn't sure, but he said, 'The president of the Christians tells Bush not to fight in Iraq and said not to kill. So why doesn't Bush listen to him?'

I began trying to explain Bush's view of Saddam Hussein and the question of Iraqi weapons of mass destruction. The old man had about as little patience for pro-war arguments as I had, and soon interrupted me. 'It's written in the Qur'an that the war that will end the world will be fought over riches under the earth of Iraq.'

'Really? In which sura?'

He stopped nodding. 'Why do you want to know?'

'I have a Qur'an with me and I'd like to check that passage. That's quite interesting.'

'Why would you read the Qur'an if you're not a Muslim?'

'Because I want to understand Islam. Look, you just told me that the Qur'an predicts the war. I'd like to verify that. Can you tell me in which sura you find that quote?'

He kept his eyes on mine but didn't answer. I repeated my question.

'The Sura of Victory,' he answered, after an oddly prolonged silence. 'But you're not a Muslim, so you shouldn't be reading the Qur'an. If you read it without faith you will disbelieve it.'

'But how can one become a Muslim if one doesn't read the Qur'an? In every Arab country I've been in people have asked me to read the Qur'an in the hope that I'd become Muslim.'

'They should not have done so. They're wrong.'

'Then how does one become a Muslim if not by reading the Qur'an?'

'Your father has to be a Muslim.'

This was untrue, and I told him so.

'Well, *arshadak Allah* [May God guide you rightly] and give you faith.'

'*In sha' Allah* [If God so wills it]. But still, as far as I understand it, there's no prohibition against non-Muslims reading the Qur'an. Such a prohibition would make no sense.'

'Becoming a Muslim is easy. You should become one. Now. Just say these words from the Qur'an and believe them.' He raised his forefinger. '"*Qul huwa Allahu ahad, Allahu samad. Lam yalid wa lam yulad, wa lam yakun lahu kufu'an ahad.*" ["He is God, one God, the Everlasting Refuge, who has not begotten and has not been begotten, and equal to him is not any one."] God had no son, no son! You *mustn't* believe God had a son. Repeat after me, "*A'udhu billah min al-Shaytan al-rajim!*" ["I take refuge in God from Satan the Accursed!"]'

'I'm not a Muslim, so I can't say the words. I don't believe them.'

'But say them and *believe* them. Right now!'

'No, as I just told you, I —'

'*Say* them! Just say them like this.' He repeated the sura, raising his forefinger again and closing his eyes, adding, 'Follow *al-sirat al-mustaqim* [the straight path]! *Follow* it!'

'I'm sorry; I just told you that I don't believe the words and I won't lie by —'

'I don't want you to go to hell!' His voice rose. 'Just say and *believe* these words! What is so difficult? SAY THEM RIGHT NOW!'

'No! I just —'

'"*Qul huwa Allahu ahad —*"'

'Please, let's change the subject!'

He leaned into my face. 'Okay, then, say the *Shahada*!' The *Shahada*, the Testimony, is the statement that all Muslims must make at least once in their lives to affirm their faith, or that non-Muslims recite to enter Islam: 'I bear witness that there is no god but God, and Muhammad is the Prophet of God.' 'SAY THE *SHAHADA* OR YOU WILL GO TO *HELL!*'

'Look, the Qur'an says, "You have your religion and I have mine"! Please, stop. I'm not going to talk to you any more about this.'

I turned away. I sat, steaming, and tried to think of a way of explaining my refusal to make a false profession of faith. 'Look,' I said, 'we were just talking about war between Muslims and Christians. But how can Muslims and Christians be friends if Muslims hold such uncompromising beliefs and don't accept other people as equals? Think about it.' He didn't answer, but his eyes drooped with contrition and he seemed to understand something: he had not expected my distressed outburst. I didn't regret my words. 'With such extremism, can there be peace between Muslims and Christians?' I asked.

'Why, yes,' he replied after a pause, returning to his nods. 'We're all sons of Adam, are we not? Just as the Qur'an says, the only difference between us is in piety. Man is brother to man – in piety.'

'In piety.' But what about those who have no faith? The Qur'an abounds in references to the flames awaiting the kaffirs. Had I told him I had no religion, I would have placed myself well beyond the bounds of tolerance Islam established for 'People of the Book' – Jews and Christians. The Qur'an enjoins tolerance toward followers of the two celestial religions that preceded Islam, but not toward atheists or adherents of Hinduism or Buddhism or other 'Godless' faiths.

This man wanted nothing but my salvation – which was precisely the problem, the root of the danger, and at least the ostensible primum mobile of all the violence jihads had brought about. He would not accept me as I was because his religion assigned him the sacred duty of rightly guiding me. Our worldviews could *never* be reconciled. The only way out for me was to stop the dialogue and turn away.

We talked no more, and I stared out the window, eager for the ride to end.

Later that day, in Kano, I checked the Sura of Victory for the reference to the war and the wealth buried under the soil of Iraq, but I found nothing of the kind. If he really knew where the quote came from, he had not trusted me enough to tell me the truth.

# 12

## TORTURE IN ZINDER

Two rusty oil drums sunk crookedly in powdery earth on opposite sides of a two-lane road, a wire marked with a fluttering blue rag strung between them – the Nigeria-Niger border. The morning I arrived in a taxi, the sun was shining soft and cool, bathing the Sahel in an almost alpine resplendence that augured a *douceur de vivre* I had not expected to experience until I reached Dakar. The Nigerian soldier ensconced in a lawn chair in the shade of a nearby neem was asleep but smiling, as if dreaming of home somewhere in the hot jungly south, where there was no Harmattan, where fruit ripened on luxuriantly foliaged trees and palm wine fermented in bulging umber calabashes.

My driver, a grumpy old Fulani, tooted his horn. The soldier started awake, his smile disappearing, and hoisted himself from his chair. He trotted over and lifted the wire. We drove the last potholed yards down the road into Niger, where the tarmac narrowed from two lanes to scarcely more than one, but smoothed out.

I was out of Nigeria! Before the oil-drum border, my departing formalities had involved a typically Nigerian potpourri of false drama, imperious officials, and bewilderment. A half-hour earlier, we had reached the shed-and-shack assemblage that was the Nigerian frontier post. The customs officer there waved us past, but at the door to the next shed an immigration officer stepped out and pointed at me. He was a giant fellow in a peach-yellow uniform, with pear-shaped hips and a round cranium that looked like a cantaloupe with facial features. Remembering the shouting interrogation to which I had been subjected on arrival in Nigeria, I cringed and climbed out.

Inside the shed, another officer, a short, sleepy man in a Windbreaker zipped up to the neck against the morning chill, took my passport and sat down behind his desk. He flicked through its pages with some urgency, and shook his head.

'What's the problem?' asked his fruity superior, who towered over me, smiling. They exchanged a few words in Yoruba; these were southerners.

'What *is* the problem?' I asked.

'You are leaving finally?' the official in the Windbreaker said, holding up my passport.

'Yes.'

'But you are leaving *finally*? Go and no coming back?'

'That's right.'

'Because you got only visa single-entry. I cancel it and you don't coming back.'

'I understand.'

He glanced down at my passport and then up at me and smiled broadly, his pearly grin communicating to me something weightier than concern about my travel plans. Was I supposed to offer him a bribe? For what? I had just seen how my taxi driver dealt with Operation Fire-for-Fire soldiers and I felt emboldened. They had flagged us down every ten miles since we left Kano. 'Tiefs! Tiefs!' my driver exclaimed each time after he had stopped for them, ignored their outstretched palms, and waited until they let us go. It seemed that if your papers were in order and you showed resolve, they wouldn't persist.

So, I returned the official's smile and stared back. He then sighed and clunked his stamp on an empty page and drew a line through my visa, canceling it. 'Okay, my friend,' he said, slapping the booklet on the counter in front of me, 'go to health check. Good travels!'

I walked out and across the sand to the next shed. There I

found the health-check officer, who could have been the twin brother of the obnoxious official who had berated me at the Ngala frontier.

He took my passport and looked up from behind his ledger, bellowing, 'You a journalist?'

'A travel writer.'

'What you writing about Nigeria?'

'I'd like to write about how friendly people are here, how good the food is, and how much I like it here.'

'You like it here?'

'Yes, I do.'

He handed me my passport and said something in Hausa to a morose officer slumped behind another desk in the back of the room. That one cleared his throat and commanded, 'Vaccination!'

I gave him my World Health Organization card, a bedraggled booklet, taped up and yellow-leafed, showing every vaccination I had received since 1987. Page after page was inked with notations indicating shots against yellow fever, typhoid, tetanus, diphtheria, polio, typhus, two strains of meningitis, hepatitis A and B, cholera, and even rabies, plus marks for malaria prophylaxis and a few other things.

He pored over all of them, but they didn't suffice.

'Have you had vaccination?'

'In fact I have, as you see. They're all listed there.'

'What vaccination here? What the date?'

I leaned over and politely pointed out the dates for my meningitis and yellow fever vaccinations – the ones I took to be most important for Nigeria.

He studied them and frowned. I smiled confidently. If he was angling for a bribe, he wasn't going to get one.

He flicked through the last pages. 'Expired for meningitis?! Expired?!'

'No, if you —'

'Expired!'

I pointed out the date in December.

'You got dollars for us?' demanded the first officer.

'I'm sorry: I live in Russia, so unfortunately I don't.'

'You got some Russian money then?'

'In fact, the ruble is a soft currency, so it's inconvertible.'

'Show me some.'

'I don't have any on me. But I do have traveler's checks.' These I knew wouldn't interest him, so I took them out. He looked away. The checks settled it for the health-check officer too, who returned my card. They wished me well and I walked out. I got back in the taxi. We drove up to the wire border and awoke the snoozing soldier.

Once we crossed the border, Niger's poverty relative to Nigeria became painfully apparent: cars, even beat-up taxis like the one in which I was riding, were few; gone were advertising billboards; absent were women in flamboyant boubous and men in regal caftans. Here, dusty-haired stick people in tattered smocks wandered barefoot at the roadside amid a desiccated wilderness of sand and neems. Only the tarmac signaled that we were not in the fifteenth century – or the fifth century, for that matter. According to the United Nations' Human Development Index, Niger is, after Sierra Leone, the least-developed country in the world.

But life would have been easier here in the fifth century, to be sure. When independence came in 1960, Nigériens had only one crop: groundnuts. Eight years later uranium was discovered, which allowed a modicum of development (mostly in the capital, Niamey), but at the same time a drought hit the Sahel and killed a third of the country's cattle. Ever since 1968, Niger has been drying up and blowing away, deteriorating in every measurable way. Primitive farming techniques hasten desertification; in the past twenty years alone, the Sahara has advanced a hundred miles south, eating away at what little arable land there is, which is all under cultivation now and covers only 4 percent of the country's five hundred thousand square miles. This means that Niger cannot feed itself. Forty percent of Nigérien children under the age of five weigh in below normal, and 20 percent are emaciated; large segments of the population for months at a time eat fewer than one meal a day; increasingly, for many, bark and leaves are the only food. To make matters much worse, the population of 11 million expands by 3.3 percent a year (the average woman bears 7.5 children – the highest birthrate on earth), but real GDP growth lags behind at 1.9 percent. This ensures a steady drop in average per capita income, which, at $170 a year, is now 30 percent less than what it was in 1983. Average life expectancy now stands at just below forty-two years, and almost half the population is fourteen years old or younger. Foreign aid, mainly from the European Union and France, accounts for 60 percent of the government's budget.

Though Niger is now ruled by a democratically elected president, frequent coups and civil wars have scared away foreign investors, and the possibility of future turmoil looms large. Even the country's name, a truncated version of Nigeria, seems to conjure up the specter of trouble. Hausa make up about two-thirds of the population, and they are separated from their brethren in Nigeria by a porous and artificial border that the colonial powers left behind. Though it hasn't yet, radical Islamist fervor in Nigeria could spill over into Niger and threaten the country's secular government.

With a population of twenty thousand, Zinder, once the capital of the Damagaram sultanate, is the only real town in Niger's vast Saharan east. It appeared to be asleep when I arrived. Up and down sandy roads crisscrossing neem-crowned hills only the occasional moped beeped and bounced, and pedestrians were scarce. I settled into a bungalow at the Hotel Damagaram and went out to drink a Coke in its pleasant garden. For the first time since leaving Chad, I relaxed.

When the sun began to fall, I hired a moped to take me to the Pacifique Bar, the most popular place in town, according to my hotel receptionist. In the garden there I took a seat and marveled at the calm: the neems soughed above, stirred by a breeze free of the exhaust fumes that suffocated the Nigerian cities from which I had come; and the Nigériens walking into the bar appeared far more tranquil than their cousins south of the border.

No one came out to serve me, so I got up and went over to the bar, which was inside an adjacent concrete hut. A shapely young

woman with long, glossy straightened hair and purplish lipstick
was nursing an infant at her ample breast. I asked for a beer.

Looking a bit tired, she got up, still holding the baby. Jostled,
he lost his suckle; thick drops of milk dotted her swollen nipple.
With her free arm, she reached under the bar, pulled out a bottle,
and placed it on the counter. The baby whined and squeezed the
nipple, and milk dribbled out. I paid and took the bottle.

'*Vous êtes Français?*' asked a big man wearing a safari suit and
sitting in the back behind a tabletop rampart of empty beer bottles. A naked baby sat at his side and flapped his arms. Both the
man and the baby had puckered, sweaty faces.

'No, I'm American.'

'American?' He burped. 'One of those ones educated in
Montreal, no doubt.'

'No, just an American.'

'Well' – he took a vigorous gulp from the bottle in his hand –
'aren't you afraid to be here? Bush is protected but you're not.
You're just a citizen. The whole world hates America because of
what Bush is doing.' He emphasized his last words with a pointing thrust of his bottle, which ejaculated foamy beer. His receding
elbow just missed the baby's head.

'I don't feel I'm in danger here. Zinder seems peaceful.'

'Oh, *we* are peaceful.'

The man introduced himself as Ahmad, and, grabbing the
baby and plopping him down the other side of the bench, asked
me to have a seat with him inside his beer-bottle fortress. His
French indicated solid schooling. In fact, he was an engineer.

Ahmad waved his bottle again, and more foam flew. 'All it
would take is for one Arab to find out you're here, and he could
toss a bomb at you. Bush doesn't care about what happens to you
or to his citizens all over the world, and Americans are everywhere. You *are* in danger.' He burped raucously and scared the
baby into a crying jag. 'Look, America is rich and has everything,'
he shouted over the screams. 'Does it really need Iraq's oil too?
Don't you have enough riches? Why do you want to attack the
poor?'

If his voice was loud, his tone was deliberate and inquisitive, not angry; he genuinely wanted answers. He drained his bottle and shouted in Hausa for another beer, and the nursing bartender obliged.

I told him that I could not justify or even fully understand why Bush wanted to attack Iraq, though I tried to explain how much things had changed in the United States since September 11.

'Oh,' he said, 'bin Laden is just a figment of the imagination. You know what I think?' He sucked down a quarter of his new bottle in one gurgle. 'You know who *really* did September 11.'

'Who?'

He pulled back and regarded me with puzzled eyes, as if startled by my ignorance.

'Why, Al Gore! It was the Democrats who carried out September 11 – for revenge. After Bush stole the elections, who knows what's in Gore's heart?'

'I don't really think Al Gore would —'

'That's how we see it, anyway. Here, one who's been cheated takes revenge. I mean, why do you think the Germans are refusing to join America in the Iraq war? They want to avenge their defeat in World War Two. Look, I don't like seeing dead people. I don't like war. I don't like blood.' The baby giggled. Ahmad finished his beer and placed it at the end of the row of bottles. 'I just want peace. Say, you want to go to another bar? I'm moving on to a place with women.'

I thanked him very much for his invitation but declined.

'Okay, okay. Look, when you get to Niamey, go to the Moustache Hotel. There you can have beer and all the women you want. Just drink and take women, all day. I go there when I'm in Niamey. Goodbye!'

He stood up and shook his head, scattering sweat drops, and tottered toward the door to step out into the now-dark street. The baby regarded his departure with equanimity. I returned to the garden, where a small crowd had assembled to watch a game show on French television. People were laughing and sipping their beer, and I thought about how in Nigeria shari'a had expunged such natural human cheer.

\*

Throughout its history, Zinder, like the rest of Niger, has known little besides suffering and blood, whether under local rule or a foreign yoke. Until the French took over in 1890, the town was a major center of commerce for the Sahel with one main commodity, slaves, which local tribal leaders obtained for the world market by raiding neighboring peoples. Sitting astride the caravan route leading north to Tripoli and south to Kano and the Atlantic, Zinder supplied slaves to North Africa, the Middle East, and the Americas. Islam forbade the enslavement of Muslims, but the sultans of Zinder bent the rules and ordered the pillaging of recently converted tribes. Male slaves could bring twelve dollars in Kano or a hundred in Constantinople, and women could fetch almost twice these amounts. The few nineteenth-century European explorers who made it to Zinder told of the commerce on their return home, and the French used halting the slave trade as a pretext for colonizing the region.

The next day I awoke to a blazing sky and torrid, still air – worse heat than anything I had known since arriving in the Sahel. Wondering what had happened to the cool, and attributing its disappearance to the proximity of the Sahara, I got dressed and went out to tell the hotel clerk that I was looking for a guide to take me to the sultan's palace. He sent out word, and two candidates soon showed up at the gate.

One of them was a young man in a ski cap and baggy Arab trousers, with a spaced-out, menacing dullness in his piss yellow eyes and three days' growth on his chin. He shook my hand and slit his lips in a snarl, revealing blackened spikes of teeth. He did not impress me as the kind of fellow I wanted to spend the day with.

The other candidate was a manic skinny fellow with a perky afro and jug ears. He introduced himself as Isa – Arabic for Jesus. Isa was dressed in a clean plaid shirt and clean jeans and was polite. Young Hausa in Niger, I was to see, tended not to wear traditional dress and were in general less pious, or less overtly Islamic, than Muslims in Nigeria. The interconfessional strife that so plagues Nigeria is unknown in Niger, partly because Muslims make up 90 percent of the population and don't have too many people to fight with.

Isa was relaxed about religion. 'Oh, yes!' he said. 'Christians drop down and pray when they hear my name!'

I laughed.

'I'm an official guide and have my papers from the police to prove it.'

'So do I,' said his louche rival.

Surprised that there even could be official guides in Zinder, I asked them to show me their papers.

The louche one pulled out a laminated card and held it up. I bent over to read it, but he tried to pull it away. I managed to snatch it from his hand. It read, OCCUPATION: FARMER.

'This is just your national ID card. It says you're a farmer.'

Keeping his yellow eyes on me, he took the card and shoved it back into his pocket. He stiffened up and looked as though he might object – violently, even – to my stern appraisal, but he said nothing.

I turned to Isa. 'What about your papers?'

'Oh, the police are just about to issue them, any day now. Really. Really!'

I doubted that – he was probably just a poor illiterate kid, judging by his French – but he seemed kind enough, and all I wanted was someone to walk me through Zinder's unmarked streets to the palace. I decided I would hire him, so I bid a gracious farewell to my potential assailant. Isa and I reached a deal for his fee and shook hands.

An hour later we were standing outside the thirty-foot-high mud walls of the sultan's palace – more of a casbah, actually – greeting Tanimoune, a cousin of the current sultan, Aboubacar Sanda. In his forties, Tanimoune was barefoot and wore a white smock and a red fez; he looked more like a poor master's servant than a royal's relation.

Out of respect for the sultan, and although we would be walking on hot sand, Isa and I took off our shoes and in stocking feet followed Tanimoune through portals into the palace grounds. The sultan's bodyguards, seven glum, hulking men in robes of red and green Christmasy hues and matching turbans, with

meter-long sabers dangling sheathed at their hips, stepped aside
to let us pass, and we walked through a low-ceilinged hallway out
into a courtyard – an empty sand lot. The mud walls radiated
heat, and the sun drove us to a shady corner.

Tanimoune recounted the history of the palace in French
while sucking lustily on a cola nut. Of course, darkness reigned
during the centuries before the Arabs brought Islam. The first
sultan was a Yemeni who established the dynasty that rules to this
day. The Yemeni tried to impose Islam on the locals, with only
limited success. Tanimoune was fuzzy on dates, but it seems light
shone on Zinder only with the successful proselytizing of the sixteenth sultan, who reigned starting in 1736.

The heat started getting to me, making me somewhat queasy
and disoriented. As sweat beaded and trickled into my eyes, I
found myself almost delirious and fixating on my guide, who
worked his tongue around gobs of red nut pulp as he delivered his
history lesson. Saliva welled up behind his gums. Turning his
head aside, he paused and spat out red flux; his scraggly beard, I
noticed, was speckled with red dribble, and his teeth were red.
Flies buzzed around us but seemed to be bothering only me, and
I stomped my feet as they bit my ankles.

'We had many punishments in the old days,' he said. 'Come.
Over here is the room of the ants.' He opened a low metal door
that gave onto what looked like a mud closet. 'After we'd filled
the room with red ants, we'd throw in the prisoners who'd committed lesser offenses. The ants would cover their bodies, biting
and stinging.' He sucked his nut. 'The screaming would never
stop.' He spat.

Isa fidgeted and glanced gleefully to see my reaction – was I
getting the blood and guts I paid for? I felt a wave of nausea and
put my hand against the wall to steady myself, but then yanked it
away because of the heat.

'And that's the scorpion room,' Tanimoune said. 'We would
put buttered meat in the room and leave the door open all night.
In the morning the room would be filled with scorpions, black
and red and as big as your hand, feeding on the meat. Then we'd
throw in the prisoner. The first scream would come, the second,

the third. The scorpions would jump all over him; you see, they don't fear people, our African scorpions. After the fourth sting he'd die.'

The ghastly description enlivened Isa. 'It's terrible, being bitten by a scorpion, terrible! I've been bitten on the finger. My hand burned like it was on fire, I gushed sweat, my head spun, and I started gasping and vomiting, my whole arm swelled up. The agony lasted three days.'

Flies covered me, and I swatted and stomped. The air was stifling and I felt an urge to flee. I needed oxygen and cool; I felt dizzy.

Tanimoune walked us farther into the palace, deep through chambers and tunnels and into another hall to an area of raised earth at the end of a sun-drenched walkway leading to a cemetery. He halted and extended his arm to stop me. 'Holy ground, forbidden!' he said, explaining why he could not take us to the tombs. 'And here, on this raised earth, we would tie the hands of the prisoner behind his back and force him to his knees' – he made a tying motion and shoved an invisible captive to the ground. 'The executioner would come in carrying a huge knife. He'd grab the prisoner's head by the hair' – here Tanimoune reached down and seized his imaginary victim by the forelocks – 'and take his knife and slit his throat, sawing back and forth, until he'd cut off his head.' He released his victim's corpse and stepped back, as if avoiding the blood spewing out of a severed jugular.

The barbaric act seemed all at once sickeningly real. I took a step back myself and leaned on the wall, here at least cool in the shade, and, steadying myself, looked at this 'royal,' a barefoot man with juice in his beard, calmly relating horrors that made up the history of his family!

'That is truly horrible,' I said, finding no profound words to express my disgust. I felt as if the heat and his gruesome tales were defeating me, and I was ashamed of my weakness.

'But that was all before we had Islam. Islam forbids us to kill.'

I straightened up. 'What? What about all the stoning and caning for adultery?'

'We wouldn't adopt shari'a here. The Qur'an forbids killing.'

It does not forbid killing as lawful punishment, of course. But the killing and misery didn't stop with the entrenchment of Islam: that much I knew. I had read European travelers' accounts of sultans in Zinder hacking open the chests of their live victims and ripping out their hearts, of flocks of vultures flapping down out of the neems to tear shreds of flesh from the dying. And the slave trade, conducted under 'enlightened' Islamic rule, cast uncounted multitudes of Nigériens into the hands of my own ancestors, my own God-fearing Christian countrymen. In my own land they succumbed to tortures and humiliations and deprivations they never knew on their own continent. No matter how one looked at it, those born in Zinder and around it had suffered fates almost too gruesome and grievous to be imagined, and my country had benefited by it.

Finished with the palace and Tanimoune, Isa and I toured the town. The sun was now lethal. Nomads drove bellowing, mangy camels and flocks of scrawny goats, kicking up clouds of acrid-tasting dust; lean oxen with three-foot racks mooed and dragged carts manned by starving drivers in rags; babies lashed to their laboring mothers' backs cried and slobbered; butchers hacked at bloody hunks of meat, stirring up clouds of carapaced black flies; merchants squatted in the dirt, picking their noses and shouting to passersby to come sample their wares – balls of stinking bark that looked like feces. Isa said they made great soup.

But then on our walk around town I spotted Tuareg – the blue-robed desert nomads of Berber blood who throughout the 1990s had fought a war with the government (both here and in Mali) in an attempt to carve their own state out of the Sahel. Scattered across the Sahel and the Sahara, the Tuareg number about a million in all – of whom a half-million inhabit Niger, three hundred thousand Mali, and two hundred thousand Algeria. They speak a Berber dialect known as Tamashek. Though many are dark-skinned, even black, the Tuareg consider themselves white and hold themselves racially superior to black Africans; in fact, historically the Tuareg have enslaved Africans, a practice rumored to continue in remote parts of Niger.

I stared, transfixed, at the Tuareg in the market and thought of the months I had spent wandering in the Moroccan Sahara two years earlier with Arab nomads. Memories of desert purity and familiar faces overcame me, and I was seized by a desire to see how Tuareg life differed from Arab life. Just before we returned to my hotel for lunch, I asked Isa if he knew any Tuareg.

'I know a prince who is related to the chief of the Tuareg in our region. I'll introduce you.'

At three that afternoon Isa and the 'prince' arrived at my hotel. The prince appeared to have been boozing: a reddish film covered his yellowed eyes and his speech was slurred; his beard was speckled with remnants of his lunch, and he smelled of sweat. Tuareg usually wore gallant and flowing desert attire; the prince was in a Rastafari hat and a T-shirt. His jeans were soiled.

'Wanna see the chief?' he asked me in French.

'You're the prince?'

'Certainly am.'

'Well, yes. If it's possible.'

Isa whispered to me, 'Don't give the prince *anything*, okay? No matter what he says.'

We walked down into Zengo district – the oldest part of town, or so Isa said. (In a town where every house is made of mud, one may be sure little is much older than the renovations of the last rainy season.) We passed a house marked number 188, with a sign in French over the door saying: HAVE CONFIDENCE IN THIS HOUSE: IT IS THE FIRST BUILDING IN ZENGO.

'Oh, by the way,' said Isa, stopping, 'this house is a historical monument.' The prince concurred.

'It looks the same as the other mud houses,' I said.

'No, it's old, really old. Come see!'

He shouted through the open door, and a young woman all in veils and wraps came out. She smiled bashfully when she saw me and retreated a step or two. Isa said something to her and she tensed up and appeared to refuse, but he pleaded and she waved us inside. We walked through the doorway into a courtyard, all sand like every other one in town, in fact like every other one in the Sahel.

There we found children covered with flies and a couple of women kneeling over a cooking fire. A tiny ancient woman sitting in the sand in a smock began smiling and waving and shouting at me in Hausa, and Isa translated: she was ninety years old and the daughter of a local marabout (Muslim saint). She was honored, *so* honored, to have me as a guest in her home.

Why? I thought. All she knew about me was what she saw: that I was a white man and therefore probably a son of one of the nations that once enslaved her people.

Her reception suddenly seemed astonishing. Whence all this goodwill toward strangers, and white strangers at that? Again I wondered why I had been so well received in the Sahel, even though my country was calling for war on Muslim countries and had enslaved millions of black people for centuries. Still, I felt good that my presence gladdened someone, especially since I was in such a foul mood myself.

She pulled an ID card out of a pile of oddments and paper scraps and showed it to me. It read, in French, DATE OF BIRTH: APPROXIMATELY 1930. PROFESSION: HOUSEWIFE.

'See!' Isa said, pointing to the birthdate. I saw no reason to point out their shared miscalculation of her age.

'I have no teeth!' she said, waving her arms and baring her gums and laughing. 'I have many children! I'm a great-great-grandma!'

The babies began crying. They were covered in flies and mucus and dirt, and so had reason enough for distress, but perhaps my strange, pale presence made them nervous. I felt I didn't want to stay longer. Isa whispered to me, 'Please leave her a gift.'

I did this, and after thanking her copiously for her hospitality, we left with a bow.

Parked in front of a mud house with a concrete floor, the Land Cruiser was marked CHIEF OF THE TUAREG. The prince knocked on the house's door and we walked inside, making half bows of courtesy and then taking off our shoes. We stayed squatting and stooping until a man in the shadows waved us all the way in, to plastic chairs lined up in front of him.

'Sit in that chair, nearest the chief,' said the prince. 'You're honored here.'

I sat down and my eyes adjusted. In front of me on a goatskin floor cover sat a fleshy man of pasty complexion, bald and unshaved, in light blue robes and white sirwal trousers. His feet were dirty, and he picked at his incurved toenails. With despondent eyes, he asked, in Tamashek, what he could do for me.

The prince explained to him that I had spent a long time with Arab nomads in North Africa, and that, if possible, I wanted to see how Tuareg lived here.

He wiggled his nose. He opened his lips to reveal infected gums and made a series of pained grimaces.

'You know Jim?' he asked me through the prince.

'Jim?'

'Jim. The American. He was in Peace Corps. A long time ago.'

He pulled aside the goatskin mat and coughed up phlegm and hawked it onto the floor. He replaced the mat over the gob.

'No, actually, I don't.'

He grimaced and again showed his infected gums.

He and the prince exchanged a few words. The prince began thanking him, and I did the same, though I had no idea why. The chief turned lugubriously away, and the prince pointed toward the door.

We were to come back tomorrow and the chief would take us out to his Tuareg camp in his Land Cruiser.

Isa showed up at the hotel the next afternoon. So did the prince, whom at first glance I took to be as stoned or drunk as the day before. But I reconsidered: his breath smelled of nothing alcoholic and he expressed himself clearly. It appeared that some people in Niger had accents that made their French sound intoxicated, and many for some reason had bloodshot eyes with yellowed whites all the time.

They took me back down into Zengo district to see the chief, who looked as infirm and sad as he had the previous day.

Now, I assumed, would come the tough part – the bargaining – for the chief was sure to charge me for any favors. I was ready to pay a decent fee to cover his time and expenses (gas for his Land Cruiser, for example). He and the prince began bantering, but soon I saw the chief looking grave and shaking his head. The prince began pleading. The chief raised his forefinger and spoke in agitated tones, saying, 'Mirriah, Mirriah' and something about the prefect.

This didn't sound like bargaining. 'What's going on?' I asked.

The prince slurred his words. 'He says he's the authority, the chief of the Tuareg, and he can't allow you, a white, to visit his camp without letting the local authorities know you're here. It would raise suspicions and he'd have problems.'

Since I last saw him, he must have reflected on the visit I wanted to make and decided there was something fishy about it.

'Fine. We can do that.'

'Explain your mission to him,' the prince said.

I turned to the chief. 'I'd like to see how the Tuareg live, Chief, since I've spent so much time with Arab nomads in Morocco. I'd like to see the differences between the lifestyles of Tuareg and Arab nomads.'

'But why see the Tuareg?' he asked.

I repeated what I had just said, with an elaboration here and there.

My answer only seemed to evoke more and graver suspicions. He shook his head and blurted out, 'Prefect! Prefect!'

The prince clarified. 'You must have official permission from the prefect to see the chief. Who authorized you to come here?'

'I'm not sure I know what you mean' – though I had a sinking feeling I knew just what he meant. 'You brought me here. You're the prince, right?'

All at once I sensed a bureaucratic tangle, and I felt a pang of hopeless déjà vu: Was this going to be Maiduguri and the shehu's palace all over again?

'I have a visa for Niger. It's all I need.'

It wasn't enough for the chief, though, who got more and more upset, pausing now and then in his head-shaking address to peel back the goatskin rug at his side and empty the contents of his sinuses onto the floor. He pointed at me and accused me of

coming to him without authorization. I would need to be authorized by the prefect before he would take me anywhere.

I tired of this. 'Please tell the chief that I meant no harm, that
I had no idea I needed a permit to visit him.' I thanked the chief,
apologized again, and we took our leave. I abandoned the idea of
visiting the camp.

The next day, Isa called in sick. The prince came to the hotel,
though, wearing a knit skullcap, a new Hawaiian shirt, a freshly
laundered sirwal, and sunglasses. I took him aside. 'Look, I've
been thinking. You're a Tuareg prince, right? Can't you take me
out of town to see Tuareg who aren't so bureaucratic? After all,
weren't you all desert warriors? What happened to your independent spirit?'

He positioned his sunglasses atop his head. 'Why, sure I can. I
thought you only wanted to go with the chief. Why don't we go to
Mirriah, that village the chief was talking about? It's just north of
here. You can meet all the Tuareg you like there.'

An hourlong ride in a *taxi brousse* ('bush taxi') minibus landed
us in Mirriah, standing amid blocky pink clay houses on powdery
pink, utterly flat clay earth. In the shade of nearby neems, boys
sitting cross-legged swayed back and forth, chanting verses from
the Qur'an engraved on palm-wood slabs; girls led little flocks of
goats out to pasture. Beyond the houses loomed the great baobabs
of the wild Sahel.

'The Tuareg are in the market, selling milk,' Isa said.

'In the market? But what about their camels?'

'Oh, these aren't desert Tuareg here. Some of us have settled
to raise animals and sell milk. We even speak Hausa.'

We walked through the market – straw-roofed stalls and piles
of groundnuts and millet and sorghum, overseen by Hausa peddlers. It was not market day, and little was for sale. But even on
market days little might be for sale if there was a drought, as
there frequently was.

'There they are!' the prince said, pointing to several unveiled
women in royal blue robes and blue and yellow scarves, squatting
over calabashes of milk and pots of butter. Behind them stood a

couple of old men in the sky blue robes, their heads wrapped in indigo-stained tougoulmousts (turbans, in Tamashek). One of the young women was gorgeous, with chocolate skin and delicate doll features, silky black hair flowing out of her white scarf, and a baby nursing at a bulbous, uncovered breast.

We approached, and I greeted them with '*As-salam 'alaykum*.' They responded halfheartedly and looked to the prince, as if for an explanation. He began pointing to me, and saying 'Nasrani' and something about Arabs and Morocco and the Sahara, and the United States.

The nursing woman covered her breast. Her girlfriend put her hand over her butter pot; the third woman hid her calabash under a cloth. I thought I heard them say, 'CIA!'

The men came over and asked what was going on. The women replied, and the men assumed grave, even alarmed, expressions, and pulled their tougoulmousts up over their mouths, leaving only their eyes exposed. They began pointing far away, toward huts at the edge of town. There was more talk of the CIA, and no one would look at me.

Soon the prince was wishing them farewell and walking away. I followed him.

Out of earshot, I asked what had happened.

'They were suspicious and didn't want to talk to you. They thought you came from the CIA to spy on them.'

'*Why?*'

'Their way of life is different from others' here. You might learn about it and report to the CIA.'

'What would I report? They're milk sellers, for God's sake. Why would their life interest the CIA?'

'Their life's different, as I said. They're afraid you'd report on them and tell their secrets. So they told us to go find some Tuareg on the edge of town. That was their way of getting rid of us.'

At first, their fears seemed absurd and baseless. Perhaps they had heard of the CIA and decided a white man in Niger would probably work there, for who else would visit their miserable country but a well-paid spy? But I thought again. With the United States about to attack Iraq and hunting Muslim terrorists all over the world, my white skin, nationality, and presumed Christian faith put me squarely in the enemy camp, and any association with me might be fraught with danger, especially to a people as recently embattled as the Tuareg. If I could have spoken to them without a translator, I might have managed to win their trust, but I couldn't, and so I had to accept their erroneous verdict.

Dispirited, the prince and I caught a *taxi brousse* back to Zinder.

# 13

# FETTERS OF BRONZE
# IN AYOROU

The rising sun inflamed the glassy expanses of the Niger River, setting aglow phantoms of mist wandering along the grassy banks, warming doves to coo and kingfishers to caw. Herons, silhouetted against the gilt waters, stood poised in the shallows, waiting for a perch or crawfish, their heads cocked, their pincerlike bills aimed to strike. Afar, by islands reedy and low, pairs of bulbous eyes and twitching, oblong ears popped above the currents, and with a gurgle sank away; hippos were feeding. Above all, against a vault of lambent turquoise, eagles and ospreys soared and dipped on the new day's updrafts.

I stood marveling at the sight. At last I had reached the river primeval of West Africa, the waterway connecting the jungle highlands of Guinea with the Sahara of Mali and the Sahel of Niger and, finally, the oil-rich delta of mangrove swamps on Nigeria's Atlantic coast. Twenty-six hundred miles in length, the Niger is the third-longest river in Africa (after the Nile and the Congo), though it becomes navigable only some four hundred miles from its source, near Bamako. The Niger was for centuries the lifeline of the Malian and Songhai empires, linking the great cities of Gao and Timbuktu with the forest people to the south, but much about it remained mysterious to Europeans until the Scottish explorer Mungo Park determined that it flowed east in

1796, and some forty years later a pair of Englishmen, the brothers Richard and John Lander, ascertained that it debouched into the Gulf of Guinea. For me, now, the waterway marked progress: it was the halfway point in my trip across the Sahel.

I had just arrived in the fishing village of Ayorou, on the Niger's banks, to attend the weekly market, a celebrated event in West Africa that draws traders from as far away as Nigeria and the Ivory Coast. Accordingly, the *taxi brousse* I had ridden from Niamey was packed with Tuareg from the desert, Hausa and Zarma from Sahelian Niger, and an assortment of boisterous Nigerians who gave themselves away by addressing me as '*Masta!*' while I was taking my seat. Also aboard were Songhai in loose white turbans; they were smaller in stature than the giants with whom I had mingled since Chad. Ayorou was in fact a Songhai village; that is, it belonged to members of the ethnic group that in the fifteenth century founded an eponymous empire that stretched over what today is Mali and Niger.

Now, sleek, motorized wooden canoes known as pinasses chugged toward the shore where I stood, coming from both up- and downriver. I had expected pinasses to resemble the rough-hewn gum-tree pirogues of the Congo, but I was wrong: fifty feet long and black-hulled, their bows and sterns decorated with intricate geometric designs of blue and white, yellow and red, pinasses are floating embodiments of the long history, multi-ethnic civilization, and polychromatic artistic panache of West Africa. Piloted by lanky boys in floppy hats and baggy trousers, the pinasses were loaded low to the water with sacks and crates, the wares of traders arriving early for the market (which would be held the next day) from Mali, just to the north, and Burkina Faso, just to the west. The news that a pinasse had hit a rock and capsized the previous night had been bruited about Ayorou all morning – a reminder for me that if I chose to take a boat to traverse the two hundred miles northwest to Gao, in Mali (as was my plan), there would be risks. The rains were long gone, the river now low.

To escape the crowds arriving on pinasses and see something of the river, I hired a wiry local fisherman named Mazou to paddle me in his canoe around the nearby villages. We set out, keeping a wary eye on the feeding hippos.

'If we got close they would attack us,' Mazou said, in French, leaning into his oar stroke. 'Those ones there, they're mother and child, so they're dangerous. To kill them, we have to throw harpoons from far away.' At the moment the hippos looked anything but dangerous, lolling about in the slow-moving water, eyeing us languidly before submerging their heads to forage on bottom grasses. 'Often they smash canoes and smash the people in them,' Mazou added. 'How many villagers have died!'

Harpoons on the sandy village beaches attested to the danger; frequently, he said, men had to do their duty and battle hippos that had killed their loved ones.

About half a mile upriver we pulled into Goungou, Mazou's home and the settlement from which Ayorou had developed. Stepping carefully around harpoons and then traipsing over a crunchy carpet of goat pellets, we entered the gray-orbed village. With their smooth lines and rounded edges, Goungou's cupola-style houses looked to be built of glossy cement but in fact were made from a sturdy mix of mud, manure, and millet chaff called banco that, not surprisingly, stinks until it dries in the sun. Everywhere women were pounding millet with pestles, lugging bundles of branches for firewood, carting sacks of grain, or stirring pots bubbling with fish stew. Men lounged in the shade of neems, chatting and sucking cola nuts and gazing at the water.

Within Mazou's walled home complex stood a banco house and a beehivelike granary where millet was stored; fishing nets covered the ground in messy coils; goats and chickens sniffed and pecked at the rubbish scattered almost everywhere. All this livestock, gear, and grain attested to Mazou's relative wealth. In villages away from the Niger's banks (and out of range of markets like Ayorou's), people ate leaves and bark, at least during the lean months before the harvest, when food supplies had been exhausted. But even these meager meals came only once every other day after villagers had already stripped their trees bare.

It didn't have to be this way. Though the land could be cultivated if irrigated with river water, no one farmed. To farm would violate labor-averse male traditions, and women had enough work to do already gathering leaves, bark, and firewood and raising the ever-numerous children. Yet it was the women and children who went hungry: according to these same traditions, men ate first and women second, and children got the leftovers. In fact, often the only 'food' children got was a drink made from millet husks and untreated river water. The effects of this diet and pecking order showed in the builds of people I had seen on the way to Ayorou: men were healthy-looking (or almost), women thin and haggard, and children emaciated, with balloon bellies and match-stick legs.

The wind picked up, which would make paddling difficult, so Mazou and I returned to Ayorou.

I had put up in Ayorou's sole hotel, the riverside Amenokal. One of my guidebooks described it as '4-star . . . quite incongruous to the town.' The guidebook was sadly out of date, for the Amenokal was now quite congruous: dilapidated, with running water and electricity the memories of earlier generations, the Amenokal was now inhabited by more mice and lizards than humans. The man-ager, a soulful youth who appeared ashamed to take the eight dollars a night that the sign in the lobby announced as the room rate, explained to me that the local electric company had gone bankrupt and the hotel's owners had quarreled and split up; hence the disrepair. The only water the Amenokal had for drinking, cook-ing, and bathing came from the Niger, and he offered to supply me with buckets of the brown soupy flux for my bath and meals.

At dawn the next day, a high-voiced clamor of fierce haggling arose outside and was punctuated now and then with ululations and festive shouts and screams and donkey braying. Spirals of dust poured over the wall around the Amenokal and seeped under the door to my room. The market was beginning, and I awoke eager to go out and see it.

There was a rapping on my door. I climbed out of my mosquito net and answered it.

'Your water, *monsieur*!'

A young man spiffily dressed in loafers, pressed trousers, and a white shirt wrestled a sloshing bucket past me and into my bathroom, leaving a smelly brown trail. I had not seen this fellow before, and that plus his alacrity aroused my suspicion. With the exception of the manager, employees at the Amenokal (and elsewhere in Nigérien hotels) budged from their usually supine positions only after much pestering and monetary inducement.

He handed me a folded piece of paper. As he did so he assumed an aggrieved expression and lowered his head.

'I'll pay the bill when I leave,' I said.

'Oh, *monsieur*! But this is not the bill!'

I opened the note. It was in French. 'Dear Esteemed *Monsieur*! It is with the greatest regret and utmost shame that I approach you in my hour of need to effect this highly embarrassing démarche . . . a medical emergency has arisen . . . dearest mother in direst peril . . . in urgent need of medicine which we cannot afford . . . financial constraints compel me to . . . I request the most insignificant sum of . . . will accept said sum in cash dollars U.S. or Euros or hard-currency equivalent . . . thanking you in advance . . . expressing my most distinguished sentiments of gratitude . . .'

I looked up and noticed he was ogling my open travel bag. He quickly lowered his eyes and put on his frowny face again.

Almost all foreigners in parts of Africa where aid workers or tourists abound (Niger belonged to the former) find themselves confronted by such transparent ruses – which is what I took his 'démarche' to be, especially given his upscale dress and vaudevillian grief. It is easiest on the conscience just to give in – I always feel guilty refusing – but doing so encourages tricksters and rogues and devalues the work of honest people.

'I'm sorry, I can't help you.' I handed him back the note.

He took it. 'Oh, of course. I see. But . . .'

'I'm sorry.'

'I understand. *Monsieur*.'

He massaged his eyes and slowly walked out, sidestepping the fecal splotches of water, and slammed the door.

I got dressed and left the room. A little while later, I saw him laughing and joking with friends by the hotel gate.

He got the last laugh, or I assume he did: later that day, with twelve hours of desert travel behind me, I discovered someone had stolen the clothes I had left in an unlockable segment of my bag.

Mazou had arranged a guide to the market for me, a Songhai in his twenties named Hassane. I met him by the hotel gate. He was illiterate, but he spoke French well enough to explain himself. He had a broad smile and earnest eyes, and took the business of guiding seriously, which made sense: besides fishing and goat herding, there was little else in Ayorou to do.

The sun was intense, the wind brisk. We walked onto the sandy barrens in the village center and straight into a dust-cloud melee of carts and merchants and hooting Land Cruisers. First I noticed a procession that was oddly cheerless on this uniquely happy day: arriving on donkeys loaded with firewood were barefoot women in blue robes with slit sides that let their droopy breasts show; they wore their hair in dirt-encrusted cornrows and chattered to one another in Tamashek. Around their dusty ankles hung half-pound rings of engraved bronze.

'The Bella,' said Hassane. 'They're the slaves of the Tuareg.'

'Slaves?'

'Officially they're free, but really they're not. They have nowhere to go. The Tuareg captured them in raids hundreds of years ago and took them into the desert. Now they do the cooking, cleaning, and animal herding for the Tuareg, and give their masters massages. The Tuareg do no work, you see, by tradition. Those ankle bracelets are engraved with the family's insignia. The Bella can only marry one another.'

I wanted to talk to one of the women, but when we approached they skittered away. Socializing with outsiders was either forbidden or not customary.

'They look miserable,' I said.

'Yes, they have many diseases. They gather that firewood and sell it for their masters.'

'And the government does nothing to help them?'

'The government doesn't care. After all, the Bella don't vote and have no money. They live way out in the desert where no one but the Arabs and the Tuareg can go.'

Toward us down the pistes were ambling herds of goats and sheep and cattle, kicking up clouds of dust that were borne away by a hot and now rising wind. Walking out to the animal market, Hassane and I passed Bella men in white turbans, each carrying a blanket folded on his left shoulder; this was their bedding, and they never parted with it. They herded goats and were going to sell them for their Tuareg masters.

We reached the animal market – a series of fenced-off lots just behind the stores around the central lot. There, turbaned customs officials with badges on their robes chased goats and goat owners, shouting and gesticulating and waving papers. The state taxes livestock, but in Niger, where no one has a sense of civic duty – that is, reason to trust the succession of thieves and generals who have ruled them – taxes have to be collected in raids, and revenuers use the market to catch people and assess who owns what. Nearby, trucks were hissing and roaring, latches were being thrown open, and cattle were being marched up gangplanks for the two-day drive to the Ivory Coast or Benin, Hassane said, where tsetse flies hindered raising hoofed animals.

Back in Ayorou's center, merchants had set up rows of Pastis 51 bottles filled with peanut oil; boisterously sensuous Christian women from Togo, unveiled, their bountiful hips and bosoms stuffed into colorful African wraps, laughed and stirred pots bubbling with aromatic spaghetti and rice, fish and meat; they were the market's restaurateurs and served merchants for the most part. Around the market's edges, grim Tuareg stood over disks of salt brought from mines in Taoudenni, deep in the Sahara north of Timbuktu; Songhai women hawked disks of red clay that Songhai use to decorate houses for weddings and Bella use to tint skin red for feasts.

We walked on to the riverside, where pointy-bowed pinasses bounced off one another in a terrific jam of nautical traffic. 'The Nigérien Port,' Hassane said. There wasn't much for sale: just piles of green gumbo and orange pumpkins, olive and crimson straw mats for dowries. From there we doubled back into a warren

of huts and stalls and arrived at the 'Yoruba Market,' – an empo-
rium of manufactured junk and ancient, dusty, no doubt
long-expired medicines, all from Nigeria. We threaded its stands
until we came to the Malian Port, where the grandest pinasses of
all were chugging in to slide their hulls ashore, loaded with bales
of grass and sacks of animal feed. The elaborate designs on the
hulls filled me with enthusiasm for Mali, where I was headed
after the market, and made me eager to get on with my trip.

Back in the center, trucks had pulled up and men were unloading sacks of millet, rice, and sorghum. Many wore the flowing
darra'a robes of the 'Arib nomads with whom I had traveled for
months in the Moroccan Sahara.

'Arabs,' said Hassane. 'They control the economy here; they
have the money and the transport. They take food out to remote
villages. They don't like us Africans and won't marry their daughters to us.'

'Where are they from?'

'From here.'

'They don't have Land Rovers going to Gao, do they?'

Soon after arriving I had started thinking about how I would
arrange my onward travel two hundred miles northwest to Gao, in
Mali – no easy matter. Throughout the nineties the Tuareg rebellion had raged in the region, and bandits were still said to prowl
the desert. Hence, there was little public transport aside from
the pinasses, which could take days and were now hindered by
low water. But there were also, rumor had it, trucks that made the
run, and four-wheel-drive vehicles.

'The Arabs are the *only* ones with Land Rovers going to Gao.
Trucks break down and take days to get there. But these Arabs
are too greedy to take that long. They take good care of their
vehicles and they *fly* once they hit the desert! Why, with a four-
wheel drive like that one' – he pointed to a nearby Toyota Land
Cruiser – 'you can be in Ansongo [in Mali] in three hours and in
Gao in five. Say, that Arab over there is from Mali. I know him.
He'll be going back today. You should talk to him. But be careful:
they're deceitful and racist.'

In a storefront next to the Toyota sat a man in a darra'a robe, with eyes adamantine and coal black glinting above the abundant folds of an 'imama (a turban similar to the Chadian kadmul in length and voluminousness, but dyed indigo). Rather illogically, his darra'a encouraged me to think I was about to meet a friend, some genial if distant relative of my 'Arib guides.

I went over and greeted him enthusiastically, speaking Arabic. '*As-salam 'alaykum!* I'm wondering if you're going to Gao this afternoon.'

He pulled his 'imama down to reveal spiky teeth and a goatee. His name was Abdullah. His Arabic sounded Moroccan. '*Wa 'alaykum as-salam*. I'm going near there. In an hour.' He squinted at me. 'Why?'

I told him I needed to go to Gao. He said he would take me as far as Ansongo, his home, and I would have to pay a lot for a seat in the cabin, or else I could sit with the Africans in the back. He wanted no less than twenty thousand francs (about thirty-five dollars) for a space in the cabin – far too much, from what I had heard, but since the only alternatives were trucks or pinasses, I wasn't inclined to argue. He added with a snicker that I found puzzling, 'I hope all your papers are in order, because I don't want any trouble at the border.'

We shook on it. His hand was all gold rings and bone. As I was about to run back to the hotel for my things, he yanked my elbow.

'I give you my *kalam inglizi* [English word] that we will leave at twelve-thirty,' said Abdullah. 'Don't be late.'

His words sounded threatening, but I was happy to hear them. Who ever thought of aggressive punctuality in Africa?

# 14

# GAO

Taking abdullah at his 'English word,' but suffering some misgivings about his attitude, at twelve-thirty I showed up at the storefront ready to board his pickup. A hot wind whipped the turbans and caftans of the crowd of some fifteen men (mostly Malians, but there were Arabs among them) as they grunted and jostled with one another to climb atop the sacks and crates loaded in the truck's rear. Abdullah's assistant, a lanky Songhai whose turban covered all but the slits of his mean, dust-reddened eyes, collected fares, snatching francs and shouting at the men as they boarded, now and then yanking them off this or that crate, ordering them away from the cab, and striking them if they failed to heed him.

Hassane shook his head. 'That Arab doesn't respect human life. He will fly and he won't care how many people fall off the back!'

I could hardly doubt him, and I now accepted that every departure in Africa would set my stomach churning. Again I was about to put myself at the mercy of a person I hardly knew and head to an unfamiliar country, but I, for sure, was the lucky one this time: I would sit in the cabin while the others suffered sun and grit and the disdain of this martinet fare collector.

I handed the Songhai my fare and gave him my bag. He slapped at a pair of passengers, who strained to make space for the bag without tumbling from their perches. Hassane dutifully secured it. I then went around and swung open the cabin door and climbed onto the passenger seat. The Songhai came over and stabbed with his bony forefinger at the middle seat, keeping his eyes on me until I moved, and then he returned to fare collecting.

Hassane leaned in the window. 'You could take me with you, you know. I once traveled to Bamako, so I know the way.'

'I wish I could, but I'll have to manage on my own.'

'Well, may God keep you safe from bandits!'

There was no point in my offering to exchange addresses, for he was illiterate. Since I had already paid him, a handshake was all I could give him now.

Shoving Hassane aside, a gray-bearded Arab flung open the door and climbed in next to me, wheezing. His sky blue darra'a robe seemed to fill half the cabin, and as he slammed the door his elbow struck me in the solar plexus. Saying nothing, he adjusted his turban so that only his eyes showed, and stared ahead. The wind was now driving walls of dust down the lane and through our open windows; I coughed and covered my mouth.

A passenger leaned on the cab roof above my head, and it buckled loudly.

'Get off my roof!' Abdullah shouted, his eyes fixed on the culprit, as he walked around the front of the truck clutching the wad of francs his assistant had just handed him. He shoved the money into an interior pocket of his darra'a, yanked open the driver's side door, and jumped aboard. He threw the truck into first, and his fist, clenched around the gearshift, struck my leg.

Hassane turned away, shielding his eyes from the blowing dust, and we pulled out slowly, honking to scatter the Bella and goats ahead of us, inching over the bumpy sand, honking some more and edging alongside herds of oxen driven by more Bella in filthy robes. Soon we passed the last straw huts of Ayorou and picked up the piste heading north to the border. The Sahel now presented a blazing tableau of sand flats and thorn trees more barren than anything I had seen since Erg du Djourab; the already stunted acacias shriveled into bushes, spiking with brown a landscape and sky glowing equally like molten zinc, thanks to the incandescent clouds of dust. I kept expecting Abdullah to hit the gas and 'fly' as Hassane had predicted, but he was more reasonable than that. Our load meant that not only would we not fly, but we would hardly exceed twenty miles an hour.

'Jelal,' Abdullah said, his words muffled by his turban. 'Je-*lal*.'He smirked. 'What are you, Lebanese or something?'

'No, American.' He said nothing. 'I spent a couple of years in Marrakesh. I was wondering, are your ancestors from Morocco? I've heard that —'

'How should I know? We're Arabs from Mali and that's all we know.'

A few minutes later he glanced over at me. He asked me again what nationality I was, and again I told him I was American.

'Well,' he said, 'Bush is sowing hatred for America all across the world. He doesn't care about future generations of Americans. They'll have no peace. A powerful country should be generous and big-hearted, but Bush isn't like that . . . America should think about preserving peace in the world, not just about attacking Muslims.' He paused. 'If you're American, *really* American, then you must be rich.'

'I'd drive my own Land Rover to Gao if I were.'

'You'll never find a car for Gao in Ansongo. Let me drive you there. My price is a hundred and fifty thousand francs.'

'That's two hundred and fifty dollars for a sixty-mile trip. It's too much.'

'"Too much!"' he said, repeating my words as if mocking me. He snickered. 'American, I'll have you know that the piste is all beat up, and rough on my truck. You're wealthy, so you'll come around to my price. Especially when you see Ansongo.' He smirked again. 'Or maybe you're not a *real* American?'

The other Arab looked over at me: I was the nervous cynosure of two pairs of suspicious eyes.

In sixteen years of traveling in Arab countries, I had never encountered such contempt, and I was as puzzled by it as I was unnerved. I have often thought that if I were to land penniless in Tunis or Tripoli, traditions of Arab hospitality would ensure that not only would I not suffer, but I would probably grow fat on proffered food and sleep soundly as a guest in people's homes.

We passed the next two hours in uneasy silence, and then arrived at the frontier. After brief formalities at a border shack, we said goodbye to Niger and bounced down the piste into a ravine and began climbing a bleak hillside of reddening dust and rock, its sun-gilt salients slanting over the river just to the west. A half-hour later we spotted a tank positioned atop the ravine's northern bank, its gun pointing down at us – the Malian border, and a lethal reminder of the Tuareg rebellion that had devastated an already destitute land.

'We couldn't have driven this piste alone a couple of years ago,' said Abdullah. 'The Tuareg would have killed us and taken my truck. Back then if you wanted to go to Mali you could go only once a week, in a military convoy. Say, you're not going to cause me problems at the border, are you?'

'I told you, I have a Malian visa and a passport.'

'I don't want any trouble. I don't need any delays.'

We pulled over the rise, bumped past the tank, and drove toward a couple of straw and mud huts. Beyond them stood a scattering of ramshackle restaurants and shops – the border village of Labezanga.

We stopped by one of the huts.

'Well, get out,' said Abdullah.

The old guy next to me climbed down and so did I. The Arabs piled in the back regarded me with eager eyes and greeted me with 'As-salam 'alaykum,' and I shook their hands, grateful for their kindness and suddenly feeling much less alone. Still smiling at me, they got down and walked, clutching their ID cards, with Abdullah toward one of the shacks. A round-headed bald man whose belly and fat biceps bulged in his navy blue uniform waved at me to come to the other hut.

'You have to see the chief!' he shouted. 'Venez!'

Inside the hut sat the chief immigration officer – another paunchy bald man with a round, oily face. Had we been in Chad, I would have taken him to be an overfed Christian from the south. Statistically Mali and Niger resemble each other in almost every miserable respect (with populations of about 11 million, per capita annual incomes of $210 and $170 respectively, and life expectancies of forty-something), and the two countries share a similar postcolonial history of military rule, coups, Tuareg rebellion, and recent 'transitions to democracy,' but Mali at least has fertile agricultural land in the southwest. Perhaps the officer hailed from there and had not suffered the malnutrition that wizens faces, stunts growth, and dulls minds across the Sahel.

He stuck out his hand and waved for my passport.

'Oh ho! An American!'

He flipped through the pages until he got to my Malian visa. He then reached for his stamp. I asked him to stamp a page that already had markings on it; I was running out of empty pages.

He froze, holding the stamp poised above the page. A twinkle enlivened his eyes. He cleared his throat.

'So you want a service? I'm *happy* to oblige. *Very* happy.' He plunked the stamp down on an already-marked free page and took the passport and examined the stamp at arm's length, as if marveling at his artistry. He looked up at me.

'Thank you,' I said.

He began flicking through the pages, all the while frowning and stealing glances at me from under his sweaty brow. Then he set the document aside and turned to other papers.

I reached for my passport.

'Oh, no! Not so fast,' he said, deftly pushing it just beyond my reach. 'You requested a service. You asked me not to stamp a blank page. *N'est-ce pas?*'

I straightened up.

'The charge is seven thousand francs' – about twelve dollars.

'What?'

'Seven thousand.'

I told him this was an outrage, which rankled him, and his voice hardened.

'Look, your president gives my president millions of dollars in aid every year. But where does it go? I don't see a single dollar of it. If I were doing this job in the States, wouldn't I be making a good salary? Would I be sitting in a straw hut with a sand floor? Look at the conditions I work in. You don't want to *know* how little I'm paid.'

Sand blew in the door and set flies on the walls buzzing. His stamping a marked page hardly qualified as a 'service,' and I was really not averse to helping him out with a reasonable donation. But he made a demand (and an excessive one), not a request, and this prompted me to hold my ground.

'Why don't you complain to your government? Ask for what you're owed.'

'Come on!' he replied. 'That kind of talk is for America. My government doesn't listen to anyone. Look, you're rich. You asked me for a service and I performed it. So I deserve payment. Seven thousand francs.'

The wind blew more sand through the straw walls. We winced and covered our eyes. His brazenness inclined me to refuse, but this man was my own age, and I felt sorry for him. He had glanced at my passport and seen stamps from countries all over the world, and what would he see before he died? Maybe the road from his village to the capital, and from the capital here. Moreover, where aid was concerned, he *did* have a point. Where have the billions of dollars given Africa since independence gone? By all indices most countries on the continent are poorer than ever, hungrier than ever, more war-ravaged than ever, and sicker than ever. To point out that the United States is proportionally the stingiest donor of foreign aid in the developed world (giving less than 1 percent of GDP, and half of that goes to Israel) seemed beside the point.

But in any case, aid has been drying up. After the cold war ended and Africa lost its strategic significance for the West, aid per capita dropped from thirty-two dollars in 1990 to nineteen dollars in 1998. Recent Western promises of debt relief go largely unfulfilled. 'Trade, not aid!' is now a popular slogan in the United States, but Africa attracts less than 3 percent of all foreign investment on earth, and subsidies paid by the U.S. and European governments to their farmers (which make African produce uncompetitive in Western markets) amount to more than the

GDP of all African countries combined. Some countries are enjoying modest economic and political progress (Senegal, Mozambique, and Uganda among them), but chances are that, elsewhere, for men like the customs officer sitting in front of me, or the common folk riding in the back of Abdullah's truck, things are getting worse.

I handed him three thousand francs. He slid my passport across his desk.

Sheltering from the wind, Abdullah's passengers were huddling on the truck's lee side, Africans in one group, Arabs in another. A few were having trouble getting through customs, Abdullah told me, so we would have to wait.

One Arab, a young man whose short stature and cheerful eyes set him apart from his tall, brooding fellows, introduced himself to me as Hamid.

'Since you're a rich American, you should give to the poor,' said Hamid. 'Start right now by giving each of us a thousand dollars!' Laughter from the others, but Abdullah didn't crack a smile. 'Give for the sake of the afterlife!' he said. 'Don't you worry about the Last Judgment?'

'He's a Christian,' snapped Abdullah. 'They have no afterlife.'

'What? Of course we do,' I said, reflexively assuming an identity I usually avoided.

'Oh, then give us a thousand dollars and save your soul!'

'Unfortunately in Christianity we don't have the zakat [the Islamic obligation to give a percentage of one's income to the poor]. My giving money to you won't get me into heaven.'

All the Arabs laughed, but the Africans, Abdullah's paying freight, sat in cheerless silence. Maybe they didn't understand Arabic, but their countenances told me there were other, deeper reasons for their grimness. The Arab-Islamic infiltration and conquest of the Sahel, late and incomplete though it had been, had left scars. Why *shouldn't* Africans regard the Arab presence here as just as 'imperialistic' as colonization by the West? Arabic in the Sahel was once just as foreign as French, as the borders and country names now in vogue. But I had already seen that calling the presence of Arabs here unjust amounted to attacking Islam and was impermissible; hence the Africans suffered their anti-Arab grievances with downcast eyes.

A half-hour later the men emerged from customs and were free to go.

As the day waned the Harmattan returned, and the sun hunkered low to the horizon in a red glowing sky. We creaked over the piste heading north into the desert, alone in the Sahara. The gritty gales and desolate land combined to suggest we had abandoned the habitable world and were cutting into wilds through which no human had ever passed. Abdullah's hard eyes reflected the truth: here death lurked, and only those with merciless acumen and much experience could be trusted to get us to safety. The piste faded in and out with the blowing sand; we bounced up one hill and down another, on and on, with each new vista vaster than the last, darker than before, more barren than ever.

'You'll find no car in Ansongo,' said Abdullah. 'Take my offer! A hundred and fifty thousand francs.'

'That's too much. I'd rather spend the night in Ansongo.'

'There's no hotel. Settle with me now or you'll be sorry.'

'Give me a reasonable price.'

He said nothing for a while. Then, 'Look around you!'

We were passing through Ouatagouna, a village well marked on my map but really nothing more than a few blocky clay hovels amid which lone Arabs walked hunched against the wind, their robes flailing, like shades in some sort of Arabian Hades.

As dusk came on we drew into Ansongo. Kerosene lanterns glowed in the Harmattan-hazed gloom; houses were dark masses of stone and mud; the few shrouded Arabs and Malians about didn't look hospitable. Maybe I would end up spending the night by the piste, wrapped in my blanket, waiting for a truck to pass.

We pulled up to a general store lit by a single lantern. The passengers climbed down from the back, shook off the dust, and dispersed into the gloom.

Abdullah cut the motor and jumped out. He unfurled his prayer rug on the sand.

'Where should I go to wait for a truck?' I asked him.

'God save you!' He turned away and positioned himself at the head of his rug, cupping his ears for prayer.

I decided I would walk out to the piste and wait for a ride there. But Hamid came up to me.

'There's an inn up at the square, and Land Cruisers going to Gao stop there to eat, so you might find a car out of here tonight.'

He was right. A few hours later two Tuareg pulled in and sold me a seat in their Land Rover. By midnight I was in Gao.

Obscured by the Harmattan, dawn in Gao the next day was barely perceptible, and noon, sunk in dust, the sun hanging dim but hot in the smoky sky. Walking out of my hotel, I took two breaths and coughed. Suddenly, I was fatigued with the trip and felt like crying out. How wretched the Sahel was, with this parching wind! Environment had to play a role in a people's culture. If the Mediterranean sun had fostered the agora gatherings and symposia of ancient Hellas by creating balmy environs in which philosophers and bards could mingle and create, what could this Harmattan do but drive Sahelians indoors and force them to fret over their belabored breath and itching eyes?

Convinced of this, early that afternoon I stood atop the tomb of the sixteenth-century Songhai king Askia Muhammad and surveyed Gao. It was hard to imagine that the place ever looked much better than it does today, though it used to be bigger; it has probably always been a spread of square mud houses under a browned-out sky. The landmark tomb of Askia Muhammad has always been a lump of clay reinforced with crooked, unfinished crossbeams; the royal graveyard next to the tomb, a vacant lot scattered with rocks for tombstones.

Yet Gao was supposed to be a city of legend, and may owe its decline to the Arabs. The capital of the Songhai kingdom in the seventh century, Islamic since the eleventh, seat of the Songhai Empire by the beginning of the sixteenth, Gao, sitting on the northern shore of the Niger, was in the Middle Ages, along with Timbuktu, reputedly one of the wealthiest cities of Muslim black Africa, where slaves, salt, and gold were sold and from where caravans departed for journeys across the Sahara. Askia Muhammad even adopted the title of caliph of the Sudan (*al-Sudan* being originally Arabic for '[Land of] the Blacks') after making the hajj to Mecca. Later he expanded Songhai dominions east to Niger, west to Senegal, and south to Hausaland. Gao once boasted seventy thousand inhabitants – more than three times its present population. But in 1591, Moroccans, eager to seize the Saharan trade for themselves, and equipped with firearms (unknown then in the region), crossed the desert and conquered Gao and Timbuktu, putting an end to Askia's empire, whatever it looked like, and poverty and misery were to follow.

Finished with my surveillance, I crept down the tomb's narrow crumbling steps, crawled through a mud passageway, and emerged on ground level. There I found Isa, the local youth who was my guide. By way of introduction, Isa had told me his name belonged to one of the greatest Muslims – Islam recognizes Jesus as one of the prophets who preceded Muhammad – but that this Jesus had anything to do with a faith called Christianity he had no idea, unlike my guide of the same name in Zinder.

We continued our tour. The caretaker youth had asked us to remove our shoes to walk around the grounds of the tomb. I obeyed but shook my head at this rule, which the Sahelians here and elsewhere had certainly imposed in imitation of the household practices of their former French masters – but the French would not have asked people to remove footwear to walk in socks on thorn-studded, pebbly earth.

Isa and I reached the gate and donned our shoes. The caretaker came up and asked me if I wanted to hire his pinasse and make a trip out to Askia Muhammad's village, a few miles up the Niger. I asked him what there was to see.

'The caliph was from there.'

'Right. But did he leave behind a palace? Or a house?'

He looked puzzled.

'I mean, did he build anything there or here, or anywhere else, that one should see?'

'You've seen the tomb.'

'He didn't build his own tomb, did he?'

'Askia was the caliph. Gao was the capital of his empire.'

'I know, but what is there to see in his village?'

'His descendants. Maybe. I'm not sure.'

'Thanks, but no thanks.'

I said goodbye to him, and Isa and I walked back out into the Harmattan dust devils twirling on the street. Like the caretaker, Isa could offer me no reason to visit Askia's village and didn't seem to know much about the caliph. One might turn to Gao's men of letters for more information, but I wanted to know to what extent this caliph's legacy, if he had one, survived where it counts: among common people. Now in Gao I had thoughts of Sokoto all over again. Caliph! Empire! Grand words for a man who left nothing behind but impoverished domains and a pyramidal pile of mud and wood.

So little in the Sahel had been embellished in any way: aside from the pointy adobe machicolations on some houses in Kano, mud bricks were mud bricks; logs served as crossbeams; what literature existed was mostly in Arabic, and consisted of historical records and treatises on Islam. In 'empire' after 'kingdom' after 'empire' across the Sahel, I was finding goats and donkeys and people eking out a meager life on nearly dead land. Sahelians were none the better for their rulers, past or present.

Again the question posed itself to me: Had Islam slain what creativity the Sahelians once had? To answer yes would be to refute history. Arabs had invaded North Africa and Spain too (among other places), but the indigenous peoples there had found inspiration in Islam for architectural and cultural wonders. Why had not the Sahelians?

Climate and geography seem to provide an answer. North Africa and Andalusia are much more fertile than any land I had traveled through since landing in N'Djamena, and droughts, so frequent and lethal in the Sahel, are rarer and less devastating there. The resulting material prosperity provided inhabitants with the means to create and develop. Also, the indigenous peoples of North Africa and Iberia – especially Berbers and Jews – began interacting with their Roman and Phoenician rulers long before the Arabs invaded, and had already assimilated elements of those civilizations. The peoples of the Sahel, however, had always dwelled in isolation, separated from their neighbors by huge distances and daunting terrain.

Yet what transpired through my reflections was one unassailable fact: Arab and Western civilizations had always been superior to those of the Sahel in science, armaments, letters, and discipline. Starting in 1591, this superiority granted the outsiders victories from which the vanquished Sahelians never recovered.

The next day I sat in a restaurant near my hotel, awaiting a lunch of kebab and fries. A young, unwashed white couple in shabby jeans and sandals walked in and began ordering their meals loudly, in fluent Songhai. I heard them speak American English to each other. They were standing next to my table, so I asked them if they were working with a humanitarian aid organization.

They were. I asked them to sit with me and told them that I myself had worked with the Peace Corps. Their fluency in Songhai suggested that they were serious about their assignment; their familiar and blunt manner of dealing with people here showed they had adapted well – maybe too well – to their new home. Immediately something else became apparent: their personal hygiene and manners reflected longtime residence among people for whom cleanliness was no priority.

Our food came and we started talking. We agreed that Americans knew little of Africa. The woman was garrulous on this subject: 'People in the States don't understand anything about Africa. They look at everything through their own eyes. When I go home on vacation, people hear I work in Mali, and they say, 'Oh Mali! Isn't that the country where they practice female circumcision?'' She took her forefinger out of her nostril and examined its tip. 'I say, "Yeah, so what?" They say, "It's barbaric!"'

'They're right,' I said.

'Well, I say, "Look, *you* women wear high heels. To me *that's* barbaric!" I can't understand why any girl would wear high heels just to make herself more attractive to a man.'

'Wait,' I said, putting down a fry. 'You're comparing wearing high heels to cutting off a little girl's clitoris and sewing up her vagina without anesthetic?'

The man joined in. 'Oh, I was against it too, because I thought it was oppressive to women, but now I know that women themselves perform it.'

'Yeah,' interjected the woman, 'it's a ritual. It's just part of the culture. There's a lot behind it – it's not as simple as Americans think. We can't judge it as something black or white. It's just their own culture. We just can't judge them from our own perspective. Americans don't have a *clue* about female circumcision, but they get all upset about it.'

'And that's wrong,' said the man. 'Because the women do it themselves.'

There *was* something to 'get all upset about' – and especially in Mali, where the singularly savage form of female genital mutilation known as infibulation is practiced. Infibulation involves, usually without using anesthetic, slicing off the clitoris, cutting away the labia minora, and sewing up the vagina. (Less severe variations of this butchery involve removal of the clitoris alone, or the clitoris and labia minora.) Mud poultices are frequently slopped onto the wound to stanch bleeding. For the most part, local women with no medical training perform this butchery with razors, scissors, kitchen knives, or even broken glass, usually at puberty or before, and the 'ritual' marks a girl's initiation into womanhood. After the operation, the initiate is, quite understandably, never the same again. If she survives (sometimes victims bleed to death or succumb to infections), she may experience pain during intercourse for the rest of her life; it goes without saying that her sexual desire is cast away with her excised flesh. Which is the point, of course. If women do the mutilating, men 'benefit' from the certainty that their wives won't be inclined to fool around. And if the men have any doubts, they or hired hags affirm a bride's virginity by using their fingers to rip open her stitched-up vagina on the wedding night.

Though most frequently associated with Muslim communities in Africa, the practice antedates Islam and occurs among Christians as well, in twenty-two African countries, including all those of the Sahel. Most likely every woman around us in the restaurant and every woman walking past us on the street had been so mutilated. For that matter, all the women I had seen since arriving in Chad had probably been circumcised.

In many African countries, including Mali, enlightened women are campaigning (with only limited success) to stop the practice. Hence, nothing can excuse the two aid workers: they knew better, and yet they fell prey (I assume) to social pressure and accepted the reprehensible, at least where others were concerned, and betrayed those women who would do unto others what these aid workers would never have done unto themselves.

I told them that I disagreed with them, and vehemently so. They dropped the subject, perhaps taking me for just another close-minded American. We ate the rest of our meal saying little.

The conversation led me to hard-boiled reflection about culture wars, including the one now raging between the West and the Islamic world. (Female genital mutilation plays its role in this war.) As disturbing as this cultural war is now, it may – just may – end up being a good thing, if people learn of other less painful, more sanitary ways of living – as has happened among the African women campaigning against mutilation. The war could thus exercise a Darwinian effect, leading to the demise of some nefarious beliefs and harmful practices and the strengthening and spread of better ways. That is, objectively speaking, development, which equals health, human rights, and prosperity. The absence of development equates with disease, oppression, and poverty.

I left the restaurant convinced that we should judge beliefs and practices by the benefit and pleasure they bring people and defend them with the same avidity or more as those who advocate opposing beliefs and practices. We must clarify our stance and never surrender.

# 15

## SAILING THE NIGER
## TO TIMBUKTU

The Harmattan-soiled sky hunkered ashen and storm-clouded over the clay warrens of Gao and the molten-mud currents of the Niger. Gao's 'port' – a stretch of riverbank where a mess of pinasses and dugout canoes lay half-beached on mucky sand flats – bustled with donkey carts piled high with firewood, porters shouldering sorghum-stuffed burlap sacks, and gaggles of idlers whose robes and turbans fluttered in the wind, forming streaks of whipping white amid a gray-brown Sahelian vista. A little ways on, near the pinasse I had hired, two naked teenage girls, facing the river for privacy, stood knee-deep in the shallows, chattering and soaping their sculpted ebony shoulders and petite apple breasts; a Songhai mother shampooed her tiny daughter's bristly hair, plunging her head into the muddy water to rinse it off.

Since bandits haunted the desert piste leading out of Gao, I decided to travel the 250 miles west to Timbuktu, my next destination, by boat. However, with the onset of the dry season, the Niger had lowered and the ferry had stopped running, so I would have to take a pinasse. To find one, Isa had taken me down to the port two days earlier. We learned that since Tabaski (as the Islamic Feast of the Sacrifice is known locally) was soon to arrive, there remained only one long-distance pinassier in town, Omar.

We found him at water's edge. In his early thirties, Omar was a lean Songhai with a scraggly beard. With his black turban rakishly tufted, his black sirwal trousers rolled up to the knees, his belt-loop silver dagger, and a roguish twinkle in his chuckling eyes, Omar called to mind a pirate, if a kindhearted one. He moved with a pirate's swaggering grace, which made sense: a pinassier here was a Big Man. He told me in fact that he had two pinasses, the larger of which he was already sending to Timbuktu loaded with people and livestock. The smaller one was a sleek, spear-bowed fifty-footer, six feet wide in the middle, with a tarpaulin roof on a rickety stick frame over the midsection, and a modified Mercedes engine at the stern. A cord attached to bells ran from the engine area to the rudder at the bow, enabling the engineer and the pilot to communicate by tugs and tinkles.

I wanted to establish credibility as something more than a tourist, so I addressed him in Arabic, which Isa had told me he spoke. To my initial surprise, he reacted with smiles and expressions of admiration, and he tried to answer in Arabic but couldn't manage more than a few words, so we talked French and chatted for a while. After a few minutes, I told him I wanted to go to Timbuktu and asked how much he might charge.

'Timbuktu . . . hmm, well the journey is long and the river is low, so of course the trip won't be easy. We can hit a sandbank and get stranded.'

'I understand. So what's your price?'

He glanced about and smiled. 'You name yours.'

This was a typical opening ploy, but thus began a bargaining session conducted, to my surprise, without the oaths, histrionics, and feigned contempt that had preceded so many deals I had made in the Sahel. As we bargained, Omar outlined the journey's specifics to justify a high price: four days of round-the-clock travel, just enough time to arrive in time for Tabaski (which I didn't want to miss); a pinasse crew composed of a pilot, a cook, and a mechanic; and all meals (rice, meat, rice, and rice) included. For all this he wanted 350,000 francs, or about six hundred dollars. I had done my research: I multiplied the individual fare to Timbuktu by the number of people I estimated would fit in his pinasse, reduced the result by 25 percent, and made an offer of

150,000. We shook hands on a compromise figure of 220,000. This all seemed almost *too* easy and reasonable.

Broken furniture and all sorts of junk-heap oddments cluttered the bow, and I asked him to remove them. He said he would be happy to do so. 'No problem. You're the boss, and the pinasse belongs to you for the trip. I'll empty it for you. And the Mercedes engine means you'll be riding in luxury and at high speed!'

High speed? Doubting this was possible in the Sahel, and wondering about what that twinkle in his eyes meant, I left him at the port, resolving against reason to look forward to days of peaceful sailing among hippos and egrets on this giant African river.

At departure time down at the port, Omar was nowhere to be found. Two hours later, he strolled down the bank, followed by a pockmarked, wheezing old man and a half-dead donkey dragging an unsteady cart on which a rusted oil drum rolled about, threatening to break free and kill someone.

We greeted each other. 'You're late,' I said.

'I needed time to buy condiments.'

'Condiments?'

'And fuel. The Arabs in the center didn't have any, so I had to send this donkey man out to the edge of town to get gas. I need half your fare now to buy it.'

I had given him two days to buy these things, but no matter. I counted out the money and handed it to him. Followed by the cart, we made our way through a crowd of gawkers and would-be porters to his pinasse. It was not empty, as he had promised, but was now stacked above the gunwale with new rubbish and freight from the prow to just before the stern, where the engine and another fuel barrel occupied a raised portion of deck and where a hole cut in the hull (a foot above water level here, since the stern was raised) served as a toilet. The heavy load brought the gunwale's top edge low to the river and would certainly slow us down, and it left no room at all in which to move about.

'You said the pinasse would be empty.'

'Oh, these are just a few personal belongings. I'll need them for the trip.'

'You need' – here I studied the load – 'twenty sacks of millet, fifteen bales of cloth, and those variously addressed parcels and boxes and all that metal junk to take me to Timbuktu?'

He smiled and his eyes twinkled. 'Yes.'

A middle-aged fellow with a sharp jaw, salted black beard, and a half-tied turban hanging astride his long face (Bashir, the cook) and a scrawny teenager (the mechanic, who would remain anonymous) came wheeling an ancient motorbike through the mud and lifted it over the pinasse's bow, dropping it in with a resounding crash.

'Don't forget the motorcycle,' he said, still smiling.

'And where are these personal belongings of yours going, including the motorbike?'

'To Gourma-Gharous and a few other places.'

'Look, we didn't agree to this: you said the pinasse would be empty. I don't want to stop to load and unload freight or I might be late for Tabaski. Remember, I've chartered the whole pinasse.'

'It *is* empty . . . except for a few of my personal belongings.'

Next a pretty young woman in an ankle-length blue and white floral dress came mincing through the muck, pushed past me, tossed a satchel into the pinasse, and climbed aboard. As I wondered about her, a twelve-year-old boy in CIA Ray-Bans did the same.

'And who are they?'

'My wife and son. They want to see my brother in Timbuktu.'

'Anyone or anything else you're planning on taking?'

'Of course not. The pinasse is all yours.'

At these words the wheezing donkey driver sprang into action, unhitching his donkey from the cart. He dragged the braying beast toward the pinasse. It bucked hysterically at water's edge.

'Oh, except maybe for one more thing . . .' Omar glanced at the donkey.

'No,' I said.

'But —'

'No!'

He waved at the old man, who glumly trudged away, dragging the much-relieved donkey.

'Oh, by the way . . .' He shook his sleeve and out slipped a tin-selly timepiece. 'Can I interest you in this genuine not-fake and tried-and-tested real Rolex? I make you a good price. Only for you.'

I thought of the unassuming denizens of the desert in Chad, and my earnest guides in Nigeria and Niger. Without hesitation they had accepted me as a brother, bargaining reasonably with me for their fees and not exploiting my lack of experience in the Sahel.

Here with Omar, I realized that I had been lucky with my other travel companions. But then, all around me in the port, and up in the market a few blocks away, and in most places in Africa, men and women haggled hard with one another – the ritual was obligatory, and I knew this. I had expected such bargaining from Omar. Merchants in all bargaining countries first assessed their customers' ability to pay and then set prices accordingly. To a great extent, where pricing was concerned, one's perceived wealth counted more than the intrinsic worth of the product or service. Thus, in this regard my skin color signaled a crucial fact: compared with most people in Gao, I was rich. Omar would have practiced this chicanery on anyone potentially as profitable; it was up to me to stake out my territory and defend it. But I also respected the obvious and overarching difference between us: I was in Gao as a guest on an elective mission; he was destined to spend the rest of his life here, suffering injustice and poverty.

So I suppressed my indignation and climbed atop the freight, taking a seat on a carpet cast over some sorghum sacks under the tarp. Omar yanked on the cord and tinkled the bell, and the pilot at the bow wrenched the rudder free of the muck. We pulled out into the river, swung around, and headed west, toward the Harmattan-clouded sky.

An hour later we were chugging past massive swelling dunes on the southern shore, with endless reed swamps to the north. The Harmattan died, and the sky and water fused into a seamless tableau of burnished glare, blue-white and eye-splitting. To the chug-chug-chug of the Mercedes motor, I fell asleep under the tarp, with a dry, river-cooled breeze from the Sahara blowing over my cheeks.

The explorer Mungo Park likened the Niger to the 'Thames at Westminster.' Park often fell ill on his Sahelian mission, and one wonders what combination of hallucinogenic heat and mind-bending dysentery could have stirred him to make this deranged comparison. The Niger to me seemed an impossible geographic and aesthetic incongruity bearing no relation to any river I had seen: it is a waterway aflame with the Saharan sun, flowing vast and blue between dun-colored dunes and acacia-strewn badlands, assaulted at times by blasts of parching wind.

By late afternoon, with all traces of Gao hours behind us, we were floating right into Saharan wilds. Omar's son, Muhammad, donned his Ray-Bans and lay on his stomach over the sacks of grain, setting his chin on the gunwale to watch the day die. The falling sun tinted the glassy river with lava hues; cattle, their fierce horns low and wide, migrated along the banks, silhouetted black against an orange sky; herds of hippos grazed in the shallows, their backs like granite boulders floating in a sea of fire; distant crooked baobabs gave roost to broad-winged eagles; snipes and cormorants whisked past us, crying urgent messages to one another. Later, as the sky purpled with dusk, fishermen poled svelte black pirogues back to their villages or floated stationary as they hauled aboard nets filled with capitaine and catfish. On high, faraway banks, mud-brick houses sheltered people who would probably never know the Internet or television, who would never meet a doctor or a nurse, who would never ride in a car.

A nocturnal chill settled over the river. I rummaged around in my pack and pulled out a sweater and put it on; I made a cocoon of my blankets and slipped inside. A full moon rose and cast a frigid glow over the willowy silhouettes of shrouded girls carrying jugs of water on their way home from the banks. We became, I imagined, a tiny black arrowhead cutting through a moon-silvered sea.

Leaving the pilot alone at the bow, Omar and Bashir clambered to a clear spot ahead of the motor and faced east, and began rising and falling in performance of their evening prayers, their suras ringing rhythmically if monotonously out into the riverine stillness, blending with it. *Salam, salam, salam* – the word, meaning 'peace,' sounded in their prayers, and was this African river not a watery incarnation of peace? Had there ever been a September 11? Was there really a world beyond the Niger where armies were preparing for war? Moreover, was there any need for vengeance and wrath, wealth and glory? If we could only sample the peace of this river at regular intervals, imbibing it as a tonic tranquilizer, we might not think so . . . I fell asleep.

Somewhere around midnight, beyond the village of Bourem, with the moon reigning directly above us, freezing the world in frigid pallor, the engine sputtered and clanked and died, and we rasped to a stop.

We had run aground. We sat idle in midriver, the Niger's currents of liquid silver flowing past us.

I looked up. 'Omar!'

No answer.

'Omar, wake up!'

He coughed and rose from his bedding in the rear.

'Omar, we've run aground.'

He and Bashir slipped into the shallows and pushed the pinasse free of the shoal, and the mechanic groggily relaunched our motor. The pilot sat unperturbed throughout, though his error – he must have fallen asleep – certainly could have broken our propeller or caused other serious damage. Omar climbed back aboard and sat down next to me, saying nothing to him. Why not? I asked.

'It was God's will,' he answered.

'Oh, come on. Your pilot could have wrecked the motor you're so proud of. Don't you care about the money you'd have to spend?'

'Well, God disposes.'

'Does God pay for new motors here?'

'Okay, you're right. I *should* be angry.'

But he wasn't. Shortly thereafter we chugged over to the bank and dropped anchor. 'The pilot needs to rest,' Omar said. 'If we keep going he could fall asleep again and we'd hit a rock. There are bad stretches ahead.'

'Stopping's fine with me.'

I eagerly grabbed my mosquito net and blanket and jumped ashore. I set up my net on the sand at the base of nearby dunes, now pearly bread loaves in the moonlight. The river hissed as it flowed past us, a luminous, infinitely uncoiling silver snake.

The honeyed flush of dawn eased me out of sleep, as did the mournful cries of cormorants mingled with the festive gurglings of fish frolicking in the shallows. I sat up and looked out onto the river: it was a mirror of silk, now and then rippled by an errant breeze.

I jumped aboard and roused the others, and we weighed anchor.

By midmorning we were passing through a defile of cinnabar cliffs and solitary dunes. I reveled in the view, a thrilling affirmation that we were entering new terrain foretelling the exoticism of Timbuktu, but Omar, standing on the stern, rang his bell to warn the pilot: there were submerged rocks here that could destroy his pinasse if we hit one.

I fashioned a chair out of sacks of grain and positioned myself to catch the sun. Bashir the cook brought us breakfast, which was leftovers from dinner: a large bowl of cold, sand-encrusted rice studded with gelatinous scraps of gristly lamb. Bashir was benevolent and avuncular, and I liked him, but this meal was foul. I ate a few bites and then retreated to my makeshift chair.

'No condiments,' said Omar, grabbing gobs of rice and meat and stuffing them into his mouth, chewing hard to break down the gristle. 'No condiments in the market. Sorry.'

The market was full of 'condiments,' of course, but he must have skimped to save money. I was grateful for a sack of dates and groundnuts I had brought along.

At noon the sun-showered river ran like a channel of mercury through tawny wastes spreading to every horizon. Omar took a seat next to me under the awning. He switched on his tape recorder: out burst the hoarse and angry voice of an imam commenting in Songhai on Qur'anic suras. Omar fished a notebook out of his sack and opened it to lines from the Qur'an he had written out in Arabic, in looping childlike script, next to which he had inscribed Songhai translations. The imam's commentary grew so violent that I asked Omar what he was saying.

'Oh, oh, he's . . . he's just explaining what a sin it is to cut your beard or nails during the feast of Tabaski.'

'He's awfully excited about it.'

'Of course. It's a serious issue.'

Maybe the imam was really exhorting his listeners to jihad – I don't know. But if he were, could Omar be inspired to jihad? I doubted so. Islamic fundamentalism flourishes most among the urban jobless and among those educated enough to perceive the inequalities the postcolonial Muslim regimes impose on their populations with the support of the West, and he was neither. Here in the outback, what counted was tradition, and traditional Islam was anything but radical.

Now we settled into the routine of river life. Much of the day Omar's wife (who never spoke) spent squatting astern, cutting meat or sifting rice for the atrocious meals Bashir prepared. The pilot, wrapped in his turban, rarely budged from the bow or even looked back at us; I'm not sure I ever saw his face. The engineer frequently slumped over his controls, his caftan and sirwal trousers filthy with grease, his eyes dull with fatigue or rancor. Omar's son lounged cheerfully next to me in his yellow tracksuit and peered at the world through his Ray-Bans, always smiling and at times using his exact schoolboy French to translate Omar's crude patois for me.

The sun bore down. I had begun dozing off when I heard the bell jingling; the pilot was alerting the engineer to danger and shouting to slow down. But the engineer was fast asleep, his head thrown back and his mouth wide open.

We plowed lurchingly aground, and the engine went dead.

Omar got up and examined the motor. 'Hmm. Damage, real damage. We need a new spark plug.'

'How are you going to find one out here?' I asked.

'My other pinasse will be along soon. They have an extra starter. We just have to wait.'

'Ah ha. Look, if you don't mind me saying so, aren't you upset about your pilot? He seems pretty negligent. You told me how dangerous it was to navigate now, but we've run aground because your crew doesn't do their job.'

Omar only gradually got my drift. Despite his pious protestations, I insisted that it wasn't God's fault, but that mortal shiftlessness was hindering us.

He shrugged. Then suddenly, probably to appease me, he made a show of anger. 'By God, I'll dock his pay twenty thousand for that! Oh, ah, no, ah, I already paid him.'

'Why did you do that?'

He shrugged again. 'I didn't think. I guess he doesn't care what happens now.'

Soon we acquired a starter from the other pinasse and were on our way.

The next morning, after passing another pacific night on a sandy bank, we drew beneath the mud walls and riverbank houses of Gourma-Gharous. Here acacias shed their thorns on soft white sand; Tuareg and Arabs milled about among the Songhai; and there were camels, camel dung, and camel tracks everywhere. We were really in the desert now. But the scene was not quite as Islamic as one might expect: young black women squatted in the shallows, topless, soaping up their arms and faces, their breasts swinging as they scrubbed. No one paid attention.

We were not moored long before a half-dozen men gathered around the bow. They argued with Omar, pointing to his 'personal belongings' and waving papers. They were of course merchants, and they wanted their goods.

'Just giving away some gifts,' Omar told me, his voice betraying neither humor nor irony.

The unloading dragged on and on. Omar checked off boxes against scribblings in the same notebook he used for his Qur'anic notes. After an hour I lost patience. I was now paying a price in exasperation for the laissez-faire magnanimity I had shown in allowing him to take all this cargo aboard. What bothered me most of all was his presumption: Did he really think I *believed* these were his personal belongings?

I jumped up and stumbled across the remaining cargo, which no longer formed a smooth secondary deck, sections of it having already been unloaded.

'Omar, why don't you just admit you're doing business?'

He laughed and scribbled in his ledger.

'I'm serious' – I was not. 'Why don't we just split the profits?'

He waved his pen at me as if to say, 'Touché!'

'I'm just kidding, Omar, about the profits, but really, who would believe that these are your personal things?'

'Oh, but they are! Really!'

'Who are all these people, then?'

'My friends.'

My years in Morocco had sensitized me to this sort of deceit. His brazen lying bothered me because it signaled an a priori notion not supported by the Qur'an but nonetheless widespread in many Muslim countries: namely, that a nonbeliever's concerns didn't count for much, that lying to an infidel was somehow pardonable. True, here as in other Muslim countries, the Europeans had done much that was wrong, and in some way that might in part explain a certain commercial revenge. Wanting to be just, I weighed the past in deciding the present, but we live in the here and now. All of us resist injustice, and our tempers prohibit us from suffering it in silence.

'Look,' I said, 'why can't you just be honest instead of insulting my intelligence with this nonsense about your "personal" things and "presents"?'

He looked up from his ledger and smiled. 'Okay, okay, I'm sorry. It won't happen again.'

'Well, oh. Thanks, then,' I said, taken aback by his about-face: again it seemed too easy.

Still, I sat down under the awning and began feeling gratified, and I complimented myself on my forthrightness. This incident showed that, with a little honesty and gumption, there *was* hope for dialogue between cultures. Omar bickered away with his merchants, but it didn't bother me anymore.

Stevedores finally appeared to empty the pinasse of its remaining cargo, which allowed me for the first time to see what had lain beneath it: wooden slats and bamboo poles covering an inch of rancid brown crud that obscured the hull and seethed with thumb-size roaches and squirming maggots and worms.

Watching me recoil from all this, Omar smiled.

I carefully reclined on a tarp against the gunwale, inches above the larvae, consoling myself with my cultural victory if fervently fearing that should I fall asleep, I would soon be covered head to foot in vermin. But the heat was intense, and I dozed off.

Worms crawling on my face, leaving slimy trails, roaches in my hair, worms slithering into my open mouth, a putrid stench and gagging and ants on my tongue and offal . . . I tried to move and couldn't – something was paralyzing me.

I jerked awake to a clattering of wood on wood, and whispers and more clattering and wood rattling. There were no worms on me. But freshly cut palm-wood beams were being stacked all around me.

I was being boxed in by beams; stevedores were loading the pinasse with new cargo that would restrict us all to the space just under the awning. I jumped up. Omar was nowhere around.

I shook the beams encasing me and shouted to the two stevedores: 'Hey! Hey!'

They stopped loading and stared at me as if I were a madman in a cage. In fact, I was a mad man in a cage. I rattled the beams and demanded release in the least culturally sensitive terms.

They exchanged nervous glances.

I rattled the beams again and threatened to shove them overboard. They set about unloading them, tossing them onto the wet sand.

Omar returned with two men who, judging by the shock and anger that lit their faces when they saw their wood in the wet sand, were beam merchants. An argument exploded in Songhai between Omar and them, and then Omar shouted at the stevedores. There was much flailing of arms and pointing of stevedore fingers – at me.

Omar turned to me and glared.

'You made them unload the beams?'

'Omar, I'm not riding into Timbuktu in a cage. I have

absolutely, this time, had enough. I'll get out here and not pay you the second half if you say one word about these beams being gifts.'

'They're not gifts. But I won't lie. They're my *personal* beams.'

I restated my threat. We left Gourma-Gharous without the beams.

The village of Mandiakoy was an African idyll: red finches chirruped among drowsy ferns, palms swayed over trim straw huts, children played tag on powdery alabaster sand. We had stopped to pick up a pilot who could guide us through the treacherous shallows near Timbuktu, and to let off Muhammad, who was in fact not Omar's son but a cousin. In African parlance, depending on age, almost any male relative could be called 'Son' or 'Brother' or 'Uncle,' or even 'Father.'

'I have a second wife here,' Omar said to me. 'Come.'

I jumped ashore. We left his boating wife stewing in the stern, wrapped in a shawl and refusing to look at him.

We walked through a palm grove to the village square. Men in purple robes and golden turbans squatted on the sand and chatted; women in indigo gowns washed clothes and carried firewood and tended babies. Omar's house, a sturdy hut of beams and bast, stood on a plot of soft white sand; inside, it was strewn with heavy red carpets and grand trunks of polished wood – tokens of his wealth.

He and his second wife, a young woman in a blue shawl and long narrow skirt, shook hands modestly but warmly. I could see she felt affection for him, which was more than I could say about the exploited maidservant now shivering on the boat. She then went about dutifully preparing a meal of lamb, sauce, and rice for us, which we later ate in the glow of lantern light, sitting outside his hut. Men and boys came over to talk to Omar, but they said little after exchanging formalities and news. They took evident pleasure in seeing him, though, and it was clear that he was a man of standing, perhaps even *the* man of standing, in the village.

It might seem strange, but the peace I felt in Mandiakoy reminded me of villages I had visited in the somnolent, fir-scented taiga of the Russian Far East, of stone hamlets beneath the Carpathian peaks of Transylvania – impoverished rural redoubts where one would have expected misery and despair, but where the light at midday had been as soft as this crepuscular luminosity, where people were content with their idylls of trees and sky and water, as content as the inhabitants of Mandiakoy. Here as there, life went on in the most undramatic way possible, and shone superior in its diurnal tranquility to the hectic if richer existence I knew in Moscow. Yes, the taiga residents and Transylvanians had their problems, but they loved their homes and stayed there.

Mandiakoy took me back into my past. In my college years, I had made Henry David Thoreau's *Walden* my bible; I had always wanted to 'simplify, simplify.' Since each of us knows our end in advance, why not retreat into Thoreauvian isolation and seek peace in the bucolic environs for which we were created? Thoreau had written about the folly of men going to 'the other side of the globe, to barbarous and unhealthy regions' to pursue trade, but certainly he would have been pleased to see this village, among the 'barbarians' on this remote African river. Why could I not halt here and now in Mandiakoy, and simplify, simplify?

As we were getting ready to leave, we got word from fishermen that the waters had receded too far from Kabara (the port for Timbuktu) to dock there, and we would have to moor elsewhere. Omar found a boy from Mandiakoy to guide us the rest of the way. We set out.

After a night of careful navigation among shifting shoals, we pulled up at the village of Ondougouma – as close as we could get to Timbuktu. When we reached the bank, villagers, surprised to see people arriving from distant Gao, tossed out a plank and welcomed us ashore.

Omar and I let bygones be bygones. We said a civil goodbye, and I went to find a Land Rover to take me the last ten miles to Timbuktu. With the most storied and exotic of African cities rising above the acacias just ahead, I was too impatient to simplify.

# 16

# DANCE OF THE DESERT

*'Pour ne pas sentir l'horrible fardeau du Temps qui brise vos épaules et vous penche vers la terre, il faut vous enivrer sans trêve.*

*Mais de quoi? De vin, de poésie, ou de vertu, à votre guise. Mais enivrez-vous.'*

(So as not to feel the terrible burden of Time that breaks your shoulders and bends you toward the earth, you must get drunk without respite.

But drunk on what? On wine, on poetry, or on virtue, as you like. But get drunk.)

– CHARLES BAUDELAIRE

Sensing a delicate reek of Johnnie Walker, I followed red-eyed Moussa through the clay portals of Djinguereber Mosque, the architectural 'masterpiece' of Timbuktu, into the shadows. Though built by an Arab architect named El Saheli who hailed from Andalusia when that territory had reached its civilized apogee under medieval Moorish rule, Djinguereber looked to be, well, a lump of mud.

Moussa navigated from pillar to pillar across the sandy floor with the meticulously measured strides of a drunk accustomed to hiding his inebriation. He halted, and, swaying a bit, flung his kaffiyeh over his shoulder. He then leaned against a straw mat hanging over a decayed wooden door.

'The Condemned Door!' he announced in French, exhaling a

whiskeyed effluvium. 'This is what you'd call a *h-h-*' – *HICCUP!* –
'holy door. You see, in the seventeenth century a religious student
turned himself into a lion here and ran out through this door into
the desert, where he roared and roared. The congregation in the
mosque saw this, and they feared he was' – *HICCUP!* – 'mocking
Islam. So they cordoned off this door and cond-d-d-demned it.
It's quite a mystery even now. Was he mocking Islam? I can't' –
*BURP* – 's-s-say.'

'That's the mystery? You think that really happened? Surely
it's just a legend.'

'It *did* really happen. The whole congregation witnessed it.
Remember' – *HICCUP* – 'Timbuktu is the city of three hundred
and thirty-three marabouts [Muslim saints]. Miracles happen here
all the time.'

Done looking at the door, we walked out of the dark into the
wan evening light of the courtyard.

'The marabouts have great power even now,' Moussa went on
to say, inhaling the fresh warm air and appearing to sober up. 'For
example, they can give you potions that make your skin impene-
trable to knives and bullets. Sometimes this power becomes
known only after the marabouts' death. Like the time the
marabout died and was put in his casket. A thunderstorm broke
out when the pallbearers were marching his casket down to the
cemetery. A bolt of lightning struck nearby and scared them, so
they let go of the coffin and ran away. But it just hung there in the
air.'

'You believe this? Doesn't it seem a bit —'

I stopped myself. Moussa, a thirty-year-old businessman, had
struck me as a cut above the unlettered residents and *faux guides*
of Timbuktu. His correct French, his Western dress (the kaffiyeh
being a necessary oriental touch to keep off the Harmattan dust),
his reputed connections to the city's elite, and even his con-
sumption of alcohol all inclined me to expect he might think
along Western lines and ascribe to mythology the fanciful legends
of his hometown. I was wrong. But I remembered 'events' in my
own country's Bible-based culture that were scarcely less implau-
sible yet nonetheless believed by millions of Americans

(according to polls and surveys) – the Immaculate Conception
and the Resurrection, bushes burning and seas parting and manna
raining down from heaven, to name a few. So I changed the subject and asked what people in Timbuktu thought of bin Laden.

'Bin Laden?' Moussa's eyes narrowed. 'Bin Laden? We *reject*
him. We don't allow *anyone* to come to Timbuktu and preach divisions in Islam. We don't even want to *know* about Wahhabism' –
the intolerant, puritanical Islamic sect to which bin Laden
adheres. 'I know what the Qur'an says: it says *not* to kill, it says to
be *peaceful*. If a fundamentalist came to my house I wouldn't even
offer him *tea*. Look, after September 11, Jimmy Carter, a man of
peace, came here to this mosque with the American ambassador.
They asked the imam to say a prayer for world peace, and that's
what he did. That is what we believe in here in Timbuktu –
*peace*. The Qur'an orders us not to kill so much as an *ant*.' He
belched whiskey. 'Not even an *ant!*'

His rejection of bin Laden on Qur'anic grounds was encouraging, but in Timbuktu I had noticed little that was Islamic anyway.
How many exuberant teenage Songhai girls, unveiled, willow-
waisted and swan-necked in sleek cotton gowns, had I seen since
arrival? They proudly displayed their beauty. Their hair was
straightened and long, or braided into cornrows and long, falling
in robust, henna-tinted shocks over their often bare shoulders.
They gathered to gossip and giggle under the neems or strolled
gaily in sun-drenched alleys, laughing and joking and flirting with
passersby. They exercised openly the power their beauty granted
them, beauty that Islam ordains be hidden in the home, for the
eyes of the husband alone.

I wasn't the first to notice the women of Timbuktu: their
flaunted charms had shocked Arabs arriving in the late Middle
Ages. But Timbuktu's history is, blessedly, irreligious and Islamic
both. Around 1100 the Tuareg, then pagan, established Timbuktu
as an oasis market settlement, but the merchants drawn to it
(mostly from Djenné, to the southwest) suffered under their rule:
though they lived in the desert, the Tuareg continually returned
to town to extract tribute. Hence in 1330 Timbuktuans entreated
the Malian king Mansa Moussa to add their city to his domain and

protect them from their despoilers. He did, and fresh from Mecca and the hajj, imbued with Islamic zeal, he ordered El Saheli to design and erect Djinguereber Mosque in 1336.

Situated at the crux of caravan routes running across the Sahel and north into the Sahara, Timbuktu then grew into one of the preeminent centers of commerce and Islamic scholarship in Africa, with a hundred thousand residents – more than London at the time. Passing eventually from Malian to Songhai imperial rule, it acquired epithets such as the Fabulous City, the Queen of the Sudan, and The Mysterious; it hosted 180 Islamic schools, plus a university and a thriving book market – unique institutions in this then, as now, largely illiterate part of the world. Timbuktu remained primarily a commercial outpost, however, supplying the desert oases to the north with rice, butter, and manioc, and dispatching gold, slaves, ivory, musk, indigo cloth, and gum arabic across the Sahara to Arab countries and even Europe. Its Albaradiou Gates, facing the desert in the northern quarter, once welcomed sixty thousand camels laden with goods every year.

But more than to anything else, Timbuktu owes its fame to gold, the element that led to its capture, plunder, and ruin by Moroccans – and its eventual resurrection in myth among faraway European peoples. In 1591 Timbuktu fell to the troops of Sultan Al-Mansour of Marrakesh, who sought control over the West African gold trade and coveted the city's salt and slaves as well. Marrakesh's distance hindered sultanic rule, however, so from 1618 descendants of the Moroccan conquerors ruled Timbuktu independently, but they could not protect it from repeated sackings by Sahelian tribes. Within a couple of hundred years, Timbuktu's literal and figurative golden era had ended, and the city sank into famine and misery. It was precisely then that Timbuktu's gilt reputation reached beyond Africa's shores and transformed it into a lodestar for European adventurers and gold seekers, many of whom died trying to reach the city. The first European to make it and come home alive was the Frenchman Rene Caillié, a baker's son who took to adventuring in Africa at age sixteen, learned Arabic to pass as an Egyptian among hostile Songhai and Fulani Muslims, and arrived in

Timbuktu via Kabara on April 20, 1828. Caillié declared, after reaching '*cette cité mystérieuse*,' that his '*joie était extrême*.' He appreciated the unveiled women, the hospitality of the locals, and the high level of literacy, but quickly decided that the city was roughly as I had found it: an '*amas de maisons en terre, mal construites*' (a pile of poorly built earthen houses).

But I had good reason to come. My desire to visit the city dated from my years in Marrakesh, when Timbuktu had shone a remote and exotic *città del sole* at the southern terminus of the trans-Saharan caravan route beginning near the Casbah, where I lived. Then (in the late 1980s and early 1990s), traveling the route was impossible, owing to the disrepair into which the wells had fallen; later, civil war in Algeria and the Tuareg rebellion would make Timbuktu more inaccessible from Marrakesh than ever. Nevertheless, I never renounced the hope that Timbuktu would in some measure quench the wanderlust from which I had suffered for more than two decades. Now, standing in the courtyard of Djinguereber Mosque, I was wondering if I had been wrong.

After I finished touring the mosque, I asked Moussa to introduce me to the Moroccans said to still inhabit the city. He directed me to a genial fellow in his thirties named Muhammad who dressed in traditional blue darra'a robes and baggy white sirwal, just as Moroccans do across the desert. Muhammad's jug ears and bug eyes, his bulbous nose and fat stubby fingers, presented an ungainly sight that contrasted with the fine features of the Songhai and Tuareg (to say nothing of Moroccans in Morocco) and prompted me to wonder whether inbreeding was a problem in Timbuktu's reclusive Moroccan community.

Muhammad invited me home. After an unnerving moped ride, swerving and sliding down Timbuktu's sandy lanes, we skidded to a stop in the Moorish quarter. There, houses were carved out of beige limestone, with wrought stone grills on their high windows and ebony doors festooned with iron knockers – the most embellished dwellings I had seen in the Sahel, a salve to my artistically deprived eyes. Mu-hammad's house was palatial, with a high-ceilinged interior painted sky blue; its two cement floors were covered with sand in places, but elsewhere strewn with colorful carpets. In his living room stood bookcases and books (not just the Qur'an), and he told me he read for edification and amusement – a declaration that set him apart from everyone else I had met on this trip.

Muhammad and I spoke Arabic. His dialect was the Hassaniya of the desert nomads who today inhabit the western Sahara, but who for centuries had led caravans all over the Sahara. Here and there he dipped into French, in which he was comfortable when discussing subjects requiring more than workaday vocabulary.

He offered me a glass of mint tea, the favorite and fragrant green brew of Morocco. As we sipped it, I told him I had spent months traveling with Hassaniya-speaking nomads in Morocco's Drâa valley; I explained how pleased I was to finally meet Moroccans on the other side of the great sand sea.

'You are welcome,' he said. 'My family came to Timbuktu with the invasion of 1591. We have Jewish roots, and we've intermarried with the Berbers.'

These were admissions one would not usually hear made in North Africa, and I told him so.

'The Jews and the Berbers,' he said, 'were the first people to live in Morocco, as you might know, so there's nothing unusual about this. Here in Timbuktu we've always accepted other peoples. That's the African way. We've welcomed conquerors, be they French or Songhai or Moroccans, on the condition that they do no harm. We believe in trade and in loving life. Not one Timbuktuan has died fighting for this city. We just don't believe in war.'

'So there's no religious extremism?'

'Other things are more important than religion. Look, the Arabs control the economic life of Mali. They're too busy making money to be extremist. Timbuktu is a city of trade and peace, and we've always been open. You won't find many women wearing the veil here, and you can drink alcohol if you like. Ask me about bin Laden and I'll say I can't really tell you much about him, but I do know that nowhere in the Qur'an does it say, 'Kill!' because of religion. That is *not* a part of Islam, and we *don't* accept it. Criminals use religion to justify their crimes, so if you're talking about terrorism, you're really talking about a crime problem, not a religious problem.'

'But aren't people upset about the coming war with Iraq and how Israel treats the Palestinians?'

'Maybe, but who knows what Bush is thinking and why he's doing these things? Anyway, that doesn't concern us directly. You would never see an African strapping bombs to himself and blowing himself up for religion. That's just the opposite of the African way, which is the love of life. Look around you here in Timbuktu: you'll see people drinking and dancing, having a good time. That's what life is all about, isn't it?'

Muhammad espoused the commonsense tolerance and joie de vivre that infused the works of the Andalusian poets, writers, and sovereigns of Moorish Iberia, whose legacy remains the glory of the Islamic world – indeed, of all medieval Europe. It bears noting that the Moorish golden age preceded the Renaissance and the Enlightenment by hundreds of years. But in the case of Timbuktu, tolerance may have had more to do with economics than with faith. A tradition of hospitality developed to encourage traders to come and spend money. Out-of-town merchants received three days of free housing from Timbuktu's hoteliers, who made commissions on their guests' purchases in the market. Jews persecuted in North Africa fled here and played a significant role in the city's trade as well. Timbuktuans, in the end, had a good many material incentives to welcome those of different faiths and eschew any sort of puritanical extremism. The city's joie de vivre was good for business.

I said goodbye to Muhammad feeling that, for the first time since arriving in the Sahel, what I saw was meeting expectations I had formed since my years in Marrakesh.

In Zinder bureaucracy and suspicion had frustrated my plans to meet the Tuareg of the desert, but would Timbuktu's openness make things easier for me? I asked around and was introduced to a Tuareg named Ibrahim, a man in his late forties who lived in an encampment some five miles northeast of town. Of slight bone structure, with a sharp nose and gimlet eyes, Ibrahim was soft-spoken and modest, and he agreed to take me into the Sahara to celebrate the Feast of Tabaski with his family. Though he knew some Arabic, we would speak French. Tuareg and Arabs have never been on good terms, so it was best to communicate in a neutral tongue.

Every day in Timbuktu, just before dusk settled over its labyrinthine mud lanes, herders drove sheep and goats in from grazing areas outside town, raising a cloud of dust so choking and dense that at first I mistook it for smoke. So it was on the afternoon Ibrahim and I walked out to rolling white dunes marked here and there by the solitary, crooked skeletons of acacias, north of the Abaradiou quarter, at the edge of the Sahara. There we found his sons dressed as he was, in faded blue robes, their heads and faces covered in tougoulmousts of shimmering indigo. Beside them stood the camels, stately and calm, their fluffy hides as pale as the sand beneath their hoofs, their single humps outfitted with high-backed saddles of balsam-light wood striped blue and red, resting on red carpets that protected the animals from abrasions.

We loaded the camels with supplies, mounted the saddles, and began an easygoing ride north up and down dunes, the late-afternoon sun a low crimson orb, fuzzy-edged and warm but not burning, thanks to the dust clouds. Ibrahim and his sons spoke Tamashek, and I listened to its quaint and intricate inflections, which were delicate enough to resemble the twittering of birds or the speech of the enfeebled elderly. I fought drowsiness induced by the pacific breezes now astir and the dreamy twilight settling over the desert.

Two hours later, under an emergent crescent moon, Ibrahim raised his hand. We had arrived. His camp, to my eyes, appeared to be only a couple of straw huts atop a sandy knoll, ringed helter-skelter by acacias. Nearby there was an enclosure for his goats made of interwoven sticks. Dressed in a white gown, his wife reclined on a maroon carpet. Her long black hair was braided and uncovered; Tuareg converted to Islam only in the past couple of hundred years, and then only halfheartedly, so their women have never been subject to the same restrictions as their Arab sisters.

'Where are the other people in your camp?' I asked Ibrahim as we unloaded the camels.

'They're in their huts, which you don't see here, because we place them just far enough away to be out of sight. For privacy. We have eight families here.'

Later, Ibrahim went off to tend the goats. His sixteen-year-old daughter, with a baby on her arm, brought us our meal of rice and lamb. Her face looked sculpted from honeyed milk chocolate, and her brown eyes were enormous and warm. Her hair was braided and long, except for short, curly forelocks. Her gown was slit at the sides, and as she moved about, her breasts, taut with milk, now and then came into view above her muscled midriff.

The glow of the sun had vanished, leaving an enamel-hard firmament of pellucid lavender. The air was still. Across these dunes only black scarabs scuttled in search of camel dung.

After eating, I lay down and looked up at the sky. Sated, I drifted off to sleep.

I awoke to a resplendent pearly moon that glazed with clair de lune the dark acacias and softened their thorniness, washed over sleeping camels and goats to give them a statuary aspect, and ennobled the straw huts around me, banishing any semblance of poverty. How long had I been asleep? I couldn't tell.

There were cries from a distant dune.

'Come,' said Ibrahim, standing at the edge of the knoll. I arose, and we set out toward the voices.

Atop a dune men lounged in the sand, puffing on pungent, hand-rolled cigarettes, their tougoulmousts pulled up to their eyes, the indigo dye having rubbed off to tincture blue their brown skin. Beside them sat and chatted a group of some fifteen teenage girls in black shrouds, their raven hair (which, like that of Ibrahim's daughter, was cut long in the back but short in front) woven into braids and affixed with silvery bangles. Older women soon joined them, coming from surrounding camps. Among them was Ibrahim's wife, who arrived carrying a goatskin drum.

We sat down amid the men.

There was an excited twittering of Tamashek. The girls stood up, cutting phantomlike black figures in the milky wash of the waxing moon, their bangles glinting. Ibrahim's wife began striking her drum, another woman shook a tambourine, and the girls launched into spitfire clapping, beating out two distinct but complementary rhythms. Some of the girls hunkered into a hoarse and grunting refrain ('Eeh-*haa!* Eeh-*haa!* Eeh-*haa!* Eeh-*haa!*'); others sang melodic verse in Tamashek, interspersed with loose, shrill cries. Their bare brown arms and hennaed hands extended from their gowns and caught the moon's argentine glow.

Then two barefoot teenage boys leaped up, dancing into the half-circle and brandishing silver swords, their robes flailing, arms raised, feet kicking. One boy wore a tougoulmoust; the other's head was bare, oblong, and shaved. Their swords cutting the air, they dodged and parried and evaded in choreographed harmony – a war dance, a duel.

'*Em*ma! *Em*ma! *Em*ma! *Em*ma!' the girls chanted in crescendo, bowing down and clapping, rising and clapping, as if worshiping the glory and grace of these two combatants, whose cries rang out as their swords flashed and slashed in the desert night.

The boy with the tougoulmoust retreated, conceding victory to Muhammad (as I later learned he was called) of the bare head. The girls abandoned themselves to the rasping refrain 'Aho *yah!* Aho *yah!* Aho *yah!*' Adjusting their shawls, they chanted and bowed and rose, their clapping in synch with the drumbeats and banshee cries of Ibrahim's wife. The men around me lowered their tougoulmousts to deliver wavering yelps; at the base of the dune, tots did their own dance, with sticks for swords.

All at once – on what cue? – the girls segued from disyllabic grunts into a pious but no less impassioned chant, '*La ilaha illa Allah! La ilaha illa Allah! La hawla! La hawla! La hawla! La ilaha illa Allah!*' (There is no god but God! There is no god but God! There is no power [except in God]!), with solitary, chilling ululations cutting in, mingled with shouts of joy. Keeping one arm raised and held behind his head, flourishing with the other his sword of cold nacreous light, Muhammad stamped and gyrated to the claps of the women, the cries of the men.

Swaying, enraptured, by Muhammad's moves and the fluid

slashes of his sword, mesmerized by the girls' panting chants, I thought, *This* is how people were meant to live, glorying in their strength and beauty, shouting their joy into the wild night sky! *Enivrez-vous!* (Get drunk!) There is no tomorrow! There is no hell, only the much-disparaged paradise our senses can grant us *here* and *now!* Tuareg of all ages took part, found release, enjoyed the transcendental intoxication that comes from sharing passion. *That* passion is what we need – to loose our spirits and share passion!

The Tuareg danced and sang to *youth* – the gift we lose to never recover. Youth *is* a treasure, *is* a wonder, and for this we worship it. Reveling in youth's ephemeral splendor is the most genuine pleasure we can know. For what do we *really* want but to live forever, and be beautiful and strong *always*? This dance was *life*, a riposte to the deadly desert around us.

I felt as though I had been waiting all my days for this moment, on these dunes, with these Tuareg. Hours later, the moon sank into the acacias, the dancing ceased, the revelers dispersed. Ibrahim and I returned to our camp. I wrapped myself in my blanket and stretched out on the cool sand.

Five hours later, sunlight suffused the sky. I awoke to see Ibrahim milking his goats. Ululations soon rang out from dune to dune. The Feast of Tabaski was about to begin.

Ibrahim asked me to wait by his hut so that his people might pray without a nonbeliever present, and I complied. On the opposing dune, the Tuareg lined up, men in front and women in back, and performed their orisons in the usual manner. Then he motioned to me to approach.

'*Emma-emma-emma-emma!*'

The singing and dancing started anew, but it was not the same. Into the half-circle of chanting girls bounded a tougoulmoust-veiled boy in his late teens. Next a girl of fourteen or fifteen, her face smeared with indigo from her shawl, her eye whites flashing from dark sockets, came out to meet him, moving her henna-splashed hands in ornate twists and florid twirls, her wrists jingling with silver bracelets, her fingers covered in silver rings.

She raised her arms to reveal breasts quivering through slits in her black robe; on her henna-patterned toes glinted more silver bangles and ringlets. In daylight as in moonlight, exemplars of unblemished youth! With her, as she moved, was the power, power over this pleading boy. Where does this primal truth not prevail? Where is it better expressed than here, among these Tuareg, in this desert?

She would not give in to the boy, who circled her, his arms outstretched. He dropped to his knees, still gyrating, but she evaded his embrace, her eyes lowered, her face demure and impassive, her hands caressing the air, her feet mincing the sand. The boy was bowing and begging!

'*Emma! Emma! Emma! Emma! Emma!*'

Another teenager in the audience danced out and sprayed them with perfume; there was laughter, and the spell was broken.

From beneath the dune rang out yelps of '*Yiip! Yiiip!*' We turned our heads.

From beneath a faraway dune a youth atop a camel whipped his beast into a gallop, and the long-legged dromedary bounded across the sands with astonishing grace, a grace camels don't evince when walking. They reached the nearby acacia, and the camel executed a sharp turn. Soon after, another boy from beneath the same dune shouted, '*Yiiip!*' and led his camel on a similar charge, his tougoulmoust trailing. These were camel races similar to Moroccan fantasias, performed not to defeat an opponent but to display a skill.

The dances and races finished when the sun got too hot. Noon arrived, and soon it would be time to eat. Using footlong knives, fathers slaughtered sheep daubed with festive streaks of red and purple paint for the Tabaski feast. Now, near every hut, blood soaked the sand, spewing in arcs from slit jugulars, and sheep coughed and gagged and kicked.

Near our tent, Ibrahim's cousins dug a pit and tossed in firewood and lit it. Ibrahim let the blaze burn down to embers, over which he tossed a layer of sand. After the sand had heated, he placed atop it the carcass of his sheep, which he covered with more embers, plus a final layer of sand.

A couple of hours later, Ibrahim called me over to the skeletal shade of an acacia to eat with a cousin of his named Ali. (Women would eat their own separately slaughtered sheep the next day.) He first served us the liver and lungs and kidneys, and then the meat, cut in shards and placed on a tray. We ate with our right hands.

Ibrahim handed me a morsel of mutton. 'Look, you don't need to add salt to this. The way we cook it keeps the blood in, and the blood has enough salt. You'll taste it.'

I bit into the meat, which crunched with sand.

'Don't worry about that sand. It cleans out your system.'

Ali looked to be in his sixties. He wore a black robe over his pale and flaccid torso. An indigo tougoulmoust lay draped on his bald head. Having studied in Egypt, he spoke fluent Arabic, and we began talking in that language.

'My father was a chief,' he said. 'He sent me abroad to study so I could learn Arabic. You see, we have problems with the Arabs because we don't speak their language. I hoped to resolve some of these problems.'

'Have you had any success?'

'Well, some,' he said, as he gorged on liver. He licked his fingers. 'But Arabs are different from us. Arabs . . . you can't trust them. They speak words of deceit. If you're good to a Tuareg, a Tuareg will be good to you. But be good to an Arab and he'll try to trick you. Arabs sell their daughters for money to the highest bidder. But not a Tuareg. We think of giving dowries as a way to help a new family. So we give things they need, like animals. We think newlyweds should be happy together.'

I had noticed a pair of newlyweds, both about fifteen, living in a small hut nearby. The young girl had come up to me before lunch and shown me her baby. It seemed odd to see a baby whose mother still had baby fat on her own cheeks. But here people married at puberty. That was not surprising, but Ali's talk of happiness was: *happiness* is a word not often heard in societies in which families marry their children to advance their own interests.

'You saw the newlyweds? We built them that house. That's our tradition. That way, they can start their own life and be happy.'

I asked him about the bad blood between the Tuareg and black Africans. There seemed to be little interaction between the two groups.

'We enslaved the blacks. When independence came we let them go, but they still hold a grudge against us. But look at them: they're undisciplined. They marry four wives and have forty children, never thinking about whether they have enough money to feed them. So the children go hungry and get sick, and their daughters turn to prostitution. No Tuareg would live this way. Look at the cities here: they're filthy and diseased.'

The old prejudices had hardly diminished, and it was easy to see how wars could begin here. We went on talking about the past, about how the Tuareg once ruled the sands over which Arabs led the caravans.

'Always,' he said, 'from Cairo to Zagora [in Morocco] the sands have belonged to us. Hundreds of years ago, when the emperor of Mali traveled to Mecca with a thousand camels, each camel was loaded with a hundred pounds of gold. He had to take a Tuareg as his prime minister to get him through the sands the Tuareg ruled. Otherwise he would have been robbed.'

After our meal the heat grew intolerable and we retired to various plots of acacia shade for a nap.

When the sun began dropping, Ibrahim roused me. His sons were saddling the camels, and it was time to go. I said my goodbyes to his family, and we headed back over the sands by which we had come, toward the jagged clay skyline of Timbuktu. It would soon be time to move on to Djenné, the jewel of the Sahel.

# 17

# DJENNÉ'S
# BITTER WINDS

The sky was a lowering canopy of copper, and every breath I took scratched my throat. Once again the Harmattan was battering the Sahel, ripping through tumbledown villages, lashing dust clouds over patches of budding grass, driving lizards into their lairs and squirrels into their nests. Clamping wide-rimmed straw hats to their bony heads, Fulanis, their faces streaked with sweat and dirt, whipped stumbling donkeys ahead of lopsided carts or carried water from wells in crude amphorae. Repeatedly, as my taxi creaked down the cratered road toward Djenné, I thought I glimpsed in the whirlwinds the spiked mud walls of the city's Great Mosque – by all accounts the most splendid extant example of Sahelian architecture – but the Harmattan was deceiving me. Each time we drew near, the mosque's walls dissolved into fata morganas of flying dust; its crossbeams degenerated into acacias withered and black; and its faithful turned out to be impoverished villagers, laboring specters of despair in a howling dustbowl.

This, and I was expecting for the first time in my trip to see green, for Djenné sits on a floodplain, in the Sahel's southern savanna.

All at once we turned off the road, trundled down a piste into an acacia grove, and pulled up to a muddy waterway – a tributary of the Bani River on whose banks Djenné sits. There was a single-engine ferry waiting there, and it seemed like a gift from another planet, a miracle. On cue from one of the deckhands, we inched aboard it, the deckhand waved to the captain, and we chugged across the river. A short while later we were driving over the market square, past the Great Mosque.

The Soninké people founded Djenné in the eighth century as a fishing village. It came into its own five hundred years later, when its king, Koi Kounboro, converted to Islam and made it a nexus for the West African gold trade as well as a seat of Islamic scholarship. In the sixteenth century, after having passed from the Mali Empire to the Songhai, Djenné succumbed to Moroccan invaders, who embellished the city with their artful dwellings but eventually did little more than preside over its decline. Nevertheless, not all has been lost, and even today Djenné retains an aura of gravitas and grandeur. The Great Mosque, a soaring fortress of umber clay, with a roof of spearlike crenellations (reminiscent of those atop Kano's palaces: Djenné in fact originated the Sahel's architectural style), dates only from 1905, though it is said to replicate a structure that King Koi Kounboro built to celebrate his conversion to Islam. The beauty of the Great Mosque has not gone unnoticed by outsiders: in 1988 UNESCO placed Djenné on its World Heritage list. Unfortunately the mosque is closed to non-Muslims, so I would see it only from the outside – a major disappointment.

Muhammad's meaty shoulders bulged under his purple caftan, which rustled luxuriously as he loped ahead, guiding me down Djenné's powdery lanes. We were going to see Imam Ibrahim, the brother of the great imam of Djenné, whose predecessors' holy remit once extended across much of the Sahel. Muhammad, I noticed, pronounced Djenné '*gyinney*,' which resembled 'Guinea' enough to remind me that European explorers misapplied the city's name to the entire West African littoral, and even named three African countries after it. If this was a mistake typical of callous colonialists, it bespoke Djenné's importance in Sahelian history.

We passed a clutch of pint-size urchins washing red-brown calabashes in the sewer. They ran up to me, chanting, '*Sadaqa! Sadaqa! Allah! Sadaqa!*' I gave them what I could. Dressed in filthy smocks, barefoot and dusty-haired, and big-bellied from malnutrition, they looked straight out of a Unicef poster – except for their identical, well-finished calabashes. I asked Muhammad who they were.

'They're students,' he said, 'here at our Qur'anic school. You see, their parents send them here from other cities because Djenné is holy. They live with their imam, who feeds them and teaches them about Islam, and gives them those calabashes, which they use to eat with and collect alms. Begging is part of their education. To learn humility.'

We found Imam Ibrahim standing outside the door to his house, a banco-smeared palace built of softball-size, roundish clay bricks. Wearing an emerald green caftan and a kaffiyeh checkered red and white, tall and stout and abundantly bearded, Imam Ibrahim personified a type of oriental pomp the likes of which I had seen nowhere in the Sahel. I wondered how he could eat so heartily and watch his ragamuffin pupils starve.

Muhammad told him I was an American; might he spare a few minutes to talk to me? He frowned and nodded, and motioned us into his blue-walled reception room, where we sat down on straw mats. Though the imam conducted services in Arabic, he chose to speak Fulani and allow Muhammad, who was also a Fulani, to translate into French.

'Respected Imam, thanks so much for taking time to talk to me. I'm honored.'

Averting his eyes, he grunted and sniffled. 'You Americans, you've really set about attacking Islam and Muslims. God should rule this earth. But you Americans have adopted the role of God, dispensing justice and acting as judges.'

'This must anger a lot of people here in Djenné,' I answered, 'as it does in the West.'

'Well, it's not up to us to be hostile to you because of who you are. We don't have the right. God does. God will do His work alone.'

Muhammad's eyes hardened and his voice hoarsened. 'We always counted on America to do the right thing, to *solve* the world's problems. But Bush has a tiny brain. What are we supposed to do when America *creates* the problems? What are we to do? Tell me!'

'You Americans attack Arabs everywhere now,' said the imam. 'Arabs can do no right in your eyes.'

'I've seen some hostility in the Sahel toward Arabs,' I said. 'After all, they came as invaders and wrecked the African empires here.'

'There is no hostility. We are not against the Arabs. The Qur'an gave them the right to conquer and enslave people who wouldn't accept Islam. So that's what they did here. We're now a hundred percent Muslim.'

'One *hundred* percent!' said Muhammad. 'We allow no missionaries here – you won't find one – and no other faiths.'

Despite Muhammad's agreement, the imam amended his assessment of Islam's hold on Djenné. 'Still, really, many people here deviate from the faith. They begin adopting Western ways.'

'What do you do about it?'

'Nothing. In the Qur'an this is all written. It says at the end of the world there will be many wars, many religions, but few believers. Everything now gets worse and worse, according to God's plan. Even here in Djenné. I'll give you an example. Once, we had five thousand people in Djenné, and water sufficed for all. Now we're between sixteen and twenty thousand and everyone's fighting over water. The government is planning to build a dam upstream, which will hurt us even more by keeping the river away, but that doesn't answer the question 'Why doesn't it rain?' The answer is simple: God has decided it won't rain. God has made his decision. Now, please excuse me.'

He stood up and directed me to the door. My meeting was over.

Just as fundamentalist Christians interpret current events as signaling the approach of the Final Days, so do many Muslims. It is not surprising that exponents of the planet's two most popular faiths should speak of the earth's end with resignation, as did this imam, or even with righteous glee, as do evangelical preachers: both creeds posit the Apocalypse or Day of Judgment as the beginning of eternal bliss for God's chosen and a plunge into perpetual hellfire for the rest of us.

In Mopti, where I had stopped for a few days before coming to Djenné, a French journalist had given me fifteen copies of *Le Petit Prince* to deliver to a schoolteacher friend of his named Oumar. So, with books in hand, I asked Muhammad to take me to his house. Schoolteachers in the West might not necessarily count as intellectual luminaries, but in Africa they are often the only educated people in town, and I was eager to get his perspective on Djenné. Certainly with him I expected to have more in common culturally than I had with the imam, or even with Muhammad.

Oumar was a fit man in his thirties with nappy hair and an affable grin, as well as spry eyes that exuded irreverence and a fervor of some sort; before he spoke, I felt he had something to say, and his Western dress told me he was no traditionalist. He welcomed us inside his courtyard and set up chairs for us under a neem. A television in the corner showed hazy images of the Malian president and foreigners inaugurating an aid program. Oumar's wife was clattering about in a clay side room, and malodorous cooking smoke was pouring out its low door.

Oumar examined the books I presented to him and smiled. 'Thank you. I'm going to give them as rewards to the students who work the hardest in my class. Books are too expensive for most parents. So, how do you like Djenné?'

'It's beautiful, and I can see why the UN made it a World Heritage site.'

He rolled his eyes.

'Is something wrong?'

'Heritage site! Come *on!*' He shook his head. 'The UN *condemned* this town and all of us in it by making it a Heritage site. Think: you can't build anything here in cement; you can't build anything modern. Your ceiling is banco and falling on your head, but you have to repair it just as they did in the ninth century, so it falls down on your head three days later, and so on and so on. And if you so much as widen your door, the police come and take you to court. 'Everything must remain the same here! Follow traditions!' Well, people were a lot shorter in the ninth century, so the doors are the wrong size now. And why should we do something just because our ancestors did it, or because our elders demand it be done now? Why? Is that what the UN stands for? Backwardness? Crazy, it's crazy! No one invests here because you can't build anything, so our youths flee to Bamako and Abidjan to find work. Is that progress? Tourists *love* Djenné, because it's ancient, which means full of mud roads and mud buildings. But would they want to live in a city like that? How would you like to live in New York if it hadn't been repaired since the eighteenth century?'

'You have a point,' I admitted.

I mentioned that I had just visited the imam. Oumar wasn't impressed.

'Their mentality is the mentality of this town: they're against education. 'No!' they shout, 'education is kaffir!' We're supposed to respect their opinion, for some reason. On account of tradition. What's worse is the people here. The Fulani are herders and the Bozo are fishermen, so they don't see any need for their kids to go to school. The Fulani send their kids out in the bush to herd animals, and Bozo teach their kids to fish – that's all. All this means our level of education is the lowest in the country and never gets better.' He kept shaking his head. 'Well, okay. I'm not always against tradition. It can do good. See this arm of mine?' He pointed to his left bicep. 'I got in an accident and crushed the bone. I could have gone to a hospital, but it cost too much, so I chose instead a traditional village healer. She took a chicken, held it in front of me, and snapped both its legs. 'When this chicken walks again, you will be healed!' she declared, and then said a few incantations over my arm. She was right: a few days later, the chicken jumped up and walked, and my useless broken arm was healed that instant. Without even a *cast*.'

As I tried to fathom how an educated person like Oumar could leap from a reasoned critique of tradition to professing belief in a cruel and ridiculous practice, a woman's voice rang out in Fulani from the kitchen. He stood up. 'Ah. Come with me. My wife has made something you *won't* want to eat.'

He took me inside the side room and waved away the foul smoke emanating from a pot on a Buta-gas burner. His wife, sweaty and smiling and squatting next to the pot, pointed to its contents – a green and bubbling, vomitlike porridge called bouilli with ingredients said to include millet or rice, but with a stench that belied such an innocuous-sounding recipe. (I never found out what made it so noxious-smelling.) I had eaten bouilli in Chad and found it repellent, and wondered if I might not feel compelled to sample some now or risk offending his wife.

Oumar laughed. 'Now I know you would *never* eat this bouilli if I asked you! It's disgusting, isn't it?'

'Oh, no, I wouldn't say that.'

'Don't worry–I *know* you think it is. I'm not going to make you eat it.'

He led me back out into the courtyard and invited me to meet him the next evening at his school for a more leisurely talk, with no threat of bouilli. I accepted and left him and his wife to their meal. I resolved to query him the next day about his mix of traditionalist and progressive beliefs.

In the morning, Muhammad offered to take me to the Fulani village of Senissa, a few kilometers outside Djenné, to meet his friend the chief. Transport would pose a problem. For safety reasons, I decided not to take a communal baché (the name for pickup trucks outfitted in the rear with *baches*, or tarps, to provide shade for passengers): bachés were always overcrowded and invariably in rotten, even perilous, repair, and their drivers frequently sped whenever the roads were good. Where the roads were bad, the jolting could, and at times did, toss passengers out of the rear like loose sacks of grain. Muhammad smiled at my refusal, perhaps finding it persnickety, but he agreed to search out a baché that I could hire privately; this would assure us seats in the cabin and some authority over the driver.

Near the Great Mosque we found the only baché not in

communal service that morning: a destroyed Peugeot 404. No glass survived in its window frames; a dusty hole gaped where the dashboard dials should have been; its wire-mesh seats had lost all their upholstery; and to open the doors, one had to yank on wires protruding from where the handles had once been and then administer a few judicious kicks and encouraging punches to the sides. The owner was a bleary-eyed young man who appeared to be suffering from malnutrition and wore a frayed, snot-encrusted ski cap and almost transparent shred-remnants of a jacket and jeans.

It was a windy day, hence a dusty day. We rattled past the Great Mosque, clanged out of the center of town, and banged onto the dry Bani River floodplain, where the sun enflamed the Harmattan, transforming it into a skywide nebula of tawny glare that pained the eyes. I put on my sunglasses, but since we had no windshield, dust soon clogged their panes and I had to wipe them off every few minutes. The whole Sahel seemed to be blowing away, with starveling villagers clutching rags to their bodies as they trudged through the gritty gale, with bony cattle nosing dead weeds and looking up to moo in distress.

At the far edge of the plain, women with floppy babies strapped to their backs were bent over, harvesting golfball-size onions by hand, struggling to yank the runty vegetables free of the baked earth. Above them rose Senissa – a mess of banco houses on a patch of high ground. We drove up to their base. Muhammad and I got out at the mouth of an alley and started walking.

We shielded our eyes from the dust and sun. Babies cried in doorways, their faces caked in dirt. Boys stood about dazed and naked, remnants of their ill-cut umbilical cords poking out of distended bellies, their fingernails broken and black, their toenails eaten away by fungus. Now and then a stench of excrement hit us. Young women with sacks on their heads trudged past us, the pale soles on their bare feet cracked, horizontal tribal scars running beneath their eyes, their mouths ringed with what looked like blackened flesh.

'What's wrong with their mouths?' I asked, queasily regretting having come.

'They're slaves,' Muhammad said.

'Slaves?'

'Right. Farmers use ash to scar their daughters' mouths when they're young, which shows who they are, what status they have. Farmers are slaves to the nobility, the Fulani herders, who are the *true* Fulani. A slave can't marry a noble Fulani.'

'You're a noble Fulani?'

'Of course.'

'But how can there really still be slaves here?'

'Slavery is a matter of caste, not legal status. Once a Fulani slave, always a Fulani slave.'

An old man walked up to us in a ratty skirt, with a frayed college sweatshirt draped like a shawl over his head; the face peering out from beneath it was speckled with flecks of white beard, cheerful and gap-toothed and curious. He was the chief, and, smiling, he invited us to his house.

The chief was in his late seventies, but spry and lucid. His house consisted of a couple of banco rooms behind a low wall enclosing several goats and an inventory of rusted farm tools. All in all, he seemed as bad off as the other villagers.

We walked inside the main room and sat down on a mattress near the door. His wife was feeding a rice cake to a limp and sickly tot; another young woman was nursing an infant as she ate her lunch, scooping up gobs of rice with her bare hand and licking her palm clean of the grains. Scar tissue mottled the skin around her mouth. Apparently, the chief could be a slave, as long as he ruled slaves.

Children spied me from the street and came running inside, their faces smeared with mucus and drool, and grabbed at my hands and cheeks, shouting, '*Toubab! Toubab!*' (White man!). I couldn't help myself: I recoiled, pulling my hands out of their sticky grasp and lifting my face out of their reach.

Muhammad smacked the tots. 'Get away from him! Haven't you ever seen a *toubab* before!'

For the first time on this trip, the filth and distress I was seeing inclined me to thank my host and run. But I stayed. I felt ashamed of my weakness for the obvious reasons: I would leave, and they would remain. I felt agony at the thought that they lived this way always, and who in the outside world really cared?

The chief pulled out a box stuffed with postcards sent by previous foreign visitors, mostly European doctors and aid workers. As I examined them, a little boy came in. The boy's face was covered in drool and crud, as were his hands. He grabbed my hand and I flinched again; he reached up to touch my mouth and I pulled away. I felt terrible denying him affection, but no matter what I thought and how I reasoned, I couldn't help myself.

The chief saw me and smiled compassionately. He said in French, 'It's terrible here now. Since 1973 no drought has been this bad. Neither the Bani nor the Niger flows by here anymore, and they used to fill the plain outside the village. We had no harvest last year at all and are living off grain donated by the government.'

The boy began crying; the tot eating the rice cake joined him; the flies swarmed in and the wind picked up, blowing dust into the room. The chief arose. 'Why don't I show you the village?'

'Okay,' I said with feigned indifference, trying not to show how grateful I was to him for the surcease of misery he was proposing.

We walked outside and set off down the alleys.

'This is our brand-new mosque,' he said, pointing to a nondescript mud edifice.

'You really needed to spend money on a new mosque?' I asked.

'Everyone in the village contributed to it. We *have* to have a mosque. But you're right: we don't have enough money with this drought. Why, we couldn't even throw a party this year to circumcise our girls.'

The dust gusted into our faces and we squinted in unison, and I turned away from him. My gaze fell on an old woman curled up nearby in the dirt, a pile of bones in rags. I felt something bubbling in my gut: even thinking about female circumcision now made me feel ill. But I couldn't help asking, even though I knew the answer.

'So you circumcise girls in this village?'

'We circumcise them one *hundred* percent!' Muhammad answered. 'That's right: one *hundred* percent!'

'*Why?*'

'Because the Qur'an tells us to,' said the chief.

'No, it doesn't,' I said. 'Nowhere in the Qur'an does it say to circumcise girls.'

'Abraham had to do it to his son on God's command, so we do it. It's even written in the Old Testament.'

Muhammad seconded this: the Bible, he said, ordained the circumcision of both men and women.

'I'm sorry,' I said, 'but the Bible does *not* say girls should be circumcised. It says in Genesis, 'Every *man* child among you shall be circumcised . . . circumcise the flesh of your foreskin,' but as a sign of the covenant between Jews and God. It has nothing to do with other peoples. Girls don't have foreskins. You're completely wrong.'

'Well,' interjected Muhammad, 'we do it one *hundred* percent here. It is *obligatory*. It is our *tradition*, and so we do it.'

The chief pulled his sweatshirt shawl around his head. 'Okay, okay: it's not in the Qur'an. But it's in the Sunna.' (The Sunna is the accepted Islamic way of life, determined from the Qur'an and the sayings of the Prophet Muhammad.)

I would not relent. 'I'm sorry, but even the Sunna does not say girls have to be circumcised.'

'It says it's *preferable* to circumcise them, so we do it,' the chief replied. (As far as I knew, he was right about this.) He grinned as if remembering rollicking good times. 'Look, we throw a big party for the ritual. The parents invite all their relations, who bring gifts of rice and money. We get the girls and boys out of bed at five in the morning so they're still sleepy and don't know what's going on, and bring them to the village square. A blacksmith cuts the boys' – here he made a snipping motion – 'and a griot [a female folk singer or storyteller] cuts the girls.' Here he made a series of much more elaborate and ghastly carving and slicing motions that finished with a chop. He smiled again. 'As long as the griot doesn't make a mistake, the girls will be okay.'

'And if she does make a mistake?'

'Why, we take them to the clinic.' He chuckled at me, as though addressing an obtuse bumpkin who was arguing that the earth was flat – or at least arguing something in which he didn't believe.

'But some girls die as a result,' I said. 'Why do you do it if it isn't obligatory and they could die? *Why?*'

'The marabouts *tell* us to do it, that's why. We follow tradition here. If a girl wants to become a woman, she *must* be circumcised. If she's not circumcised, she'll run wild. This is our *tradition.*'

We reached our baché. I felt anger alternating with despair. The chief would make life in this miserable village even harder for half its inhabitants because he enacted without questioning a suggestion written in a text a thousand miles away, thirteen hundred years ago. How many lives had been ruined or ended across the Sahel on account of this 'suggestion' in the Sunna, or the misperception that God ordained circumcision for both sexes? Citing 'tradition' could never justify the practice or mollify my reaction to it. It was better for me just to leave.

Feeling like an outraged alien, wanting to quit the trip and abandon the Sahel, I thanked him and handed him a few francs for his hospitality. We drove, creaking and sputtering, back across the riverbed into town.

That evening I left Muhammad behind and went alone to see Oumar at his school, a cavernous low cement building at the edge of town giving onto the floodplain. After visiting the chief, I needed to talk to Oumar. I wanted to express my alienation and see what he had to say about it. I needed to resolve my reactions to Sahelian rituals by talking to Sahelians themselves.

Oumar invited me inside his classroom to have a seat. We chatted about why he came here in his off-hours: the school gave him a place to collect his thoughts away from his family. After a while, I told him about my meeting with the chief.

'Well, the chief has it wrong,' Oumar said, his face showing what I took to be sympathy for me. 'Religion,' he said, 'hasn't got anything to do with this. The Qur'an does *not* tell us to circumcise a girl. Our marabouts used to say that circumcising men was a matter of hygiene, and girls a matter of religion. We now know better.'

I was relieved. Where tradition was concerned, although he

condoned harm to chickens, he was reasonable enough not to advocate mutilating members of his own kind. But to my puzzlement, some sort of disgust began screwing up his features.

'You see,' he said, 'a *bilakorou* is, well, how can I put it?' He shifted in his seat.

'What's a *bilakorou*?'

'Oh, sorry. An uncircumcised woman. A *bilakorou* is a . . . a *disgrace*, lower than . . . than' – his voice thickened – 'lower than a *donkey*.'

'What!'

'We circumcise girls because of the dire consequences that result when we *don't*. No one but *no one* would marry a *bilakorou* because she would be filthy and emotional. They must cut off her thing or she can't control herself and she'll be no good for family life.' His voice trembled. 'She would be lower than a *donkey!*'

'But the other day you said that blindly following tradition is no good.'

'This is a matter of identity, not tradition. To be a true Fulani, a woman *must* be cut. We will *never* abandon this ritual. To abandon it would mean abandoning our identity. No matter where a Fulani is, in Mali or America or Europe, even if he has had an American passport for ten years, he *must* circumcise his daughters. You see how bad the drought is?'

'Yes. So what?'

'Well, we say it's bad because we're abandoning our traditions. It's a vicious circle: the drought means people are too poor for the circumcision, which means the ritual is abandoned and the drought gets worse. God is getting angry, you see. We need to do *more* circumcising around here, not less. We have a saying, 'No matter how long a log sits in the water it will never become a crocodile.' A Fulani woman is a Fulani wherever she is, and she *must* be circumcised.'

'Look, aren't there foreign organizations working here to stop this?'

'Oh, them. They can teach us new farming techniques and all that, and give us aid, but don't let them dare try to stop us from circumcising our daughters. We will *never* abandon the practice.'

'But have you ever thought about the agony it causes the girl? Being sliced up with a razor or piece of bottle glass? By a griot who doesn't have any idea of medicine or hygiene?'

'The pain is good for them: it tells them they've passed from one stage in life to another.'

'So you were circumcised, I take it, and learned from your pain?'

'Of course I was circumcised. But my parents were educated, so they had mine done in a hospital. I don't remember a thing.'

Frustrated, I changed the subject as a prelude to parting, and soon we said goodbye.

The next day the sun rose hot and stoked the Harmattan, infusing the windblown dust clouds with fiery light. Following trails across the floodplains, ox- and donkey-drawn carts rolled slowly toward the square beneath the Great Mosque, loaded with Fulani and Bozo villagers. It was the weekly market day. People would arrive from as far afield as Burkina Faso to sell their wares here and buy their supplies.

Muhammad and I arrived early at the market to watch. Near the square a Fulani woman in her thirties stood by a jeweler's stand assaying a bracelet of blue and red beads. She presented a magnificent sight: tall and long-necked, she had fastened her shoulder-length, cornrowed hair with silvery spangles; a necklace of gold cowries on a leather cord hung from her collar; abundant purple robes lay draped over her chocolate-colored arms and turquoise tassels hung from her sleeves; and she wore gold rings in her nose and ears. She delivered her commands to the merchant with queenly aplomb: she found this bracelet unsatisfactory (Muhammad translated for me), and what else had this lowly jeweler brought for her to try on?

Looking at her, Muhammad waxed proud. 'The Fulani noblewomen are beauties. Their skin is naturally clear and rich-toned. The Songhai are also beautiful.'

'You're right. But it must be hard having such long hair with all this dust around.'

'That isn't really her hair. It's a hairpiece, and it comes from the Arab countries.'

Ahead of us, the Qur'anic-school toddlers, so covered in dust that in their ash-colored smocks they resembled ghosts, fought over rice cakes a merchant was handing out. Other boys pushed carts as big as they were or blew dust from merchants' wares and tidied things up.

'The merchants adopt their favorite students and treat them like sons. It's common here. That boy you see there will get a meal and a few francs for helping him out.'

We walked on. Fulani nobles dressed in blue or green caftans were arriving, dragging goats and calves. Most sported straw hats with leather cones and tassels, variations of which announced their status with a precision lost on me; others wore red and white kaffiyehs; and the poorer ones had on coarse cotton turbans dyed with indigo.

Just beneath the ramparts of the Great Mosque, a Fulani woman squatted and sprinkled water over cola leaves, on which she then arranged an assortment of magenta-colored nuts; girls irrigated piles of carrots and jumbo-size tomatoes and onions. Bozo fisherwomen lugged baskets of smoked perch to sell to buyers from Bamako and Ségou, where fish is a delicacy; another woman shooed flies off pungent balls of sumbala bark, which could be mixed with onion and pepper to make a sauce for fish; men sat in the shade by balls of si, a sort of butter made from a tree; a calabash merchant arrayed her merchandise from San; a seller of millet sifted her golden grain; a man presided over mounds of green tobacco that could be chewed or smoked.

Everywhere we went we saw surprising evidence of the region's bounty, drought or no, both natural and man-made. There were piles of coconuts from Sikasso, baguettes from local bakeries, and what looked like stacks of logs that were actually raw yams. In the far part of the market Chinese sandals and Nigerian medicines enjoyed strong demand, and a hide merchant sold goatskin wallets into which he had sewed tiny pieces of paper bearing verses of the Qur'an for good luck. There were dates from Gao and Algeria and piles of glittering gum-arabic crystals strewn over dark blue cloth. Beneath awnings pots of oil bubbled with farani dough balls; pubescent girls wandered about with trays of bananas on their heads, emitting plaintive cries. Just off the square, a roguish-looking teenage boy threatened a terrified if enchanted circle of children with a six-foot boa constrictor, drumming up business for his panoply of traditional powders that were supposed to cure malaria, colds, dry skin, infertility, and impotency.

The crowd multiplied. The din from the mule carts and human carts and bellowing oxen and shouting children deafened; the incense burned by spice merchants mingled with the scent of urine and dung and clouds of dust to rasp at nostrils and hinder breathing; the clamor of Songhai, Fulani, Bambara, Bobo, Sarkolé, and Bozo, all languages of Mali, mixed with shouts in More and Dioula from Burkina Faso and confused the ear. Adding to the clamor were the cries of a crazy woman, who was wrapped in a filthy robe, with unwashed hair. She rooted about in refuse heaps, searching for a meal.

'She's a Burkinabé' (from Burkina Faso), said Muhammad. 'They say she walked here from Burkina Faso. People take care of her, though. They give her leftovers.'

Little in this market resembled anything I had seen before in the Sahel; much came from beyond Mali's borders. These borders were, of course, the creations of colonials. Yet at least here, unlike elsewhere in Africa, the borders did little to divide the peoples within them.

Nor did much here originate in the West. This market embodied a truth about Africa: no matter how much globalization affects the developing world, this one continent is in many ways untouched. That seemed positive at first, but then, probably every woman around me had suffered mutilation, and Fulani men and women both were still divided into castes of slaves and nobles. Isolation lets the good traditions survive, but also the bad.

# 18

# DEATH IN THE SUN

Just outside Djenné I boarded a bus to take me 225 miles southwest to Bamako. Away from Djenné, the narrow, raised, two-lane tarmac down which we rolled cut through terrain that greened appreciably, with grass sprouting through ever more fertile soil, and scrub brush thickening into groves. About a hundred miles farther to the south began the tropical regions of Mali, with fruit trees and forests, vegetation that would eventually coalesce into the mahogany and rubber jungles of Liberia and spread out into the cocoa plantations of Côte d'Ivoire. Liberia! Côte d'Ivoire! These names evoke Africa's promising past and failure-ridden present. Founded by freed American slaves in 1847 and once amazingly stable, Liberia since 1980 had slid into a cycle of coups and civil war; Côte d'Ivoire had been West Africa's most prosperous and conflict-free country until the military takeover of 1999 and the outbreak of civil war in 2002. Now and then the Western media reports on these debacles, but mostly, as hundreds of thousands of people die and millions flee their homes, they turn away.

Back on the highway to Bamako, my bus slowed. On the steep southern slope of the roadbed just ahead of us, a young woman was struggling to her knees, with twigs in her hair, clutching a baby. She raised her arm to wave at us and fell back into the grass. Behind her, blue and yellow caftans and blouses were scattered in the grass and trees. We all turned our heads and puzzled at the sight, and the driver pulled over.

The sun showered the scene in noontime glare, and there was silence. Some fifteen yards beyond the woman, a baché lay upside down between two acacias, its windshield gone and its grille caved in, its wheels spinning slowly, steam pouring from its engine. With its every surface dented and decrepit in a way that suggested decades of wear, the baché must have been in scarcely better repair before the accident than the wreck that had taken me to Senissa. I turned and looked out the rear window. Fifty yards behind us, a wild crescent of skid marks hinted at what had happened: the baché had been speeding when a front tire had blown out and sent the truck careening across the opposing lane to fly off the raised road and travel some forty feet through the air. Judging by the trail of wreckage the baché had left, it crashed down into the thorny branches of the trees, disgorging the human cargo huddled in its rear and then overturning and rolling for some distance.

Our bus driver and his assistants, along with a French woman carrying a doctor's bag, got off and scampered down the roadbed toward what looked to be crumpled clothes in the shade of the acacias. A round of shouting in Bambara and Fulani and French followed, as the men seized the bloodied bodies and began dragging them up the hills, stumbling as they did so, to the voluble distress of the French doctor, who wanted no one touched before examination. The woman who had waved to us sat dazed on the slope, a cut on her forehead dripping blood, her baby motionless in her arms.

Another baché, this one empty, slowed down and stopped. Under the direction of the doctor, who ordered that no one else among us intervene or move any of the injured, the driver and his helpers started carrying the victims up the roadbed. The faces of the first ones were blank, their eyes clenched shut, their ears and mouths dripping blood. Their caftans and jackets were speared with branches and thorns, their limbs limp. The next ones had gashed thighs and lacerated backs and head wounds but were groggily alive. Soon the hot tarmac was covered with writhing and still bodies amid blood puddles. Nothing but the commands of the doctor could be heard, as well as shouted answers of '*Oui, madame.*'

A little while later, the doctor ordered three or four victims – those with clenched eyes and bloody ears – placed in the back of the just-arrived baché. Its driver and a couple of other men tossed them aboard and slammed the back door, and then drove off. Other victims were hauled or led aboard our bus.

We started up again. Just a few seats ahead of me, the doctor set about snipping away trouser legs and shirts, exposing ripped flesh, binding limbs with tourniquets torn from donated T-shirts, and bandaging cuts with dressings made from pieces of shawls, now and then raising her head to demand bottled water; this she used to clean the wounds. One man's buttocks had been split, the backs of his legs opened up, and blood was gushing onto the floor. He stared ahead in shock as she scissored away his torn sirwal to get at his wound.

I looked down at the man tossed in the aisle by my feet. He was hollow-cheeked from malnutrition, as were so many Malians. Sprawled on his side in a cheap, frayed tracksuit, shoeless, one arm tossed up over his head, he reposed with blood seeping from his mouth and ears, grass and twigs in his hair. His eyes were shut tight, as if against the sun. His blood pooled in the aisle, and passengers pulled their bags out of the way. He might have been twenty-five years old, but his dry skin, withered from a life of out-door labor, made him look older.

'Please, doctor!' cried the woman in front of me in French, pointing to him, 'this man is in a bad way and needs your attention now!'

The doctor paused in her work and stepped over. She put her forefinger to his jugular and confirmed the obvious. '*Désolée. Il est mort. Désolée.*' She returned to her bandaging.

The bus rolled and rocked on the worsening road.

'*C'est la vie,*' said the man next to me, sighing. 'What do you think could have happened?'

'The driver was going too fast and a tire blew out. There were skid marks.'

'Could an accident like that happen in Europe?'

'Maybe, but there might not have been so many victims, because probably people wouldn't have been allowed to ride in the back.'

He shook his head. 'Well, I feel sorry for the driver, but it wasn't his fault. *C'est la vie.* It was Fate.'

For my fellow passenger, as for so many people I had met on this trip, Fate ruled and man submitted. (More typically, others would replace Fate with God, whose 'decisions' would always be wise, for the best, and therefore to be accepted without demur.) Fate absolved the driver of responsibility for the death and injury he caused with his speeding, absolved the checkpoint soldiers who surely, for a bribe, let his overloaded and unsafe vehicle pass, and even absolved of recklessness the passengers, who, in a better world, might have refused to travel in such a dangerous truck. For my companion the event merited some maudlin rumination but nothing more, and no lessons were to be learned.

I glanced again at the dead man. I imagined that he had begun his day as I had, fully expecting, if nothing else, to live to see the sun set. His had been a short and hard life in a hot, dusty country, and then, without warning, he found himself hurled face-first into thorns and sun-scorched rocks. He probably had known more hardship in a day or two than I could experience in a year, or ten years. If I died here there would be inquiries, an embassy investigation, stories in the papers. His death would prompt no legal action or press coverage, if it would be recorded at all; it appeared to be the ultimate nihilistic event, death standing for nothing but itself, just as the deaths of millions across Africa in civil wars, from AIDS and from malaria and other diseases, seem to stand for nothing, and are now rarely given more than a few lines in the backs of major papers.

But this perception of death originates from a worldview that implicitly assumes the primacy of the rich (and white), the worthlessness of the poor (and black), and the discrete nature of each group. The discrepancy between the wealth of the West and the poverty of Africa constitutes an inequality largely accepted as intrinsic to the continent, an inequality that few in the West dwell on or spend time lamenting; after all, don't we all have our problems, and can Africa ever change? But it helps foster differing states of consciousness, modes of interpretation, and philosophies (the guiding role accorded to God or Fate, for example) that prompt some people to actions that are incomprehensible or unacceptable to others (reckless driving being one of them). In the Sahel, inequality and poverty spark revolt, cheapen life, and lead to bloodshed; they may someday be construed by the enlightened there as vile injustices wrought by exploitative outsiders and motivate acts of terrorism, just as in dan Fodio's day they provided justification for jihad. All indices show the material gap between Africa and the West is widening, and the bloodshed- and disease-related deaths on the continent are increasing in number. So, what can we expect from the future?

As populations grow, the desert expands, food and water become even scarcer, and the confrontation between the West and the Islamic world intensifies, whatever peace existing now in the Sahel will probably turn out to be a lull before a regional apocalypse, the course of which is easy to imagine because in places it has already begun: emaciated hordes fleeing south from the encroaching desert, swamping settled communities and provoking their ire and violent resistance; renewed civil war; the further spread of Islamic and probably even Christian extremism (a precedent exists for the latter in Uganda, where the 'Lord's Resistance Army' purports to be fighting to establish a state based in Biblical precepts, which it somehow hopes to accomplish by the widespread kidnapping, enslavement, and rape of children); the infiltration of foreign terrorist groups and criminal gangs; and the rise of Western-backed dictators who promise to stamp them out. With nowhere else to go, millions of Sahelians, including large numbers of the sick and starving, would flee north, to North Africa and Europe. Perhaps NATO would begin patrolling the seas around West Africa to interdict refugee ships (as European states do now around their coasts). Whatever, the result would be the same: misery and rage and death for the Sahelians, a barricaded Europe, and vast territories available for anti-Western terrorism.

We drove into Bla (the next town), lumbered around its dirt alleys, pulled up to the hospital, and honked. From the doorway orderlies appeared, without stretchers. They grabbed the injured who were too weak to walk and carried them off the bus by their ankles and elbows, ignoring their gasps and cries and grimaces of agony, as well as the remonstrations of the French doctor. The dead man next to me they hauled out and tossed by the side of the road.

We pulled out of the hospital lot and returned to the main road to continue our trip. Only around sunset would we descend onto a wooded, rocky plateau toward Bamako, where a lone sky-scraper rose above leafy expanses and spreading shantytowns intersected by the serpentine, eternally sluggish Niger River.

# 19

## *MISÈRE!*

Huddled in a basin that traps heat and smog, Bamako is a wretched grid of dirt roads and sun-warped tarmacs lined with hovels of corrugated steel and rusted wire and rotting wood, overlooked by a scattering of Soviet-style concrete behemoths recalling Mali's ill-fated dalliance with the now-defunct superpower that sought to promote itself as liberator of the Third World. Rattling and jolting along in one of the city's collapsing taxis, stirring stenches from open sewers, you penetrate crowds of beggars and idle youths and hustlers; your driver honks to scatter pushcarts and their panicked proprietors; you disperse columns of women laboring bug-eyed and sweaty under sacks of sorghum or jugs of water from neighborhood wells.

The chants of the mendicants, the hyena-honks of taxis, the grunts of the women, and the oaths shouted by angry drivers all compose a cacophony of urban distress as grievous as it is vain. Vain because beyond the Sahel the voices of these people cannot be heard; their stories will never be told. They are born to live poor and die hard, leaving nothing behind; their misery, once the subject of ideologies of liberation and revolt, now inspires no one. 'The Wretched of the Earth,' Frantz Fanon called people like them in another time, but he is dead, and his oeuvre, passé. However, in defiance of intellectual fashion the Wretched remain, orphaned of Western defenders, ever leaner, ever hungrier, increasingly angry, serving their sentences, awaiting an emancipator, a commander. For now, poverty and despair banish thoughts of revolution among these masses, but later, when a savior appears, he will exploit their suffering to create an army of the enraged that will swamp coalitions of the willing, breach the walls, and storm the West. Or perhaps a few determined fanatics or seekers of martyrdom will take terrorist action on their behalf; after the carnage, it will seem impossible to fathom how such an abyss could have been allowed to widen between the north and south, between the whites and the rest, and how we could have tolerated, in a continent neighboring Europe, the deaths of millions from hunger and disease, and the radicalization of the survivors.

The French have a word that expresses more succinctly than anything in English the combined notions of extreme poverty, suffering, and impotence: *misère*. At least some of Bamako's *misère* stems from one objective factor: a population explosion. Little more than a village of 6,000 in the early nineteenth century, by 1960 Bamako had grown to 120,000, and today it has passed half a million. The explosion continues. Malian women bear an average of 7 children in a lifetime, a parturitional exploit outdone only by the 7.5 of Nigériennes. This birthrate results in a countrywide population increase of 3 percent a year, while the GDP growth rate lags behind at 1.2 percent. One conclusion presents itself: if things are bad now, they will get worse, *much* worse, in the future. And looking at Bamako or any number of big cities in Africa, one feels the most acute dread: the cities bear the brunt of population growth, just as they incubate disease and ideologies of revolt and resistance.

Is there hope in 'development projects'? Mali has been one of the most 'aided' countries on earth. For four decades now, France, the World Bank, the International Monetary Fund, the European Union, and the United States have subsidized Mali's *misère* – and they show no signs of stopping. Foreign aid makes up a quarter of the country's GDP and totals roughly $500 million annually. What have aid workers accomplished here over the past forty years? There is no satisfactory answer, as a glance at, or whiff of, Bamako will tell you. One thing is sure: with few exceptions, where development agencies were decades ago, there they are now – unless, as is often the case, their 'host countries' have slid into such economic collapse and political anarchy that aid workers are forced to flee aboard the warships and aircraft sent by their home governments to evacuate them. Whatever, the ruins of Bamako embody a truth: most foreign aid perpetuates corruption and malfeasance, discourages countries from adopting necessary reforms (for example, switching from the cultivation of cash crops, such as tobacco and cotton, introduced by former colonial masters, to food crops), and renders irrelevant notions of government accountability vis-à-vis its electorate, if an electorate exists. Funded from abroad, an aided government need seek no legitimacy from its citizens, who do not pay its bills.

State functionaries and bureaucrats (the overwhelming beneficiaries of most foreign aid) make up the largest part of Africa's tiny middle and upper classes, whose Western-educated youth express aspirations and an ethos that are, not surprisingly, Western and even progressive. Soon after arriving, I looked up a representative of this elite – a friend of a friend of mine, a twenty-four-year-old photographer named Ouassa, the daughter of a former Malian chief of staff. We met one evening at her father's villa. Sitting on an embroidered sofa in front of a widescreen Japanese television, I might have been in Paris or Berlin, the only reminders of Mali being the muggy air seeping in from the Niger and the scissor-legged anopheles mosquitoes whining around my ears.

Ouassa had the sculpted face and svelte figure for which Malians are famous throughout West Africa. A stonewashed denim dress brushed the tops of her slender calves; leather sandals encased her petite feet; and from behind glasses with smart gold frames, chestnut brown eyes peered out sympathetically. Her voice was sensuously hoarse, her banter dreamy, eerily plaintive, and her greetings strikingly repetitive. How was I, she asked, and how was I doing with '*la journée? et la famille? et la santé? et la fatigue? et la journée? et la famille? et la santé? et la* . . .' One did not

answer each inquiry but responded simultaneously with an echoing litany of languid verbiage, interspersed with '*merci, merci, ça
va, merci, oui, merci, et vous?*' – all the while nodding sympathetically. Salutations lasted until one party asked a non-formulaic
question or, as was more likely, the equally prolix act of parting
began. I concluded that this ritual must have been inherited from
North African Arabs – at least I had encountered the same in
Morocco and the Western Sahara. Its purpose was the same on
both sides of the desert: not to ascertain the true state of a collo-
cutor's health, family, etc., but to commiserate and comfort, for in
Mali, as in North Africa, no one dared assume life was going well,
and complaints were reserved for God alone. In her greetings, at
least, Ouassa had retained her Malianness.

Ouassa and I took a taxi out to a nightclub where a friend of
hers was singing in a band. Darkness now hid the capital's *misère*.
Cooking fires on the corners cast ovals of orange on chatting clicks
of sidewalk-dwellers; the neon lights of cafés in the center tinted
the dirt roads and wrecked asphalt with impressionistic shades of
blue and green; and a huge moon glowed red and primeval over
all, reminding us that the bush was near, and that Africa was a
place of astonishing beauty, at least outside its cities.

The nightclub at first seemed like a Western parody. Its interior was done up in red leatherette; its lighting was Age of
Aquarius ultraviolet; its musicians wore Shaftian leisure suits and
Stevie Wonder sunglasses. Ouassa nodded greetings to her friend
on the mirrored stage, who raised his chin and crooned out
'Feelings' with a nasal Bambara twang that set the speakers crack-
ling with excessive decibels and false notes. Ouassa gazed
admiringly at him, enchanted by the lyrics in the unfamiliar language with a cachet far cooler than that of French, which is now
out of favor (if still in use) among young and hip Malians.

Wanting to plug my ears to 'Feelings,' trying to ignore the
sticky grip of the leatherette, and noticing the black-light glow of
the pale Sahelian dust on my dark shirt, I felt nonetheless unex-
pectedly relaxed and at home. I don't deny it: it was talking to
Ouassa that set me at ease. Between us there was no tension, no
gaping cultural divide, for her family's wealth and status had

permitted her a Western education. She was creating, doing something she was excited about – a luxury, in Africa – which I could understand and appreciate. She was a product of her class, almost as different from the Wretched outside as I was.

'I'm young and I want to exercise my profession,' she said in French, after ordering a cup of tea. 'I don't want to get married right now. You see, I've spent a lot of time with whites – with French people, that is – and I've adopted their way of thinking.'

'I didn't know there were many female photographers in Africa.'

'There aren't. It's been terribly hard to make a living. How many times have I been stiffed! How many times have I shot a wedding and then been paid five thousand francs instead of the twenty thousand we agreed on! I've quit doing a lot of work. Men just don't take me seriously here. They say it's not a woman's job.'

To make a living, she told me, she now sends her photographs to a friend in Paris, who sells them there in a gallery with some success.

A waitress brought Ouassa her tea and spoke to her in French with an unfamiliar accent. Ouassa asked her where she was from. She stiffened up and answered the Ivory Coast. She had reason for apprehension: in the past few years, Malians had come under attack in the Ivory Coast, where the regime had proclaimed a nationalistic policy of *Ivoirité* (in the coinage of the country's president) that incited Ivoirians to blame their economic problems on guest workers, many of whom were from Mali. As a result, thousands of Malians had fled home, and resentment of Ivoirians was running high in Bamako.

I waited for Ouassa to reply to the waitress, wondering, with some trepidation, if her progressiveness would turn out to be a veneer, as had the progressiveness of two of her upper-class friends earlier that evening at a café. Then, I had asked their names and where they were from. It turned out they didn't know each other.

'Ah ha!' said one, hearing the ethnically distinct name of the other, and leaning back and taking stock of him. 'You're my slave!'

The 'slave' chuckled, looking uncomfortable.

'Why do you call him your slave?' I asked.

'Because his people were always the slaves of my people. This is the way it was.'

'But if they're not now, why bring it up?'

Said the 'slave' in defense of his 'master,' 'Oh, it's a matter of *cousinage* [literally, 'cousinhood,' but in this case, 'relationship']. Why are you bothered?'

'I don't like what the word *slave* represents. Aren't people in Africa divided enough as it is? Do you have to bring painful history into things now?'

'This word is in our blood. It causes no offense. Really, I'm not bothered.'

'He's even *happy* to be a slave,' said his 'master.'

The 'slave' frowned and looked away. He would not, even free and even now, contradict his 'master.'

Ouassa had listened impassively to this exchange. No doubt, I assumed, she also accepted the master-slave relationship as something immutable. But when I came out of my musings in the nightclub I found her smiling and welcoming the waitress to Bamako.

'There's so much racism in Côte d'Ivoire now,' she said. 'But you have a very beautiful country. I've traveled there myself.' The waitress smiled back, and they chatted about Bamako's elegant club scene.

The singer crooned through the last verse of 'Feelings.' Ouassa asked me where I had been in West Africa. She sighed on hearing the names Timbuktu, Gao, Djenné, Ayorou. 'Oh, the bush! *Ça va un peu la-bas*. The people out there aren't really civilized. They circumcise their daughters.'

'They don't do this now in Bamako?'

She turned away her eyes. 'Oh, most still do. They don't care what girls suffer, as long as they follow tradition. Only recently have a few people on the high levels begun thinking for themselves and stopping the practice. Among the enlightened, boys are circumcised but not girls. My sister and her husband wouldn't circumcise their daughters.'

I wanted to ask if she had suffered the ritual herself, but felt to do so would be improper. That possibility pained me: she was soft and sensuous, cultured and talented. I wondered if being mutilated and deprived of libido could damage the artistic drive – or would it spark rage and alter consciousness in a way that could make for the strongest creative energy ever?

The music grew too loud to talk. The band moved on to 'Hey Jude.' They looked straight at me through their sunglasses as they performed, taking obvious pride in singing Western songs for a Westerner, and I did not deny them attention or applause.

# 20

# THE COAST OF SLAVES

The handless clock on the railway station's belfry should have told me something about how the Bamako-Dakar Express would run. But I had no time to think about it as I pushed through the grasping crowds of beggars and pickpockets throng-ing the neem-canopied rue Baba Diarra to reach the fenced-off sanctuary of the station grounds. I dashed into the station build-ing, a cavernous structure that resembled a New England church, made of chipped red brick but streaked with soot as if damaged by fire, and ran smack into a motionless queue of fifty or so sweat-ing and stolid Malians waiting in front of the ticket window. To my astonishment, they parted and waved me to the front of the line, straight to the ticket seller, a safari-suited fellow reclining in his chair, studying the ceiling with the pensive look of a philosopher-king on his glistening face. For some no doubt arcane bureaucratic reason he was not selling tickets to the people in front of his window. On seeing me, however, he leaned forward and smiled broadly.

I asked him for a ticket to Dakar. He sung the praises of the Express, of its first-class sleeper, air-conditioned and of European provenance, the closest thing to luxury travel one could experi-ence in West Africa. He told me – and here he made eminent sense – that as the main train of one of the few railroads in the Sahel, the Express was a matter of national prestige for both

Senegal and Mali; it would not be allowed to run like some bush-battered baché. So, I came away expecting to depart, for once, if not necessarily on time, then at least on the scheduled day, and to reach my destination without undue risk to life or sanity – wildly grandiose assumptions for the Sahel in any other circumstances.

The next morning, under a hammering shower of sunlight portending the hottest day I had seen so far, I lugged my bag into the station lounge and patted away the perspiration, somewhat incredulous and certainly mournful: this was the last time I would be going anywhere in the Sahel. It was now late February, and the change in weather signaled an ending of both season and ordeal (I had chosen to travel in the cool dry season) and brought on nostalgia for the people I had met since landing in N'Djamena. Where was Mahamat now? Was the peace holding in Fada and Faya Largeau? Had the shehu's secretary waited for me to leave Maiduguri so he could have Ezekiel fired? At that possibility I shuddered with nervous guilt and turned away from my reminiscing.

Ahead was Dakar, a well-off city of sea breezes and haunting music and colonial-era villas. I forefelt the relief it would offer: there, for the first time in months, I would be beyond the reach of the Harmattan, able to breathe air free of the rasping dust with pervasive grains that had now browned almost all my belongings and, I sensed, worked their way into every alveolus of my lungs. But Dakar reminded me that further disorientation awaited. From there I would fly to Paris, back into the rainy, foggy European winter. From France, a month later, I was scheduled to leave for snowbound Moscow. I grieved for the demise of what had been, after all, a discrete stage in my life, replete with kind and generous people whom I would probably never see again.

This was so painful to contemplate, and such a recurrent feature of my peripatetic life, that I wondered if it would not be better to forswear traveling and cleave to the people and places I knew well. The years were passing, each one adding to a gallery of faces I missed, faces of people whom, if I could ever convene them, I would have no way of reconciling in my life, so disparate were their nationalities, religions, homelands, and languages. Only my wife in Moscow was a constant.

Thus regretting the trip's end, I walked toward the exit for the railway platform, but there the station guard told me that – could it have been otherwise? – there would be a delay of 'only' nine hours. Departure, he said, was 'certain' at six-thirty that evening. I sat down, took out a book, and waited.

At six-thirty there was still no train, and the deadening heat of the long day mingled with a pungent humidity to discourage even the beggars from their chants, the hawkers from their rounds. I asked about the new delay, but the guard, now slumped in a sweaty heap on a platform bench, seemed reluctant to suggest that a train of any kind would ever leave this station, and the strange absence of passengers confirmed his reticence. Rainy Paris and snowy Moscow all at once looked impossibly far away and infinitely desirable. I wondered if I should not just hire a Jeep to make the six-hundred-mile trip to Dakar. But I renounced that option, which would mean a two- or three-day ride, taking survival supplies and possibly even a guard. The road between the capitals of the two countries had fallen into such disrepair that it would be quicker, easier, and safer, if not cheaper, to fly to Paris and from there to Dakar. So I would just do as Africans would do: sit down and wait, and ask no more questions.

Two hours later, as streetlamps cast milky, mosquito-dotted orbs of light into the humid dark and people began wandering onto the platform, an ensemble of coach and sleeping cars, ancient and malodorous, hissed and clanked into the station, dragged by a grimy diesel engine. As the train squealed to a halt, I puzzled over the three or four small, lightweight cattle cars (loaded with sheep) situated between the heavy engine and the even heavier passenger cars. My childhood experience as a model railroader told me that when you put light cars between the engine and heavy cars, trains derailed on curves. No one shared my concern, however. I joined the crush by the car doorways and fought my way up the steps. Immediately, once I was aboard, copious sweat spouted from my pores: the sun had beaten down on the cars all day, and they had soaked up enough heat to melt wax and addle brains.

To welcome passengers aboard, the engineer cut the lights, leaving people scrimmaging toward their places in a sweaty-limbed, curse-filled blackness. I had a flashlight, though, so I found my cabin quickly and settled in. It was not a 'luxury cabin.' The entire car appeared to have been rescued from a railway junkyard – but a junkyard in Europe: signs and warnings and instructions were written in French, German, and Italian.

A jolly-looking man of around fifty, half dressed in some sort of uniform, came waddling down the dark corridor, humming. The conductor. I asked him when we were due to arrive in Dakar. He would not hazard a guess either, though 'certainly,' he said, not within the scheduled thirty-six hours. On hearing that, I sat down, depressed, on my bunk, but it puffed dust and I jumped up again – it was too hot and filthy to sit on. I walked out into the aisle and stared out the window, and waited. The heat was dizzying, and, despite the dark, it wasn't abating.

Somewhere around eleven o'clock the electricity blinked on, there were whistles and the screech-slamming of doors, and the train shuddered into motion. We were soon rolling out of the station and into utterly dark bidonvilles on Bamako's outskirts.

I returned to my cabin to go to sleep and lay down on the bunk, resigned to suffering. Its sagging mattress precluded comfort, as did the heat and the moths fluttering around the inextinguishable ceiling light. When it seemed nothing could get worse, we hit the open Sahel and in through the windows poured clouds of tawny dust.

Lying on my bunk, I drifted into a heat-induced delirium of remembrance and rumination. Though I had passed through five countries, I remembered tribes and dead kingdoms and antagonistic religious groups and individuals but not nations, because there were no nations: nowhere in the Sahel did ethnic or linguistic territories correspond to national frontiers. All of the Sahel's states were the bastard creations of French and British colonial rule, with the emirs and sultans who were once the frontmen for foreign domination now providing the same service for shaky federal governments in the capitals.

We look at a map of West Africa and see borders with country names, some sort of order. For Sahelians, these borders are the walls of the houses the colonial powers built. But why have they not reconfigured their walls to suit their own interests in the forty-plus years they have had of independence? In fact, over the past two decades walls have been coming down across the continent, but hardly as the result of studied consideration and mutual agreement; a bloody war for resources (diamonds and other minerals, gold, and oil) has been raging, as have battles newly intense over religion and ethnic origin. (To wit: the Tuareg rebellion in Mali and Niger; the mineral-motivated Libyan invasion of Chad; Chad's multitudinous ethnic and Muslim-Christian conflicts, supported by Sudan and Libya.) But where peoples live intermingled, as they do in the Sahel, could satisfactory borders for modern nation-states be determined on the basis of ethnic or religious criteria? And in the twenty-first century, outside the framework of the nation-state, could political stability be achieved, economic prosperity ensue, investment flow from abroad, and standards of health and education improve?

No. But who was asking these questions? Most of the Sahelians I met fumed about ethnic and class rivalries and religious differences. ('Most people here don't even understand what citizenship and statehood mean,' Mustafa had told me in Kano. 'We are at heart tribal and religious more than Nigerian.') The differences, given the Sahel's history, were inevitable, but it troubled me that I found so little desire to overcome them.

Just after dawn the next day, I awoke in Senegal in bizarre comfort – my dusty skin was dry, and I was cool. We were about a hundred miles east of Dakar, rocking along beneath gloriously cloudy skies, with wonderfully chilly air pouring in through my window. Since I had covered some four thousand miles without seeing a single drop of rain, the mere sight of cumuli enchanted me, and I jumped down from my bunk and walked out into the aisle, savoring my luck, to get a better look. I poked my head through the corridor window, into the breeze, on which I hoped to detect salty harbingers of the Atlantic.

There was a thud and a bang, a nauseating lurch. I caught my balance on the curtain rod. The train bumped and rumbled to a stop.

Silence. Wind blew sand in hissing waves against the side of the car, and the clouds rolled low and heavy just above the trees.

About ten minutes passed before I noticed railway workers on the ground, streaming toward the front of the train. I went over to the car door and jumped down to land on the soft grainy earth, and, shivering in the cool, fell in with them. Sheep were bleating. Sure enough, one of the light cars in the front of the train had derailed on a curve.

I stood and stared at the crooked axles and wheels. The conductor came over and stared at the mess with me.

'Well,' I said, 'what are you going to do?'

'This is no problem. The engineer has already radioed Tambacounda. They're sending the repair car.'

No problem? I looked back at the rest of the train. From doorways here and there, passengers were tossing their bags down onto the sand and jumping out, and arguments were breaking out among them about which way to go, with railway workers slogging toward them, yelling at them to reboard.

A soldier was passing by us, holding his knapsack to his shoulder and striding south. I asked him where he was going.

'To the road. It's three kilometers from here.'

'You don't want to wait for the repair car?'

'*Repair car?* Don't believe them. Escape while you can. There's no water on this train. When the sun gets hot and that car doesn't come, everyone will be in trouble, *real* trouble.' He hurried ahead to catch up with his buddies.

'What do you think?' I asked the conductor, as wind whisked sand in our faces and the clouds seemed to lower still more.

'Ignore that man,' he warned me. 'As a railway employee I'm obliged to advise you to remain on the train. We're in the bush, you know.'

Soon a spirit of pure *sauve qui peut* came to reign. More and more soldiers jumped down and marched in anxious twos and threes toward where the road should be, and almost all the passengers were climbing out and looking around. As I wondered what to do, from the direction of a distant straw village a donkey came charging at us, splitting the dust clouds, an emaciated coachman at the reins, balancing atop the bouncing wooden cart behind the beast. Passengers swarmed around him.

I retrieved my bags from the train, threw them atop the cart, and hauled myself aboard. The driver shouted the Wolof-language version of *giddyap!*, and we charged off toward the road.

Three hours later, I was seated in a forty-seat *car rapide* – a boxy white bus that sat seven to a bench row – destination Dakar, gazing out the window at the modern town of Thiès, where lithe teenage girls in hip-hugging jeans and tank tops, Day-Glo back-packs strapped around their shoulders, were laughing and holding hands and sauntering down spotless asphalted streets; teenage boys in backwards baseball caps glided by them on rollers; women dressed in elaborate banana headscarves and tight-waisted floral dresses strolled the sidewalks. The wind set loose clothes flapping, but it carried no dust; it was pure, coming from the Atlantic, intoxicatingly fresh. Two hours after that, the deep turquoise sky – a maritime sky – spread above Cap Vert and doused the sandy land in light, and then, above hooting traffic clogging the peninsula road, there arose suddenly Dakar, a frieze of whitewashed Casablanca-style houses under a sea-spray sun and diving flocks of gulls. I felt relief and joy.

We soon slowed and got stuck in a traffic jam. I was too excited to sit still. With my bag on my shoulder, I jumped out, crossed a couple of intersections to a freer side road, and hailed a taxi.

My taxi drove me into the city, past elegant French terrace cafés and outdoor restaurants crowded with Lebanese business-men and Senegalese and French expatriates, and wound up circling above the ocean on route de la Corniche Est. From there we dropped into fresher maritime winds, into splendid, saving blue light, heading for my hotel. Beyond the last houses and rocks, giant pinasses cut through the glittering sea, crashing through frothy waves. Far beyond them, on the horizon, oil tankers were steaming north, possibly carrying fuel from the south – from Nigeria, I guessed.

But I didn't want to think of Nigeria, not now. I checked into a room with a balcony that gave onto the Atlantic. That night, listening to the surf break over the rocks below and to boats chugging in the harbor, I drifted into a sleep of profound relief.

The sun and wind never relented. Dakar was all bright light on clean glass, the smell of the salty sea, tall, exquisitely featured men and women in tailored robes, and hand-painted signs in French and Arabic announcing the meetings of the country's increasingly popular Muslim brotherhoods.

A few days later, I took a ferry across the harbor to Île de Gorée. From the dank stone chambers of the House of Slaves, wisps of foam blew through the weathered green door opening onto the ocean, which exploded over moss-mottled rocks just below. Through this door into waiting slavers some 15 million Africans were dispatched to the New World on a voyage of torture and abomination that would become known by the prosaic name of the Middle Passage.

How often had I listened to Africans calling one another slave and master! To be sure, slavery did exist in Africa before the Europeans touched down. This bondage was akin to the vassalage prevalent in Europe during the feudal centuries. Western slavery, however, was of the chattel kind, bestial and unprecedented in Africa, and engendered strife among tribes seeking to capture one another for sale to the Europeans; sparked an arms race for European weapons necessary for self-defense and the enslavement of others; rendered agriculture unprofitable and crippled nascent manufacturing industries; and deprived the continent of its most able-bodied men, women, and children, whom it dispatched to a terrestrial purgatory from which death was the only escape. Slavery halted Africa's development; the systems the colonial powers imposed dealt the Sahel in particular blows from which it has not recovered.

The subjugation of Africa goes on still, though it is effected now not with muskets and barracoons but by economic subterfuge, or, better said, sabotage. The main weapons are two: farm subsidies and trade barriers, and the West wields both while spouting rhetoric about the developmental benefits of free trade. The farm subsidies, grants from Western governments to their agricultural sectors, currently total $360 billion a year, or $30 billion more than Africa's GNP. They make, for example, cotton farming for export absurdly unprofitable in West Africa: a pound of cotton costs 23 cents to grow in West Africa but 60 to 80 cents in the United States. However, grants of $3.5 billion a year to American cotton farmers allow them to undersell their African competitors. Trade barriers keep other African textiles and produce out of Europe and the United States. Western companies continue to control African export markets, fixing the prices they pay Africans for the commodities they take from their shores. These impersonal facts and figures add up to a bleak but human truth: Sahelians will suffer in the future more than they do now, and die more than ever.

Their imams will tell the survivors whom to blame.

# ACKNOWLEDGMENTS

I could never have made it from N'Djamena to Dakar without the help of the Sahelians I met en route. Let their presence in my text serve as an indication of my gratitude.

Otherwise, I would like to thank my friend Brigitte Oddo, a former resident of N'Djamena, for her encouragement, inspiration, and hospitality during the writing of this book's first draft, which took place in her apartment in Marseille; Dominique Oddo, for his help and for recounting his experiences in West Africa; Alex Grawitz, for his support with reference materials; Captain Philippe Fouquet of the 31st Régiment du Génie of the French army, for arranging my aerial transport from Faya Largeau to N'Djamena; photographer and friend Christien Jaspars, for her stunning, inspiring pictures of Mali and the Tuareg, and her company beyond the gates of Albaradiou; Frédéric Berthoz, consul of Niger in Marseille, for providing me with a visa and contacts in Niamey; Denis Vene, ambassador of France to Niger, and his wife, Laurence, for the hospitality they showed me in Niamey; James R. Bullington, director of the Peace Corps program in Niger, for his well-researched aperçu of that country; Lauren Vlachos, for telling me about her time as a Peace Corps volunteer in a Nigérien village; and Andy Passen, U.S. consul in Dakar. At the *Atlantic Monthly* I would like to thank William Whitworth, editor emeritus, Cullen Murphy, managing editor, and Toby Lester, deputy managing editor, for supporting me during my first trip to Nigeria in 1997. Special thanks go to Lieutenant Colonel Scott Womack of the U.S. Army and Mrs. Rebecca Crispin. And I would like to express my gratitude to my agent,

Sonia Land, for her support, friendship, and thorough, effective work at this project's every stage.

For inspiration and much historical information, I am indebted to, among others, Basil Davidson, the author of *Africa in History* and *The African Slave Trade*; J. D. Fage and William Tordoff, for their magnum opus *A History of Africa*; and Karl Maier, for his masterly tome on Nigerian politics and society, *This House Has Fallen*. To Chinua Achebe, the author of *Things Fall Apart* and *The Trouble with Nigeria*, among many other wonderful books, I owe my initial fascination with Nigeria.

Quotes in English from the Qur'an are taken from Arthur J. Arberry's translation *The Koran*, published by Oxford World's Classics.